# Moving the Marginalized to the Center

# Moving the Marginalized to the Center

## Dr. Carolyn M. Byerly's Research and Pedagogy

Edited by
Unwana Samuel Akpan

PETER LANG
New York - Berlin - Bruxelles - Chennai - Lausanne - Oxford

**Bibliographic information published by the Deutsche Nationalbibliothek**
The German National Library lists this publication in the German National Bibliography; detailed bibliographic data is available on the Internet at http://dnb.d-nb.de.

**Library of Congress Cataloging-in-Publication Data**
Names: Byerly, Carolyn M., honouree. | Akpan, Unwana Samuel, editor.
Title: Moving the marginalized to the center : Dr. Carolyn M. Byerly's research and pedagogy / edited by Unwana Samuel Akpan.
Description: New York : Peter Lang, 2026. | Includes bibliographical references and index.
Identifiers: LCCN 2024021520 (print) | LCCN 2024021521 (ebook) | ISBN 9781636675015 (paperback) | ISBN 9783034352109 (hardback) | ISBN 9781636675060 (ebook) | ISBN 9781636675077 (epub)
Subjects: LCSH: Byerly, Carolyn M. | Women in the mass media industry. | Women in mass media. | Mass media and women. | Feminism and mass media. | LCGFT: Festschriften.
Classification: LCC P87.3.B94 M68 2024 (print) | LCC P87.3.B94 (ebook) | DDC 302.23092–dc23/eng/20240524
LC record available at https://lccn.loc.gov/2024021520
LC ebook record available at https://lccn.loc.gov/2024021521
DOI 10.3726/b22012

Cover Credit: Ekely/iStock

ISBN 9781636675015 (paperback)
ISBN 9783034352109 (hardback)
ISBN 9781636675060 (ePDF)
ISBN 9781636675077 (ePUB)
DOI 10.3726/b22012


Published by Peter Lang Publishing Inc., New York, USA

info@peterlang.com—www.peterlang.com



This publication has been peer reviewed.

Contact for General Product Safety Regulation (GPSR): gpsr@peterlang.com

*Carolyn M. Byerly, Ph.D.*
*Professor Emerita*
*Department of Communication, Culture & Media Studies*
*Howard University*
*Washington DC*
*USA*

Dedication

This book is for those critical feminist media scholars, such as Dr. Carolyn M. Byerly, who questioned and challenged the status quo before us, and for all those who will continue to ask critical questions and challenge the status quo.

Therefore, this book is dedicated to an exceptional critical feminist media scholar, Dr. Carolyn M. Byerly, professor emerita, Howard University, Washington, DC, for her decades of academic enquiry, doggedness, ruggedness, resilience, excellence and professionalism.

# Contents

# Foreword

H. LESLIE STEEVES AND AUDREY S. GADZEKPO

This volume celebrates Howard University Professor Emerita Carolyn M. Byerly's many contributions to feminist media studies during her nearly four-decade career. As her friends and colleagues on two continents, North America and Africa, we write jointly to highlight the global relevance of Dr. Byerly's work. We also point out that Dr. Byerly's former students span the world and in fact, a Nigerian former mentee, Dr. Unwana Samuel Akpan, has taken the lead in assembling this anthology. Throughout her career, beginning with her University of Washington master's thesis and later her doctoral dissertation on the UNESCO-funded Women's Feature Services (1990), Dr. Byerly has sought to elevate and support the work of feminist journalists around the world, as well as to identify and interrogate the constraints and challenges women face in newsrooms, and other sites of struggle within the media industries, including misogynistic language in media. Major barriers to women and feminists in journalism stem from capitalist patriarchal ownership and control, leading to Dr. Byerly's extensive scholarship advocating for research and theory on feminist political economy, while drawing also on postcolonial theory and feminist intersectionality.

Specifically, Dr. Byerly has sought to unpack global forms of masculine hegemony in journalism and how it is sustained, experiences of women in news reporting, and feminist critiques and interventions in newsmaking (e.g., 2004;

2017; 2020; Byerly & Ross, 2004). Dr. Byerly and her co-author Karen Ross (2004) argue for "a feminist political economy analytical framework to examine male-owned media industries' exploitation of women's bodies and talents to increase their own profit and the social power flowing from them" (p. 3). They also point out that colonialism is far from over and continues to bring a proliferation of media products and content from the Global North to the South and therefore also must be considered (p. 4). Further, Dr. Byerly (2017) explains how she reconciles intersectional feminism by requiring, acknowledging, and examining the complexity of gendered power relations, in terms of political economy and postcolonial thought. She argues powerfully that multiple forms of oppression still must consider issues of ownership and "structures of capitalism that allow discriminatory practices" (p. 31). Along with advancing feminist political economy, Dr. Byerly has been a leader in documenting and exposing many overlapping dimensions of women working in journalism globally, including numbers, leadership positions, experiences, and activism. She was the principal investigator of the *Global Report on the Status of Women in News Media* for the International Women's Media Foundation (2011), complemented by her anthology *The Palgrave International Handbook of Women and Journalism* (2013). The latter illuminates the nuanced pathways of women's participation in news industries across the world, highlighting 29 national case studies on women's positions in newsrooms. Feminist media activism against gender violence, and theory building on the impact of feminist interventions, are additional key themes in Dr. Byerly's work (e.g., Byerly, 2020; Byerly & Hill, 2012).

Aside from her own important scholarship, Dr. Byerly has invested considerable time and resources in supporting feminist media scholars and activists, including numerous master's and doctoral students at Howard University and at previous universities where she taught, and professional and academic colleagues globally. For many years she was co-trustee and co-coordinator of the International Communication Association's Teresa Award for Feminist Scholarship, and in 2023 her own work finally was recognized when she was presented with a well-deserved Teresa Award. She recently made a significant donation to create the Byerly Award for Feminist Political Economy. The first awardee was announced at ICA's Feminist Scholarship Division awards event, also in 2023. This donation is extraordinarily generous, and a wonderful incentive for feminist scholars, as well as a legacy.

Dr. Byerly has been personally supportive of each of us, calling our attention to opportunities relevant to our interests, and generously consulting on research. We are grateful for her many major contributions to feminist scholarship, activism, teaching and mentoring over the decades, and her friendship as well, and it is a privilege to write the foreword to this anthology.

H. Leslie Steeves, University of Oregon, Eugene, Oregon and Prof. Audrey S. Gadzekpo, University of Ghana, Legon, Accra, Ghana

## References

Byerly, C. M. (1990). *The Women's feature services and the making of world news* [PhD dissertation, University of Washington].

Byerly, C. M. (2004). Feminist interventions in newsrooms. In K. Ross & C. M. Byerly (Eds.), *Women and media: International perspectives* (pp. 109–131). Blackwell.

Byerly, C. M. (2011, March). *Global report on status of women in news media.* International Women's Media Foundation. https://www.iwmf.org/wp-content/uploads/2018/06/IWMF-Global-Report.pdf

Byerly, C. M. (Ed.). (2013). *The Palgrave international handbook on women and journalism.* Palgrave Macmillan.

Byerly, C. M. (2017). Feminist intersectionality research in communications: Origins, contributions and tensions. *Ex Æquo, 35,* 23–31. https://doi.org/10.22355/exaequo.2017.35.02

Byerly, C. (2020). Gender, media and political economy. In K. Ross (Ed.), *The International encyclopedia of fender, media and communication* (pp. 1–6). John Wiley & Sons. https://doi.org/10.1002/9781119429128.iegmc109

Byerly, C. M., & Hill, M. (2012). Reformulation theory: Gauging feminist impact on news of violence against women. *Journal of Women and Gender (Symposium Issue).* https://www.academia.edu/2247510/Reformulation_Theory_Gauging_Feminist_Impact_on_News_of_Violence_Against_Women

Byerly, C. M., & Ross, K. (2004). Introduction. In K. Ross & C. M. Byerly (Eds.), *Women and media: International perspectives* (pp. 1–7). Blackwell.

# Preface

This book is a festschrift in honor of a renowned international critical feminist media studies scholar, Dr. Carolyn M. Byerly, professor emerita, Howard University, USA. The book comprises fresh, innovative, concise, and insightful references to research, theories and pedagogy associated with her scholarship and leadership from a cross-section of her colleagues, students and mentees. It showcases comments on her critical pedagogy and corpus of feminist media investigations and theoretical postulations. Feminist discourse demands fresh and challenging theory-of-knowledge interventions and rescue, and this makes this text an essential and a cardinal interlocutor and dialogist in feminist media studies. To a large extent, this book frames and showcases genial epistemologies pertinent to locating and situating feminist media studies in the pluriverse. This book is key and essential for critical feminist media studies scholars.

Dr. Carolyn M. Byerly was recently featured in a recent interview article titled "16 Feminist Media Studies, 7 Questions about Working in the University (and beyond)." Feminist media scholarship, race and gender inequalities are major global issues that have occupied scholars around the world, especially in the developing countries, for more than half a century. Divided opinions have been churned out among scholars within this research sequence, which have revealed a lot of uncovered and unresearched ground in feminist media scholarship.

These phenomena have also been the basis for global movements in women's and LGBTQ liberation, national laws and policies, and significant changes in social mores and practices related to gender relations the world over. Indeed, the media have had a significant part to play in advancing recent public discourse, particularly through social media.

This edited volume maps the current field of feminist media research and considers its connections to pedagogy that engages both feminist theory and principles of egalitarianism as taught by Dr. Carolyn M. Byerly. The book takes a global (international) approach by including authors from several regions of the world whose scholarly interests encompass concerns about gender and racial equality in the media and who have a personal or scholarly connection to Dr. Carolyn M. Byerly.

In addition, her teaching has uniquely influenced new generations of scholars both within the United States and globally. Together, scholars, colleagues and former students have applied feminist questions and principles, expanding both research and praxis. All of the contributors to this edited volume have been influenced by Byerly's research, teaching, and/or leadership in the field.

Feminist and critical race research have developed over the last few decades through the leadership of scholars who worked in the intellectual margins of their fields. In the process, they produced a rich literature that engaged important questions about gender and race of the day, and that produced a realm of new knowledge. Beyond their scholarship, feminist and critical race scholars guided new generations of students down similar paths of inquiry through their teaching and mentorship. They also collaborated with other colleagues to establish new divisions and awards in scholarly associations, sponsor colloquia, and otherwise open the space for critical debate and challenges to the status quo. Feminist scholars have had the most difficulty gaining recognition for their intellectual accomplishments as well as the ripple effects of their research and teaching. The evidence of this is in the few books that have considered the relationship between feminist pedagogy and research or celebrated the achievements of individual feminist scholars.

The study of how media operate and how they are associated with gender inequality and equality has been the central concern of Dr. Byerly's work. This festschrift reflects on that work through a series of articles by those who have followed and been influenced by her work—peer scholars, colleagues, and former students. Contributors represent nine different nationalities and approximately half of them live outside the United States, making this a truly international project. No doubt the book is multidimensional and rich in intellectual and aesthetic content. The subject areas that this book emphasizes are the issues of gender, race, communication, media studies, journalistic practice and political economy of the media that have characterized her academic career.

This book is subdivided into five sections. Section I is the Introduction; Section II is Research; Section III is Pedagogy; Section IV is an Afterword by Dr. Byerly and Section V is a Photo Gallery. Chapter 1 is by Karen Ross, "CB: The Ultimate Feminist-Sister-Scholar," chronicles both scholars' journey into the feminist media research track; Chapter 2 by Margaret Gallagher, "A Feminist International Perspective on Women, Media and Power: Reflections on Meetings with Carolyn Byerly," address Byerly's prominent body of work on women, media and power. In Chapter 3, Meenakshi Gigi Durham explores the "Optimistic Feminist Praxis: On Carolyn Byerly's Contributions to Transformative Feminist Activism." In Chapter 4, Catherine J. K. Sandoval reflects on "Dr. Carolyn M. Byerly's Media Justice Scholarship: Centering Women's Critical Information Needs in Public Interest Regulation." Elizabeth L. Toth considers Byerly's broader range of research in Chapter 5, "In Honor of Carolyn M. Byerly: Contributions from Her Feminist Scholarship." In Chapter 6, "Carolyn the Brave: Five Lessons from a Trailblazer," Dafna Lemish enumerates instances of Byerly's academic courage. "From the Local to the Global: Carolyn Byerly's Praxis and Theory" is the title of Chapter 7, by Lana F. Rakow, as she explores the steady growth of Prof. Byerly's influence globally. In Chapter 8, Marian Meyers' "An Interview with Carolyn Byerly: Feminist, Scholar, Activist and 'Partner in Crime,'" queries Byerly on her personal politics and its role in her academic life. Chapter 9 by Ammu Joseph, "Three as for Carolyn: Affection, Appreciation and Admiration," recounts how she and Byerly's work together evolved into friendship. The last chapter in section II is titled "Never Losing Sight of the Bigger Picture with Persistence," by Stine Eckert, shows how Byerly's tenacity in her scholarship and research ultimately led to new awards for feminist scholarship.

Section III is on pedagogy, where Dr. Byerly's students and mentees reflect on her contributions to their development as feminist scholars and leaders. Chapter 11, "Carolyn Byerly: The Perfect Combination of a Sound Researcher and a Feminist Activist," by Aimée Vega Montiel, comments on Byerly's influence on her own scholarship. In Chapter 12, "Mentor or Other Mother? Byerly Feminism Meets Black Feminist Thought at a Historically Black College and University," Ashla C. Hill Roseboro ponders Byerly's mentorship of Black women like herself.

In Chapter 13, Shoaa Almalki shares her personal experience in "Finding My Voice: Dr. Carolyn M. Byerly's Impact on My Academic Journey." Chapter 14,

"The Feminist Standpoint of Dr. Carolyn M. Byerly," by Tsovinar Nazaryan, examines Byerly's feminist research standpoints. Chapter 15, "The Final Boss: Carolyn Byerly's Critical Empiricism," by Sholnn Freeman, chronicles his relationship with Dr. Carolyn M. Byerly and her role in articulating the study of critical communication research; the article also addresses the growing need for such research as the United States slides deeper into plutocracy. The last chapter under section III, "#Doyouseeme: An Academic Search for 'Self'—Inspired by Dr. Carolyn M. Byerly," by Ngoma Evelyn Moghalu, takes readers into Byerly's classroom and teaching methods. The afterword is positioned alone in Section IV. "In Finding a Synthesis," Byerly traces her intellectual roots and the sources of her consciousness about gender, race and class—the central concerns of her academic life. Section V comes as the last section, and documents select photographs of Dr. Carolyn M. Byerly's network of colleagues, friends and students.

Unwana Samuel Akpan, PhD

# Acknowledgments

First, my appreciation goes to God who gave me the inspiration for this festschrift, and He also made it possible. Second, my heartfelt thank you goes to Dr. Carolyn M. Byerly, professor emerita, as well, who graciously accepted the gift of this festschrift from me. I am grateful to you all (contributing authors) for being part of this success story, and for all we have collectively accomplished during the period of this festschrift. We all did it! As I surveyed the last couple of months of putting this festschrift together in honor of Dr. Carolyn M. Byerly; for me what stands out is not this printed copy but collegial commitment, support and of course faces—faces of the chapter authors who enriched me and sharpened me in diverse ways—especially those senior colleagues, through our email exchange. Based on the tributes poured out on Dr. Carolyn M. Byerly in recognition of her impact on humanity in the pages of this festschrift, suddenly some things I thought mattered to me no longer do, as they have lost relevance; and I have just realized that only humans last . . . I mean touching the lives of others, especially how one treats others. Therefore, I would like to express my deep appreciation to the esteemed chapter authors who responded promptly through the submission of their papers. My appreciation also goes to the Department of Communication, Culture and Media Studies (CCMS), Howard University, and Dr. Byerly's network of academic friends, colleagues and mentees for their significant show of support and solidarity. In addition, a special appreciation goes to those who also helped in the peer review process of the articles, and the editors (Niall Kennedy, Dr. Elizabeth Howard and Anthony Joshua) who all worked with me to ensure that all the Is are dotted and the Ts crossed.

Moreso, I want to apologize to anyone whose toes I stepped on while I literally hurried my way through the process of gathering and putting together the bits and pieces of everyone's article to form a single manuscript in honor of the honoree; especially those my periodic interfering friendly deadline reminders that might have been perceived as too frequent, intruding, invading and interrupting. The trespass, most likely and certainly, was not deliberate. Thank you all for understanding that we needed to get the job accomplished, and thank you for giving me all the support that made this festschrift a huge success. Finally, thank you all for honoring Dr. Carolyn M. Byerly in this manner!

Unwana Samuel Akpan, PhD

# Section I

# Introduction

# Dr. Carolyn M. Byerly: Advancing Feminist Media Scholarship Through Mentoring, Leadership and Networking

UNWANA SAMUEL AKPAN

*Whatever the young lion knows, he learnt it from the mother.*

—An Annang Proverb

## Unveiling

In the ancient Annang mythology in Nigeria, it is historicized that the lion cub gets his first hunting lessons, skills and mentoring from his mother. This mirrors the traditional belief among the indigenous Annang-speaking people of Akwa Ibom State, Nigeria, that lionesses are the primary hunters for the entire pride. Flipping through the numerous memories painted by the various contributing authors in this volume, one begins to liken Dr. Carolyn M. Byerly to the proverbial African lioness, because she has equally taught and mentored a good number of students across the world who have grown in the academy to become established scholars in their respective research tracks. They can now metaphorically hunt for themselves as a result of sitting under Dr. Byerly's mentoring. This explains why the essays in this book cover a broad spectrum of thematically treated issues, written by a diverse range of established and budding scholars around the world. These individuals, whether established or emerging in their fields, have collaborated with Dr. Carolyn M. Byerly at various points—whether through co-research, co-authorship or as students under her tutelage. Consequently, the pages of this book are rich with testimonials, highlighting Dr. Byerly's roles as a scholar, team leader, mentor, activist, teacher, and, notably, an "academic-mother." For me, it is more than an honor that those whom she once taught, mentored, collaborated and worked together with would accept to contribute chapters to this edited book; it is greatly humbling, that these scholars have taken time out of their crowded research and administrative schedules to pen these about the person of Dr. Byerly.

In essence, the essays that adorn the pages of this book are borne out of years of relationship, academic culture, nurture, conviction and fellowship from a heterogeneous range of global scholars and other professionals to pen these pragmatic streams of thoughts, themes and experiences they have all had with Dr. Byerly, at different times. The chapters are all different in style and in concept, but these texts all have some sort of originality and organic enthusiasm rooted to their callings and dealings with Dr. Byerly. Perusing through these texts and editing them, I felt a sense of feminist originality and the willing attitude of a distinguished set of scholars who actually wanted to contribute to this festschrift that honors Dr. Carolyn M. Byerly. This speaks loudly to the fact that she was indeed a good colleague, teacher, mentor and leader for so many to have accepted to participate in this festschrift honoring her. And so to me this book epitomizes the years of labor of Dr. Byerly's academic toils. Dr. Byerly is an American; hence, this work for me is figuratively premised on part of Nigeria's lyrics of our national anthem—"the labour of our heroes . . . shall not be in vain." For me, that lyric resonates with Dr. Byerly's efforts and contributions to scholarship and leadership.

The carefully selected texts in this festschrift speak to a humane and human quality that Dr. Byerly has the capacity to bring diverse people across colors together for inclusion, equity and diversity. And it is also evident in her ability to bring diverse people together in the team that she has worked and researched with as a scholar over the years. One of the authors in this festschrift, Dr. Meenakshi Gigi Durham, a professor of feminist media studies, puts it rather unequivocally, beautifully and succinctly, where she referred to Dr. Byerly as "perhaps best known for her piercing critiques of the media environment and its treatment of women and other minoritized people . . ." She further reiterated:

> Carolyn's analyses are unique in that they confront two realities at once: on one hand, the incontrovertible fact that the media environment is patriarchal

> and misogynistic, and that women and people of color face systemic barriers to both fair representation and other forms of access, such as decision-making power and ownership; on the other hand, the people who experience discrimination and bias have exceptional agency and insight, and they work tirelessly for change, in many cases effecting transformations in policy and practice to create space for new ways of making media. In this form of "double vision," making both the problems and the solutions visible, Carolyn's work exemplifies what I am calling "optimistic feminist praxis." (Durham, 2026)

Reading through this beautiful rendition by Dr. Durham, about Dr. Byerly, I thought this would be a wonderful definition of a person who has touched the lives of many, especially people of color in diverse ways unimaginable.

## How Our Paths Crossed

I had the good fortune of getting to know about Dr. Carolyn M. Byerly first on Howard University's online faculty profile in 2017 while I was surfing the internet for a perfect host for my postdoc. My first conversational contact with her was in 2018 via email when I was applying for a postdoctoral research fellowship at the Department of Communication, Culture and Media Studies (CCMS), at Howard University, a historically Black institution in Washington, DC. In her email, she was very sincere in her response. She told me that "foreign scholars have a great way of enriching our academic communities" (C. M. Byerly, personal communication, 2018). Since then, I have been using that beautiful phrase of hers each time I have an opportunity to recommend scholars for academic exchange programs. As a scholar from the Global South, I ran into some diplomatic barriers at the American Embassy in Lagos, Nigeria, in trying to obtain my visa for the fellowship in the United States. She helped to resolve it for me. Despite the several administrative hiccups, she followed my application tenaciously till I landed in the prestigious department (CCMS). Within the short time I related with her at personal and academic levels as my postdoc co-supervisor, I observed that the Irish-American critical feminist scholar is gracious in her pursuit of assisting students, especially those from the Global South, to attain their academic goals regardless of their nationality, color, creed, or religion. For me, there are few individuals I have known personally who rival the service Dr. Byerly has rendered to students, especially foreign students and scholars, faculty members, and of course the entire Howard community.

I believe the legacy of service Dr. Byerly has left behind at CCMS is worth emulating and celebrating. Undoubtedly, many at Cathy Hughes School of Communications in which the CCMS Department is housed, myself included, can proudly attest to this. During my short stay in the department, I recognized Dr. Byerly as a fearless, vocal and tactful feminist, whose feminist commitments are expressed in her research, writing, teaching and mentoring. One of the amazing characteristics of Dr. Byerly is that, if you are meeting her for the first time, she has a way of graciously amplifying the humanity of all those she comes into contact with.

## Coming to America and Memories of Mentorship

Just like in the famous movie *Coming to America*, that starred the legendary comedian Eddy Murphy, my coming from Nigeria, Africa, to conduct research in the United States, filled me with numerous incertitudes due to how Nigerians are framed, labeled and perceived globally by the mainstream media, social media as "con men" and "fantastically corrupt." I was beyond scared of being labeled or framed in a way that I am not, due to my nationality. As a social science researcher, this generalized notion has never sat well with my journalism and research orientations. I landed in the United States some days before I reported to Howard, my patriotic self struggling with these media stereotypes. I felt morbid fear at facing people of other nationalities due to my Nigerian identity. I would wonder at "all those eyes" looking at me with rapt attention. I would say to myself, "who knows what they have been reading about Nigeria and Nigerians, and who knows if they are aware that I am a Nigerian, and if they get to know, would I be welcomed?" My thoughts raced and produced a lot of questions, because I know too well that receiving an invitation does not always mean your presence is welcomed.

However, my first physical encounter with Dr. Byerly erased lots of my unfounded uncertainties, especially those perceived culture shocks, and how Nigerians are perceived. Dr. Byerly gladly hosted me in her department as a post-doc fellow, and I got relaxed, my fears of being labeled or framed evaporating like gas because of the quality of her hospitality, sincerity and the warmth in her welcome. Most times, I would stop by in her office, we would discuss quite a lot, including how Nigerians are framed globally, and she would tell me, "oh Dr. Akpan, I don't relate or deal with people based on hearsay; I allow personal encounters to create my impressions. Don't forget we are academics, we have to first test our hypothesis before we generalize them. Besides, I have great Nigerian students turned friends" (C. M. Byerly, personal communication, 2019). And I can remember jokingly agreeing with her notion; "oh yes ma'am, hypotheses are intelligent guesses after all; and besides, I would make a 'perfect sample size' in testing this hypothesis about Nigerians." And we both laughed about it as if we had known each other for decades. Only a methodological person reasons and relates the way she does, as I was especially struck by Dr. Byerly's careful attentiveness in the way she read through my initial postdoc proposal draft. The person who has the quality of careful attentiveness can patiently mentor others. This brings me to a recurring idea in this book, which is that Dr. Byerly is thorough, as expressed by most authors here. It is an ideal to which I too subscribe.

She would meet with me periodically to discuss feminist and postcolonial theory, and some other topical issues, and also assess the progress of my postdoc research. Each time I paid her a visit in her office, I would also observe her administrative ability as a department chair. Also, her collection of African portraits and carvings I met in her office were beautiful and haunting and most of all, I think that they showed me the humane and human qualities of Dr. Byerly, as accommodating. According to her, the Afrocentric portraits and carvings that adorned her office as the chair of CCMS back then were given to her by her African students . . . and again, this speaks to the fact that she is accommodating. During my stay at CCMS, she gave me the opportunity to guest-lecture in classes and public lecture once on an African cultural theme. She also introduced me to colleagues in the Department of African Studies that could aid my postdoc research on "Second Generation Nigerian Identity in the U.S. and Sources of Information," a study that Dr. Byerly and Dr. Chuka Onwumechili carefully supervised.

I cannot thank her enough for making me a global scholar through our intellectual discourse and for co-supervising my postdoc research. I believe our paths crossed for an indelible mark and palpable show of whom a mentor/academic supervisor should be: encouraging, friendly, calm, approachable, knowledgeable, skillful and welcoming. Looking at the calm manner she handled my postdoc and visa applications when they hit the bricks, I have learned a lot from her from those discouraging scenarios, and beyond the four walls of the university system, and of course beyond research. I learned boldness, calmness and hope in the face of intimidation and hopelessness from the way she handled those scenarios, and within my short stay at CCMS. After my encounter with her in 2019, my academic track has never remained the same, as her mentoring has enriched and sharpened me in diverse ways unimaginable. In one of our email exchanges, when I was informing her about my latest book, she pleasantly penned, "Dr. Akpan,

I think your coming to Howard greatly paid off" (C. M. Byerly, personal communication, 2021).

While I was at Howard University for my postdoctoral research fellowship, I recalled frequenting her office and chatted with her about sundry intellectual things, especially Paul Gilroy's scholarship that she introduced me to. We talked about Afrocentric themes, media research, leadership, management and more. She would engage me on some of my Afrocentric convictions. I recalled asking her surprisingly, "what are you doing in a predominantly Black university?" She smiled and answered, "to learn of course, and by the way, are you interviewing me as a journalist that you were?"(C. M. Byerly, personal communication, 2019). And we both laughed. I can go on and on. Fond memories came rushing back to me as I was penning this article. Those lovely memories! Dr. Byerly is an esteemed co-traveler in my life's academic journey who I have sorely missed since I pivoted from Howard University as a postdoc fellow.

She is a pragmatic teacher who took interest in me right from the time I was seeking a host for my postdoctoral fellowship. Sensing my future prospects, and interest in communication and culture track, Dr. Byerly did all she could to get me into the department. She discovered my interest in feminist media studies later, and I started reading her works online during my postdoc days. I admired and respected her feminist posture and dexterity, her feminist epistemological intelligence and her pedagogic lines of thoughts. Then I started paying rapt attention to her in one particular class she invited me to guest lecture, and I gained a lot in her communication theories seminar with her doctoral students. The effect of this exposure on me is the development of an independent mind rooted in integrity, an attribute that I owe to Dr. Byerly's vision in providing the golden opportunity for systematic research/teaching quite early in my career as a postdoc fellow.

During my postdoctoral research in her department, there were many times that Dr. Byerly and I exchanged views on various issues on teaching and in African feminist research, most especially during her postgraduate seminars and informally at other times. Under Dr. Byerly, I had the benefit of her advice throughout my postdoc research, most especially her influence on my scholarly perspective, as she gave me books written by the legendary Professor Paul Gilroy. I can add that she has helped greatly in the practical pursuit of my academic career and teaching. The legacy that has been passed by Dr. Byerly on to those of us she has supervised at one level of academics or another, most especially those of us who imbibed our culture in general and that of our research in particular. It is this phenomenon among all other academic phenomena that has been guiding my thought and also provoking in me that sense of keen observation and inquisitiveness as far as research investigation is concerned.

Byerly's epistemological view is that first, one must understand what constitutes knowledge and the in-depth study of a field of any discipline that leads to understanding and ultimately the accumulation of knowledge. Correct application of knowledge is wisdom she would always say. She is a very sound feminist media scholar, an excellent teacher, activist and mentor. She has demonstrated so far in all her words and works the attribute of diligence, hardwork and commitment to her professional calls. Dr. Byerly is versatile, productive and has an all-round knowledge of not only the academic field but from other fields of education such as culture, diaspora, history, sociology, language and so on. Throughout, Byerly has steadily maintained integrity and confidence in her research track which has portrayed her as a straightforward and focused scholar. She has a strong conviction that the "central concern of feminist movements the world over has been violence against women, both physical and sexual" (Byerly & Hill, 2012). She has never been seen bowing down to intimation. Writeups based on her research investigations on feminism and her teaching pedagogy have shown concrete elements of a high sense of scholastic productivity even after retirement.

## The Convictions that Fueled Dr. Carolyn M. Byerly's Festschrift

First, I think the greatest gift a teacher can have is the eternal gratitude of his or her students and Dr. Byerly has that, through this festschrift. I must say that reading Dr. Byerly's students and colleagues praising her, warmed my heart particularly because it reminds me of my dear mother who was a competent and dedicated teacher and taught for 30 years before her retirement. She would always tell me that "a teacher's reward is in heaven," but for some of us, we want Dr. Byerly's reward to start here on earth. Moreso, maybe this is one of the reasons Dr. Carolyn, M. Byerly, was featured as one of the 16 feminist media scholars in the world, in a recent research interview article titled, "16 feminist media studies, 7 questions about working in the university (and beyond)" (Bishop, 2021), and this further inspired Dr. Byerly's festschrift.

Second, what drove and fueled my conviction about this project was that, during my stay at CCMS three years ago, she demonstrated a perfect blend of Diversity, Equity and Inclusion in her dealings with students and faculty of color and in her postulations, and in the way she speaks against racism and inequalities in her writings. For instance, in her paper on "Feminist Intersectionality Research in Communications: Origins, Contributions and Tensions," she posits that:

> . . . also had to factor in racism, classism, ethnocentrism, national origin and homophobia that we saw in the institutional practices that surrounded and enabled the violence to exist. (Byerly, 2017, p. 25)

And this globally accepted blend (Diversity, Equity and Inclusion), one would feel it in her mentorship, leadership, writing, research, scholarship, administrative chores and corporate space relationship.

Third, most of the time, it is Herculean as an international postgraduate student (especially of African descent) to get a supervisor in the United States who is ready to take you in and supervise your thesis or dissertation. In fact, getting a faculty member who is of African descent even proves harder as some of them would not even reply to your mail. Getting a reply from Dr. Carolyn Byerly who was ready to take me in as a co-supervisor and host for my postdoctoral was entirely a miracle. This is why media scholar Mohammed observes that "first-generation college students, mentorship can go a long way to helping them more effectively deal with imposter syndrome, perform well in their study, and set off their research and careers as academics" (Jack-Davies, 2018 as cited by Mohammed, 2021, p. 136). Some African scholars recount the ordeal they went through in their undergraduate days trying to get materials and supervisors for their studies in the Global North, but I can attest to the fact that I used Dr. Byerly's personal library to gather materials for my postdoc research. She took me to African studies and Howard University library, and introduced me to the personnel and faculty members, so I could gain access to their repertoire of research materials and books. My case was different, compared to the ordeal of this scholar:

> In many graduate programs, however, very few resources are made available to students of color, especially international students, to navigate not just the culture but the academic climate. Many students go into graduate programs without the necessary guidance to prepare themselves to begin working toward publishing their research and gathering teaching and other types of professional and service experience to adequately prepare them for the job market. (Mohammed, 2021, p. 136)

Most of the time, those faculty members who embrace budding scholars in their request for thesis dissertations automatically become their academic mentors who they look up to, and this was my case with Dr. Byerly. Again, Mohammed reiterates:

> For many African students, their advisor becomes their mentor. It is usually not guaranteed that African students will get the chance to work with professors whose research interests overlap with theirs or who even study their geographical area of interest. (Mohammed, 2021, p. 136)

There are a lot of African postgraduate students out there in the United States, just wishing they could have the opportunity to be mentored by the best brains in their field, but lack the opportunity. The feminist media studies need more recruits into the sequence, especially students of color whose home country put cultural and religious barricades and ceilings for women not to compete with men. Professor Karen Ross succinctly reveals how Dr. Byerly has set structures on ground to achieve this:

> I have always appreciated CB's approach to both academic but also life more generally and her genuine desire to lift up others and this is nowhere more notable than in her involvement in the setting up of the Teresa Award—she and Marian Meyers as trustees of the fund, established with a donation from another great feminist scholar, Yoo Jae Song—and then the Helen Award for young/er scholars and most recently establishing her own award (the Byerly Award) with a focus on scholars working in the specific field of feminist political economy. (Ross, 2026)

These students of color, especially from the Global South, need to be introduced to the feminist media studies as future foot soldiers in the field. It is noted: Studies have shown that "just over 5 percent of all full-time faculty members at colleges and universities in the United States are black" (*The Journal of Blacks in Higher Education*, n.d.), and there are few data to show what percentage of the 5 percent are Black African faculty. These statistics are far from representative of the demographic of the student body in American higher education institutions (Mohammed, 2021, p. 136). This phenomenon is supported by Asante et al. (2016) observation of the difficulties Black migrants, especially African students face in securing a supervisor, in the United States. Again, Dr. Byerly's approach to encourage Black students to soar in the academia comes handy, as revealed by one of her students:

> Dr. Carolyn Byerly, former professor and chair of the Communication, Culture and Media Studies program at Howard University, mentored countless students

> across decades, particularly supporting Black women doctoral students in navigating research and careers in academia . . . Dr. Byerly emphasized empowered voices of racial and gender minorities in her graduate courses where we discussed strategies that Black women often must adopt to think and speak for themselves. (Roseboro, 2026)

Fourth, it is my conviction that exemplary leaders and people who have touched the lives of others and humanity in general in immeasurable ways should be immortalized. Sometimes, governments mold their statues at public places to honor their memories, preserve historical facts and inspire acts of courage. In academia, festschrifts are one of the perfect ways of celebrating, immortalizing and preserving the intellectual efforts and contributions of outstanding scholars who have greatly impacted and imparted their academic sequence with strong results and outcomes. A festschrift in academia typifies the conventional statues and Dr. Carolyn Byerly's intellectual prowess inspires this festschrift. The timing of this festschrift is perfect, because it comes at a time she has retired from active faculty duties.

During the long incubation and gestation period of producing this important book that would immortalize Dr. Carolyn M. Byerly's huge contributions to her research calling, I was asking myself, "how do I convince any reputable academic publisher with high rating, and strong and enduring online visibility to sign up a 'personality focused festschrift', against a 'stealth' festschrift that seems easier and common?" I quickly found an answer for that question. In the corporate world, every marketer worth his/her weight and value in gold knows that a good product with an international appeal sells itself, and this model perfectly fits Dr. Byerly's worth. Today, the rest is history.

## Contributions to the Field: Assessing Through My Lenses

The truth is, I have had very limited experience with Dr. Byerly's mentoring, looking at the short span of time I spent at CCMS, and the challenge of having to return to my home country after my study leave. But the little time I spent with her as her mentee made it worthwhile, and also, I noticed some good qualities about her.

Though she needs no introduction as a leading scholar with research expertise in the areas of feminist media scholarship, international news, feminist political economy, and race and gender in media policy; Dr. Byerly is one scholar who would not allow you to overhype or exaggerate her work or her achievements. Her writing and research investigate how women are represented occupationally in the media around the world. She has in her research over the years drawn the attention of policymakers around the globe to issues around inequalities and underrepresentation associated with women occupational, especially in the media space. She points out that "women's voices and activism in these unprecedented times of political and economic shifts merit our scholarly attention, as does our ever-changing relationship to communications media" (Byerly, 2018, p. 19). This is her research track. Her 2011 study was an eye-opener as she revealed that "women in the United States own fewer than 6 percent of radio and television stations" (Byerly, 2011, p. 24). Dr. Byerly is broadly interested in the occupational representation of women in the media, and how women are evenly represented in allied industry. For her, "in the wider society, those who hold class power are able to make decisions that create the rules and laws and determine how resources are to be allocated" (Byerly, 2018, p. 26). While critiquing the UNESCO article on women, she thematically points to some areas of gaps in the article that caught the attention of her research calling:

> The salient question to pose with this realization is how will women become full participants in their societies if they cannot affect the telling of their own stories, if society does not see the wide array of images and roles they occupy, and people cannot obtain the information they need for society's advancement by addressing gender inequality? (Byerly, 2019, p. 29)

She has widely authored, edited and co-edited books, as well as published articles in international academic journals in these areas. She has also mentored budding and established scholars in the field of Mass Communication who have greatly contributed to the body of knowledge in the field of Gender Studies, Communication, Culture and Media. She had professional experience as a journalist and public information specialist before joining academia. Dr. Byerly is one of the leading academic voices addressing gender discrimination in the media in the United States, as well as the developing countries like those in Africa. Her numerous theoretical postulations have widely been cited, revered and referenced by respectable scholars around the world as a scholar, "helping women's voices to be heard, both among each other and in the general population" (Byerly, 1995, p. 120).

I remember watching Dr. Byerly's conference presentation at the Howard's 9th Annual Social Media Technology Conference and Workshop in Washington, DC (USA) in October 2019, when she was presenting a paper on "incels," and I realized that she has a linguistic command of her research track. Among the feminist media scholars, she has distinguished herself. From one of her submissions, it appears she is one of the sort-after scholars whose work keep generating data:

> Even my own work has become increasingly data-driven in that the projects I have taken up have expanded in scope and volume, something that has required the management of information, typically using spreadsheets and requiring the coding and counting of data. (Byerly, 2018, p. 20)

Available records show that, for nearly two decades, she served on the communications faculty at Howard University, where, in her last seven years, she chaired the CCMS doctoral-level department that continues to graduate the largest number of Black PhDs in the United States. In those years, she directed more than three dozen dissertations and masters' theses, helping to shape a generation of young researchers, many of them from nations in the Global South. Her leadership work in her academic field can be seen most specifically in the International Communication Association (ICA), where she served as the co-chair and chair of Feminist Scholarship Division for several years, and then as trustee of the Teresa Award for Feminist Research for more than a decade. She has just endowed a major competitive award in ICA, the Byerly Feminist Political Economy in Communication Fund, which will support new research on the subject annually. These efforts have helped to advance critical international research on gender and media, to bring together peer collaborations, and to support young scholars in their work.

Over all, Dr. Byerly dedicated more than 35 years to teaching and research, 17 of those years at Howard University helping to build a new PhD program at the Department of Communication, Culture and Media Studies (CCMS). Her signature study, the *Global Report on the Status of Women in News Media* (2011) I have cited several times, remains the only global-level study of women's standing in news organizations and is still quoted widely. Her subsequent book, *The Palgrave International Handbook of Women and Journalism* (2013), brought together original research on women's standing in journalistic practice in all regions of the world. She is reputed to have gathered scores of influential feminist media scholars around the world on this project that up till today has no rival. In 2022 after studying her work and how she was able to pull together feminist media scholars from 29 countries to contribute articles to her edited volume on *The Palgrave International Handbook of Women and Journalism* was impressive. "This is the first book to present original empirical research comparing women's occupational status in journalism employing a systematic methodology" (Byerly, 2013, p. 3). This book broadly has an international coverage and mileage, "including country case studies from Asia and Oceania, Middle East and North Africa, SubSaharan Africa, Americas, Eastern Europe, Nordic Europe and Western Europe" (Byerly, 2013, p. 3).

No other feminist scholar working today is addressing the intersection of political economy and gender, race and nationality to this extent in media policies and practices. This is evidently felt in her research as she professes:

> In my own research, I typically adopt a feminist critical political economy theory of media, which is grounded in Marxist assumptions but which also factors in intersectionality concerns of gender and race relations. (Byerly, 2018, p. 26)

Assessing these numerous articles from her students and colleagues, one would discover that Dr. Byerly over the years had attended the building and nurturing of feminist media-focused scholars who would promote a shared ownership, gender-friendly media environment and representational narratives among media scholars and media professionals. Even after retirement, Dr. Byerly has continued to deploy her over 35 years of classroom, research and leadership experiences working with leading feminist media scholars across the world and in the United States of America. In her new role as Professor Emerita, Dr. Byerly continues to further position the feminist media studies sequence for the next phase of growth in a world as digital as ours, while building an aligned team with a disruptive productive mindset across the diverse academic cadets within the communication and media studies.

She recently completed a new book on intersectionality and political economy in the media which is billed for publication by Routledge in Summer 2024. She might have retired, but she is not tired of mentoring, writing and researching. The editor of this volume is among the emerging and established scholars in the field of Mass Communication whom she has mentored. Like myself, her former students and mentees are busily contributing to the body of knowledge in the field of Gender Studies, Communication, Culture and Media. Most of her colleagues and students who have contributed chapters in this book are university professors in numerous nations.

## Before Signing Out: A Tribute to Dr. Byerly

In the traditional Annang, Ibibio, Efik communities in Nigeria, traditional chieftaincy title holders who are females are referred to as *Obonganwan* (this means a *Woman King*); and in the neighboring Igbo traditional custom, female traditional chieftaincy title holders are called *Lolo*. These are traditional chieftaincy titles that were given to she-warriors in the pre-colonial days in these African communities. These women were audacious, daring and heroic in their dealings and confrontations with anti-feminism postures and struggles against machoism/machismo mentality in their communities. They championed the earliest feminist ideations in their community with their confrontational nature against men's activities that were repugnant to social justice and the dignity of women. Dr. Carolyn M. Byerly fits into the status and category of these historic and iconic women. Corroborating this, recently, the renowned Nigerian-American feminist and novelist, Chimamanda Adichie was conferred with a traditional chieftaincy title in her native town in Nigeria, in recognition of her service to the feminist community globally. By every extension, Dr. Byerly is what I would call a *Lolo of Feminist Media Studies* and an *Obonganwan of Feminist Media Studies.*

As she has officially retired, it comes with mixed feelings, as they always say! But one cannot but be happy that her moving on is to chart a new course, which will help make the grazing field wider, broader and richer for the many budding scholars she has been mentoring over the years. And so, for the sake of some of us, we can only bid her farewell in this new phase of hers, while some of her mentees revel in the fact that she is only an email, a phone call or a WhatsApp message away. As she has officially entered this phase, for me I see the end of an era and the beginning of another incredibly exciting research journey for her, of which I have no doubt will be filled with astonishing successes, breaking down barriers, and blazing a trail of empathy and competence. My hope is that this new phase of her life would be more glorious than the first.

Congratulations to you, Dr. Byerly, on this new and important journey of your retirement! Very grateful to have been a part (albeit a very small one) of your time at Howard– you certainly made my postdoc journey that much more enjoyable. A huge thank you to you for being a fantastic mentor. A woman who has consistently nurtured and built others to come up to her level, by bringing out the very best in them. Thank you for being a quiet dependable and witty mentor. A woman with a large heart who has invested a great portion of her life in molding many generations of media and communication students while at Howard University. Most of us will miss you; but some of us are so glad we had the privilege of learning under your tutelage. All you had imprinted in us will never be forgotten. Beyond leading this project, I would be an ingrate if I did not join your numerous colleagues and mentees across prestigious ivory towers around the world to express my profound thoughts on the immense contributions you made in making my dream of earning and holding a postdoc from the premier university a dream come true!

Dear Dr. Byerly, thank you for your humanity, humility and honor. Thank you for being one of the few ones who were approachable and helpful. The good legacy some of us as your mentees are so proud of is that we are all *Byerlys* because you are etched in our hearts forever. I also hope you find joy and peace, contentment and satisfaction as you chart a new course. This article, and by extension this festschrift is aimed at upholding the memory and legacy of Dr. Carolyn M. Byerly, a truly caring mother of CCMS, a true daughter of Howard University, and a shining ambassador of critical feminist media studies. I find immense joy in having known her and I do hope that everyone within and outside the Howard University community will too.

## References

Asante, G., Sekimoto, S., & Brown, C. (2016). Becoming "Black": Exploring the racialized experiences of African immigrants in the United States. *Howard Journal of Communications*, 27(4), 367–384. https://doi.org/10.1080/10646175.2016.1206047.

Bishop, S. (2021). 16 feminist media studies, 7 questions about working in the university (and beyond). *Feminist Media Studies*, *21*(8), 1338–1359.

Byerly, C. (1995). News, consciousness, and social participation: The role of women's feature service in world news. In A. N. Valdivia (Ed.), *Feminism, multiculturalism, and the media: Global diversities* (pp. 105–122). Sage.

Byerly, C. (2011). Behind the scenes of women's broadcast ownership. *The Howard Journal of Communications*, *22*(1), 24–42.

Byerly, C. M. (2013). Factors affecting the status of women journalists: A structural analysis. In C. M. Byerly (Eds.), *The Palgrave international handbook of women and journalism*. Palgrave Macmillan. https://doi.org/10.1057/9781137273246_2

Byerly, C. M. (2017). Feminist intersectionality research in communications: Origins, contributions and tensions. *Ex Aequo*, 35, 23–32. http://exaequo.apem-estudos.org/artigo/35-feminist-intersectionality-research-in-communications-origins-contributions-and-tensions

Byerly, C. M. (2018). Feminism, theory, and communication: Progress, debates, and challenges ahead. In D. Harp, J. Loke, & I. Bachmann (Eds.), *Feminist approaches to media theory and research* (pp. 19–35). Palgrave Macmillan. https://doi.org/10.1007/978-3-319-90838-0

Byerly, C. M. (2019). Gender equality and media structures. In A. Vega Montiel & S. Macharia (Eds.), *Setting the gender agenda for communication policy.* United Nations Educational, Scientific & Cultural Organization. https://en.unesco.org/gamagandunitwin

Byerly, C. M., & Hill, M. (2012). Reformulation theory: Gauging feminist impact on news of violence against women. *Journal of Research on Women and Gender, 3*(2), 8.

Durham, M. (2026). Optimistic feminist praxis: On Carolyn Byerly's contributions to transformative feminist activism. In U. S. Akpan (Ed.), *Moving the marginalized to the center: Dr. Carolyn M. Byerly's research and pedagogy.* Peter Lang.

Jack-Davies, A. (2018, April 30). *Navigating racism: Black graduate students need support.* The Conversation, United States. https://theconversation.com/navigating-racism-black-graduate-students-need-support-92550

The Journal of Blacks in Higher Education. (n.d.). *Black faculty in higher education: Still only a drop in the bucket.* https://www.jbhe.com/features/55_blackfaculty.html

Karen, R. (2026). CB: The ultimate feminist-sister-scholar. In U. S. Akpan (Ed.), *Moving the marginalized to the center: Dr. Carolyn M. Byerly's research and pedagogy.* Peter Lang.

Mohammed, W. (2021). Decolonizing African media studies. *Howard Journal of Communications, 32*(2), 123–138. https://doi.org/10.1080/10646175.2021.1871868

Roseboro, A. (2026). Mentor or other mother? Byerly feminism meets black feminist thought at a Historically Black College and University. In U. S. Akpan (Ed.), *Moving the marginalized to the center: Dr. Carolyn M. Byerly's research and pedagogy.* Peter Lang.

# Section II

# Research

# 1

# CB: The Ultimate Feminist-Sister-Scholar

KAREN ROSS

The routes into feminist consciousness are as many and varied as the minds in which it resides. I was a rather late bloomer in this respect and that I found my way at all is due in no small part to the person who is at the heart of this Festschrift, the inestimable Professor Emerita Carolyn Byerly who will be named henceforth in my chapter as "CB," the abbreviation and nickname which I used routinely in addressing my friend, colleague and feminist-in-arms.

I had an unexceptional but decidedly apolitical upbringing, one of a pair of twin daughters whose parents were solid, lower-middle-class homeowners who had no greater ambitions for their girl children than to get a job, get a husband, get a house, get a baby (or two) and live an unremarkable life unburdened by aspirations of imagining that there was anything more than this simple life trajectory. I dutifully followed parts of this plan, got married at 19, had a husband and a house but I eschewed the baby because in some deeply buried part of myself, I knew there *was* something more than that and that I was going to find it, taste it, live it.

Leaving that (first) husband in my mid-20s in search of myself, I became the first person in my family to go to university, sliding under the radar of the standard academic passage by enrolling onto an access course and then into the second year of bachelor's program, astonishing myself, not to mention my parents, by achieving a 1st class (honors) degree. Having been written off as a lazy and aggressive teenager, I realized much later that I was simply disaffected by the rigidity of a school curriculum that did not tolerate a more creative mindset. A year spent as a youth worker in inner London brought me up close and personal to the realities, albeit secondhand, of racism and my first encounters with and recognition of the rampant inequalities that existed then, in the 1980s (and of course, still exist in the 2020s) for everyone marginalized by their race (in this case) but also their sex, their class, their status in society. A grant then allowed me to embark on a doctoral program at Warwick University where I wrote my dissertation on the role that popular TV plays in fueling the white imagination about, and subsequent behavior toward, minority communities. I assumed that I would then spend my academic career further developing this interest, but, as so often happens, life's vicissitudes prompted me to pivot in a completely different direction, and this is where the story of me and CB begins.

I should say that I have written these opening paragraphs because there is seldom the opportunity for more experienced feminist scholars to say something about their entrance into the academy, to share their lived experience with newer generations who may imagine that we all enjoyed an easy and straightforward route into the academic world. That may well be the case for our male colleagues but so many women, including myself and indeed CB, came late(r) to the academy because they had a life before and actually, that life experience is exactly what makes us empathic as teachers, as feminists, as humans.

After three precarious postdoc years of short-term research contracts, I found myself working in the world-renowned Centre for Mass Communications Research at Leicester University which, at that time, was under the careful stewardship of Professor Anabelle Sreberny who sadly passed away in January 2023. Although we didn't always see eye to eye, I had a lot of respect for her and its was largely her prompting that encouraged me to take my first foray into the world of feminist research after I had been complaining about how my local media framed me very differently to my male colleague when we were out campaigning to be the local councilor for our town. Turning my attention to the ways in which mainstream media reported on other political women led to my first publication on the topic (Ross, 1994), quickly followed by three further publications, two of which were co-authored with Annabelle (Ross, 1995; Ross & Sreberny-Mohammedi, 1996, 1997).

Scarcely without noticing, I had become a feminist media scholar and with this newfound passion, kindled not only by my early publication success which was amazing for a relatively newly fledged academic, but because suddenly my professional, private and political selves collided and then settled into a satisfying and mutually reinforcing research agenda. It was with this newly forming feminist consciousness that I took a flight to Taiwan to present at my first-ever international conference. It was here that I first met CB. Together with another (male) scholar from the United States, we three were the only non-Taiwanese speakers attending the conference, and we had the rather weird experience of spending the entire conference (which felt like a week but was probably only two or three days) with our own personal translator sitting behind each of us, whispering in our ears. I still have a photo of me and CB from that conference, leaning against some highly decorated wall and looking impossibly young.

What I appreciated then and have done so ever since, was CB's non-patronizing kindness toward a younger and relatively inexperienced colleague who was still developing her voice. She introduced me to the world of feminist media theory and after we had each returned home after that conference, she invited me as a visitor to Radford University where she was then teaching. As well as working with her students, I also got to hang out with her and her partner at their home since she insisted I stay with her instead of some anonymous hotel. She didn't just talk the talk of sisterhood, she practiced it in ways that most of us would like to emulate, but rarely do. During that visit, I got to learn about CB's activism, especially prior to her taking up an academic career and was a little bit in awe of what she had achieved compared with my meager political efforts which largely focused on developing strategies to combat dog waste on pavements and enforcing desist notices to noisy neighbors.

While spending time with colleagues outside the explicitly academic context may seem nothing more than enjoying entertaining social discourse—and we certainly enjoyed a lot of food, walks and laughter—telling each other our stories, our hopes and aspirations, both for ourselves but also for the world can foment a real shift in our thinking. And so it was with me and CB. She always pushed me with her "but why?" questions, often in response to some glib comment I had made about wanting to be an elected politician or an activist or a university president. She got me really thinking about what it meant to be a feminist, not just in the context of research but in the real world, in our relationships with other people, how we act in our communities. Sometimes, you meet someone by chance and you just hit it off and so it was with me and CB. We hit it off in Taipei and we consolidated that liking as academic colleagues into a liking as human beings and, as it turns out, my following her lead into a lifetime's commitment as a feminist.

After Radford, we kept in touch irregularly and we got on with own projects but in 2001, I attended my first International Communication Association conference in Washington DC and, through CB's generous brokerage, was first inducted into the joys, sisterliness and enormous fund of collective wisdom and knowledge which was the Feminist Scholarship Division. To use a very modern idiom, I found my tribe. What I discovered was a whole world of feminist research endeavor that went considerably beyond my own interest in women and representation. By then, I had got involved in the Global Media Monitoring Project which started in 1995 and is about to celebrate its 30th anniversary in 2025, first as the UK coordinator and then later also coordinating the European team. What I had already begun to realize was that there was a relationship between representation and production and that the political economy of the media was inextricably linked to sex-based disadvantage through the wielding of male power and control. What I hadn't realized at that point was the importance of CB's own work in this particular area, how she was in the vanguard of scholars analyzing this crucial element of media ecology through the lens of feminist theory (see Byerly, 2002, 2004, 2011). She was also among the first scholars to look at the contributions that women media professionals were making to the wider news landscape (Byerly, 1995, 2000).

In the early 2000s, possibly 2001 during that year's ICA conference, Jayne Fargnoli at Blackwell asked us if we would like to edit a collection of essays on women and media. I can't now really remember how the conversation started or who was approached first, but the upshot was that me and CB decided that we would do it and the resulting book project further consolidated our working relationship. You never really know someone as a colleague until you start working with them, relying on them to do their bit of a shared venture.

When you are working across continents and time-zones, that relationship can get pretty strained but actually, it was a truly enjoyable experience, working alongside CB as co-editor, and with a group of great feminist media scholars who all submitted on time, their chapters needing the lightest of light touches and the whole thing brought together by us in less than 24 months (Ross & Byerly, 2004). Phew! Such was the success of both our working relationship and the book that Jane suggested that perhaps we would like to write a "companion" text, where we could explore the ideas and practices of women and media in a richer and more expansive way, perhaps identifying some kind of schema to elucidate different forms of action and activism within the gendered media space.

We had been thinking along exactly the same lines and so our second collaborative book project took off (Byerly & Ross, 2006). It's one thing to bring together a collection of essays as editors, but it's quite another to work on a monograph where authors have different experiences and expertise, different styles, different ways of writing. But we did it and we did it pretty well. Or rather, Carolyn provided the intellectual thinking and creative heft to develop what we went on to call the Model of Women's Media Action in which we identified four pathways to action. I was more focused on providing the scholarly background and context as well as undertaking some of the interviews that informed the development of our model. That book is still in print as I write this chapter in 2023, a testament to the importance of that model as a way of thinking about how and in what ways women have agency in different media contexts.

As a consequence of listening and talking with CB about the politico-economic aspects of media systems and thus upskilling myself in this aspect of gendered media relations, I felt confident to tender for a project being funded by the European Institute for Gender Equality to explore the extent to which women occupied senior positions across a range of large-scale, mainstream media outlets. I won that tender as PI and worked with two other fantastic women scholars—Claudia Padovani (University of Padova, Italy) and Erzsébet Barát (Central European University, Hungary)—in shaping the project, and then with a further 25 wonderful women scholars in the other (then) EU Member States who undertook the fieldwork in their respective countries (2012–2013). This was the first all-EU analysis ever to be undertaken and produced both an important dataset and several publications (Ross, 2014; Ross & Padovani, 2016), but also taught me several things about myself including how to be both patient and diplomatic.

As it happened, I was once again following in the footsteps of CB's own scholarship in this broad area because the year before, she had undertaken a global study that had looked at the experiences of women media professionals, first published as a technical report for the Women's Media Foundation and then as an edited collection (Byerly, 2013). Our combined scholarship in mapping the location, employment terms and status of women media professionals, with both European and global perspectives, incorporating both surveys and interviews has shone a light on the gendered working practices of media organizations including gender pay gaps and other discriminations, but also a range of positive initiatives such as women's leadership training and equality policies which are both implemented and monitored. Our academic lives have crisscrossed over time and space but always with a strong feminist ethos guiding our work.

While the discussion so far has looked at CB's contribution to the research literature and its influence on my work, I would now like to turn to the other crucial aspect of doing feminist scholarship and that's the bit about us, as human beings, how we actually practice what we preach, how we incorporate a feminist sensibility in our relations with others, how we act in real life, not simply how we apply a feminist lens in the academic work we do. Although I admit that I'm rather biased and of course, this is something of a generalization, I *do* think there is something special about the community of feminist media scholars which is about a generosity of spirit and the giving of time which feeds us and makes us feel welcome, whatever our generation, however sporadic our meetings. In the same year that our monograph was published, CB organized a one-day, ICA pre-conference in Dresden which showcased feminist news scholarship and activism from across the globe. These moments of sharing, both of new ideas and thinking but also of experiences (good and bad) are precious in building a community of interest and practice which prompts not only confidence in our own work but also opens up the possibilities for collaborative working as it has done so fruitfully between me and CB.

I have always appreciated CB's approach to both academics and life more generally and her genuine desire to lift up others, and this is nowhere more notable than in her involvement in the setting up of the Teresa Award—she and Marian Meyers as trustees of the fund, established with a donation from another great feminist scholar, Yoo Jae Song—and then the Helen Award for young/er scholars and most recently establishing her own award (the Byerly Award) with a focus on scholars working in the specific field of feminist political economy. This latter is merely the latest example of CB's commitment to supporting both feminist scholarship but also a scholarship focused on political economy, not just with warm words but with her own, hard-earned cash. Speaking truth to power is easy enough to write in the pages of a text or in an Insta post, but actually doing something concrete to support feminist scholarship is rather less in evidence.

I am one of the recipients of the Teresa Award (2013) made at the ICA conference in London that year by the Feminist Scholarship Division, and all the more wonderful because my friends and family were able to be at the ceremony. Ten years on, I still remember the glee that CB took in telling some embarrassing stories about my various indiscretions which had somehow slipped into our many conversations over the years, but it was all good. I attended the Teresa Awards before and since my own event and they have always been joyous and collegial occasions, serving to reinforce the power of a connected and committed feminist collective which is mutually nurturing and respectful. We can learn from each other whatever our experience, however many books we've published or papers we've written. Who knew that in 2022, our students would be getting their news from TikTok? Well, some of our young/er colleagues saw that particular writing on the wall way before many of the rest of us did! That's the point, right? To support and encourage the next generation to boldly go where we have not been before and, at least speaking for myself, are not so interested in going anyway.

Even though CB is now, allegedly, retired, she still seems as busy as ever. As I write this chapter, she is fully involved in writing her fifth book, this time taking an intersectional approach to the political economy of communication by synergizing three discrete but overlapping elements, that is gender, race and class, in order to construct a more nuanced lens through which to interrogate communication practices. As with all the multiple things she does, I'm sure her latest project will be full of insight, informed and honed by a lifetime of committed feminist media scholarship. I very much look forward to reading it. If this is indeed her last hurrah, it seems a fitting one, bringing together all that she has learned about, and contributed to, the field of feminist media research. It's a good legacy to leave behind: it is her superpower.

## References

Byerly, C. (1995). News, consciousness and social participation: The role of women's feature service in world news. In A. Valdivia (Ed.), *Feminism, multiculturalism and the media*. Sage. Reprinted in Sreberny-Mohammadi, A., Winseck, D., McKenna, J., &Boyd-Barrett, O. (Eds.). (1997). *Media in global context: A reader* (pp. 248–258). Arnold.

Byerly, C. (2000). Women's feature service. In E. Burt (Ed.), *Historical dictionary of women's press organizations* (pp. 265–272). Greenwood Press.

Byerly, C. (2002). Gender and the political economy of newsmaking: A case study of human rights coverage. In E. R. Meehan & E. Riordan (Eds.), *Sex and money: Intersections of feminism and political economy* (pp. 130–144). University of Minnesota.

Byerly, C. (2004). Women and the concentration of media ownership. In R. R. Rush, C. C. Oukrup, & P. Creedon (Eds.), *Women in journalism and mass communication: A 30-year summary* (pp. 245–262). Lawrence Erlbaum Associates.

Byerly, C. (2011). *Global report on status of women in news media* (Technical report). International Women's Media Foundation.

Byerly, C. (Ed.). (2013). *Palgrave international handbook on women and journalism*. Palgrave Macmillan.

Byerly, C., & Karen, R. (2006). *Women and media: A critical introduction*. Blackwell.

Ross, K. (1994). Bambi, thumper and the one in the dress: Press coverage of the Labour Party's leadership campaign—1994. *Everywoman, 110*, 12–13. Also translated into Polish, in E Oleksy (Ed.) (1999). *Mass media in civil society* (pp. 53–56). Lodz: University of Lodz.

Ross, K. (1995). Gender and party politics: how the press reported the labour leadership campaign, 1994. *Media, Culture & Society, 17*(3), 499–509.

Ross, K. (2014). Women in media industries in Europe: What's wrong with this picture? *Feminist Media Studies, 14*(2), 326–330.

Ross, K., & Byerly, C. (Eds.). (2004). *Women and media: International perspectives*. Blackwell.

Ross, K., & Padovani, C. (Eds.). (2016). *Gender equality and the media: A challenge for Europe*. Routledge/ECREA.

Ross, K., & Sreberny-Mohammadi, A. (1996). Reporting the body politic: Women MPs and the media. *Parliamentary Affairs, 49*(1), 103–115.

Ross, K., & Sreberny-Mohammadi, A. (1997). Playing house—gender, politics and the news media in Britain. *Media, Culture & Society, 19*(1), 101–109.

# 2

# A Feminist International Perspective on Women, Media and Power

## *Reflections on Meetings with Dr. Carolyn M. Byerly*

MARGARET GALLAGHER

The email was innocuously titled "An invitation to participate in a festschrift in honour of Dr Carolyn Byerly." Of course, I thought. I'm so familiar with her work—this will be straightforward and enjoyable. But when I looked closely at that formidable list of publications and achievements, and started to sift through my own memories, I found it hard to organize my commentary in a coherent way. In the end, I opted for a roughly chronological account, structured around our meetings over the past 35 years. Inevitably, this results in a personal appreciation, slanted toward aspects that have coincided with my own professional preoccupations. Beyond that, I hope it pays due tribute to the prolific scholar, courageous feminist, exemplary colleague, and generous friend who is Carolyn Byerly.

## The Women's Feature Service: An International Starting Point

*Paris, France, October 4, 1989.* It is mid-morning as I wait for my visitor—an American graduate student who is coming to talk to me about the women's feature service (WFS). This UNESCO-initiated project had been set up in 1978 to create space for women journalists and news about women in the global information system; I had worked on it as a consultant in the early 1980s. The graduate student was Carolyn Byerly. This would be our first meeting, which—in that pre-email, pre-mobile phone era—had been set up through an exchange of letters and perhaps the occasional new-fangled fax. I learned later that the phone call I received that morning from Carolyn (or "cb" to use her preferred sign-off) to confirm our meeting was made from a local post office, there being no telephone for guests at her small hotel. We sat in my tiny study, drinking coffee and talking through my documents about the WFS before heading out for lunch (salade Niçoise for CB), after which Carolyn set off for UNESCO. There, for days, she combed through box after box of badly organized notes and scraps of paper and reports on the WFS project. "No xerox machines or cell phones available then, so I literally had to take notes of things that seemed to matter. . . . It was all an adventure" (personal communication, April 8, 2023). The research would be integral to her doctoral dissertation, completed the following year (Byerly, 1990).

The Paris "adventure" would mark the beginning of a lasting collegial friendship fostered by shared professional concerns which were evident in the focus of that dissertation: the absence of women in mainstream media content both as news protagonists and producers; women's struggles and strategies to intervene in news-making processes and outputs; the structural basis of media power and its effects, from the local to the international level; the role of feminist activism in challenging male-dominated systems; and an overarching belief in the value of situating studies of gender and media in the context of global patterns and movements. At a time when little media scholarship looked beyond national boundaries, the decision to focus on the globally oriented WFS—"the first internationally organized effort to interrupt global news practices that had historically ignored and marginalized women's concerns and achievements" (Byerly, 1995, p. 118)—was remarkable. This early work, and the lessons drawn from it—in particular, the demonstrable value of "news production under the control of and in the service of women" (ibid., p. 120)—would be a spring-board for many strands of CB's research and writing in the decades to follow.

## An Agenda for Feminist Media Research and Action

*Arlington, Virginia, August 3–4, 2001.* The bond created in Paris endured, though it would be more than a decade until our next meeting in 2001. In the intervening years, CB was working her way through the complicated pathways of early academic life, with successive posts at Radford University, Ithaca College,

George Washington University, and the University of Maryland, before finally arriving at Howard University as a Visiting Associate Professor in January 2002. A few months earlier, at the Freedom Forum's headquarters in Arlington, we both gave papers at the Donna Allen Memorial Symposium. It was an event to mark the activism and scholarship of one of feminism's pioneers—founder of the Women's Institute for Freedom of the Press (WIFP) in 1972 and of *Media Report to Women*, a then monthly publication whose international scope was unique in those pre-internet days. Allen's feminist activism resonated strongly with CB. At the symposium, the Donna Allen Award for Feminist Advocacy—to recognize feminist media activists who promote women's rights and freedom—was established by the Commission on the Status of Women of the Association for Education in Journalism and Mass Communication (AEJMC). Ten years later, in 2011, the recipient would be Carolyn Byerly.

Donna Allen's goal to build a global women's democratic communication system chimed fully with CB's growing conviction of the need for a feminist political economy approach to media analysis and advocacy. Her presentation at the symposium, on media conglomeration (Byerly, 2001), presaged a line of research that would become central to her future academic work. The development of her thinking on this broad topic was honed through many conference papers and presentations in the late 1990s and early 2000s, and the publication of a chapter in an early, groundbreaking collection of essays linking feminist and political economy theories and research (Byerly, 2002). In this chapter she analyzed news coverage of the fiftieth anniversary of the Universal Declaration of Human Rights, finding that women's human rights were scarcely mentioned—despite "thirty years of global feminism that have revealed . . . the wide-ranging violations of women's human rights everywhere" (ibid., p. 141).

That exclusion followed a pattern already established by feminist media research, but CB's political economy analysis went deeper, highlighting the lack of any attempt in the coverage "to raise larger questions about the gendered nature of political and economic structures within which human rights (women's in particular) are violated" (p. 142). Feminist media scholarship, she concluded, must support feminist political action by making connections between the well-documented absence of women in news coverage "and the financial and policy contexts within which coverage is defined and produced" and "by expanding its commitment to problematize women's marginalization within the political economy of world capitalism" (p. 143). Beyond this, feminist media scholarship must intensify its questions about the role of human agency in social change and in particular the contribution of women-owned and feminist-owned media in circulating "oppositional analyses and information about women" (ibid.). These conclusions, building on her earlier study of the WFS, would in effect provide a research and action agenda for CB herself.

Several publications from 2004 show the evolution of that agenda in CB's writing. For instance, analysis of media ownership is the main subject of Byerly (2004a). However, the essay ranges over much wider terrain, including the influence of corporations and corporate donors on the content of journalism education programs and curricula, the obstacles—in terms of both hierarchical status and intellectual recognition—faced by feminist scholars in the academy, and the absence of gender-specific concerns and language in media reform movements. All of this adds up to a policy sphere that is either oblivious of or resistant to feminist analysis and intervention, and to the need to find ways "to join feminist journalism scholarship and political activism" (p. 259) to achieve a more democratic media system. Another chapter from that time (Byerly, 2004b) focuses on the newsroom, highlighting the work of the feminist, gay and lesbian press and of multicultural advocacy groups to challenge homophobia and to open the media industry not just to feminist voices, but to gay and lesbian voices and ethnicities. Egalitarian news access, Byerly concludes, helps to advance the presence and power of minorities both politically and culturally and is a matter of social justice.

This approach is extended in a third book chapter from that period (Byerly, 2004c), which looks at feminist interventions in newsrooms over a 30-year period, primarily in the United States, and attempts to develop a more theorized account of masculine hegemonic newsroom culture. This culture, Byerly argues, is reproduced within male news structures "whose products influence and serve to construct public opinion, public policy, citizens' understanding of society, and their daily lived experience in it" (p. 126). Feminist interventions are therefore crucial in relation to women's rights, and specifically women's right to communicate.

## Media Conglomeration, Globalization and Feminist Political Economy

*Dresden, Germany, June 18, 2006.* Now an Associate Professor at Howard University with tenure within reach, if not yet secured, CB had a stable academic environment in which to pursue several major lines of research alongside her teaching commitments. One important baseline initiative was the organization of an international symposium on women and news, a pre-conference held in conjunction with the 2006 International Communication Association (ICA) conference in Dresden. It brought together feminist researchers and activists to explore news research and social change agendas, including that of the Global Media Monitoring Project (GMMP) on which I worked as a consultant. The GMMP's third iteration in 2005 had monitored news coverage in 102 countries, and its networking and advocacy dimensions had become increasingly important. The symposium's focus on under-investigated areas -including financial structures of the news industry, media policy, media globalization, and the dynamics of news and social change—reflected CB's growing insistence on the need for macro-level studies of media, and for analysis of women's media activism in these wider contexts. For instance, also at the ICA 2006 conference she organized a roundtable session on "Women and the Media Globalization Syndrome: Emerging Research Agendas" in which her own paper on "Dialectical Lessons in Women's Media Activism" looked at women's relationship to media globalization in terms of their organized efforts to speak through the media, and as part of a historical gendered struggle for the right to communicate. These twin preoccupations—the politics of media globalization and the place of women's media activism within global social movements for communication rights—were now crystalizing into an important body of work. Two examples from that period illustrate something of the scope of this perspective.

In a wide-ranging critique of feminist media research, Byerly (2006) drew on globalization analyses in the work of scholars such as sociologist Saskia Sassen and political theorist Zillah Eisenstein to argue that globalization processes affect women's lives in material ways, and that the globalizing media industries "present a presumed and imminent threat to women's public speech and participation in democratic processes" (p. 47). However, she argued, the overwhelming focus of feminist research on micro-level studies of women's mediated representation means that "we lack a substantial body of empirical data and theory to help us understand where females fit into the larger scheme of today's global media in terms of access to capital and ownership, employment, and decision making" (p. 40). In particular, "we have a great and troublesome silence in our literature, as well as in our activist circles, regarding the development and passage of communications policy" (p. 49). To fill these gaps, CB set out a feminist research agenda built around four lines of inquiry that should "enable women to intervene in public policy and media operations, and encourage them to establish alternative media structures that strengthen women's voice and role in public deliberation, governance, and other sites that determine relations of power" (p. 40).

The second example is an especially important and original contribution to knowledge and to feminism—jointly authored by Byerly and Ross (2006). The first part of the volume is a culturally sensitive, critical review of existing literature on women and media, but it is the second part that breaks entirely new ground. Based on interviews with 90 feminist media activists, practitioners, and researchers in 20 countries, this extensive analysis of women's media activism sets out to reveal the influence and potential of a "historically significant but under-investigated and under-theorized aspect of women's relationship to contemporary media" (p. 3). Byerly and Ross propose a Model of Women's Media Action, identifying four "pathways" through which women's agency has created spaces for both media change and social change. They argue that this is part of a broader political process in which women media activists envisage a world in which "women's influence shapes everything from culture to social policy, advancing women in the process" (p. 232). This richly documented account was a groundbreaking attempt to theorize women's media activism and its relation to social change. Much-cited, it remains unique in the literature. Some years later, reflecting on the Model of Women's Media Action, Byerly (2012) said that it "challenged feminist media scholars to pose a more complete theory to explain the dialectical process formed by women's challenges to the androcentric media industries that operated without women's interests in mind" (p. 16). Yet, she argued, much feminist research remains trapped in a static critique that privileges representational over structural issues and fails to consider how feminism has come to "embed itself in media content, media policies, or other aspects of media industries" (ibid., p. 15). This critique of what she has described as "the stasis in women-and-media scholarship" can be found in much of CB's later work (e.g., Byerly, 2013a, 2016).

## Women and the News Media: A Global Study

*Newport Pagnell, England, June 18–19, 2008.* In late 2007, CB was contacted by the Washington-based International Women's Media Foundation (IWMF) about their plans for a study of women's positions in the news media worldwide. The challenges of mounting such a huge international study were immense, and the IWMF had been wrestling with its complexities for several years. With CB's commitment and involvement, by March 2008 funding had been secured and detailed planning was underway—with CB as principal investigator. In the 1990s, I had conducted a more limited international study of women's employment in media which had not been replicated since, and which would be a methodological starting point for the new IWMF research. So it was that in June 2008 CB found her way to my home—now in England, to where I had moved from Paris—to talk through some of the details of the upcoming study. While we pored over questions of selection, categories, coding, and the problems of making international comparisons, our partners Kay and Alan explored the by-ways of the small, rural town where we lived. It was a short visit, but one that laid the ground for a continuing, intensive exchange of ideas that lasted throughout the two-year period of the global study.

The result (Byerly, 2011a) remains "the most complete picture to date of women's status globally in news media ownership, publishing, governance, reporting, editing, photojournalism, broadcast production and other media jobs" (p. 7). The study covered 170,00 individuals employed in 522 news companies across 59 countries—by far the most extensive research project of its kind carried out before or since. The 390-page Global Report is packed with data not just on occupational status, but on salaries, hiring and promotional policies, news assignments and other gendered workplace practices. It is, however, basically a technical, quantitative report. Convinced that this unique, vast trove of data deserved a level of academic and contextual analysis that had been beyond the remit of the Global Report, CB set about finding a publisher for a volume of essays inspired by the original research.

The task proved exceptionally difficult. In an insightful preface to the eventual published volume (Byerly, 2013b), CB reflected on how the problem of media conglomeration—a topic on which she herself had written with reference to the news industry—had also affected the publishing industry, "threatening the existence of serious academic work" as well as of researchers and staff employed in publishing (p. xiii). Happily, a publisher did come forward and the eventual volume, rich in data and theoretical perspectives, promises to be a solid reference work on women and journalism for decades to come.

The insights from this global study would inform much of CB's later thinking and work. In Byerly and McGraw (2020), the data were analyzed in combination with other global data sources—for example, the World Economic Forum's Global Gender Gap Index and the Global Media Monitoring Project—to examine relationships between women's position in news organizations, their standing in other social realms and their presence in news content. Tentative, but nonetheless important correlations were found—for example, supporting "the claim that women's numbers in the newsroom matter to news content about women" (p. 218); at the same time, a "ceiling effect" is in operation so that this finding is true "only to a certain extent" (p. 219). Alongside this meticulous statistical study, broader think-pieces on the need for feminist intervention in macro-level media research and in media policy studies (e.g., Byerly, 2013a, 2019a) illustrate how already-present preoccupations with macro-level media structures and decision-making processes had been reinforced by an immersion in the issues thrown up by the global study.

## Feminist Intervention in Macro-Level Media Research and Policy Studies

*Paris, France, February 28–March 1, 2013.* In early 2013 CB and myself, along with our friend and colleague Ammu Joseph, were invited by UNESCO to join a 27-member international advisory group to write material for UNESCO's upcoming report titled *World Trends in the State of Freedom of Expression and Media Development.* We three were to provide ideas and input for the gender dimensions of the Report's main themes: media freedom, media plurality and media independence. At a two-day workshop held to present first drafts of the requested material, we found ourselves in the company of eminent colleagues, not all of whom understood the need for gender-disaggregated data or indeed why gender (one of UNESCO's global, cross-cutting priorities) should be included as a focus of the Report. The final evening, over dinner at a bistro whose specialty we belatedly realized was steaks, Ammu and I admired the sang-froid with which CB—a non-meat eater—reacted to the large platter of raw steaks from which we were invited to make our choice, before sending the staff away to put together a tasty meal of vegetables. With a good bottle of wine, we reflected on lessons learned at the workshop including—a favorite topic—the blindness of most of our male colleagues to feminist media research, and the marginalization of feminist scholarship within the academy. In 2020 CB would be invited by UNESCO to contribute to a later edition of the same Report. Seven years after the 2013 workshop, a similar sense of bemusement at the inclusion of "gender" characterized the 2020 meeting, with no greater acknowledgment of feminist analysis or of the ways that "women continue to be marginalized in the freedom of expression assessment" (personal communication, March 21, 2020).

By the time of our 2013 Paris meeting, CB had been a full Professor at Howard University since 2010. In these later years of her career, she built a corpus of empirical data on women's media ownership in the United States (Byerly, 2011b; 2016 with Valentin) and on media conglomeration as a global concern

(Byerly, 2014a), and continued to develop her analysis of feminist activism and its relationship to communication policy (Byerly, 2017a). Also in this period, together with colleagues at Howard, CB produced an important series of studies and critiques of lack of progress in the promotion of race-conscious and gender-conscious communication policies in the United States. For example, Byerly et al. (2011) take a public interest perspective on media policy, analyzing the "ways in which the needs and interests of women and people of color figure into such policies" (p. 438), documenting the shortcomings in policy implementation, and critiquing the "barriers erected by the economic system that privileges the powerful few over the less powerful majority" (ibid.).

In this work, CB brought together macro-level studies of media concentration and media conglomeration with a feminist analysis of power, gender and race discrimination to arrive at a structural critique of the intersectional nature of oppression. In Byerly (2017b), she described this process and its evolution in her work, "which has reached increasingly to Marxist analysis of capitalist relations to examine the problems of gender and race in the media: For the last decade, I have been examining communication policy with respect to its enablement of media conglomeration and the further marginalization women and racial minority ownership in the United States. . . . In all cases, these macro-level inquiries have taken me face-to-face with the structure of capitalism in which those in the powerful elite class have been able to dominate by financing their candidates for public office and in doing so also affect communication policy to serve their interests" (p. 30). This focus and these themes would be brought together and further developed in CB's late career book-length study of intersectionality, political economy and media (Byerly, 2024), marking the summation and integration of many varied strands of analysis pursued over the previous several decades.

## Walking the Talk of Feminist Activism, Research and Policy Intervention

*Mexico City, May 27–28, 2015.* Twenty years after the 1995 World Conference on Women in Beijing, CB and I were guest speakers at an international forum on Gender, Media, ICTs and Journalism. The forum was organized by Aimée Vega Montiel, a researcher at the Universidad Nacional Autónoma de México (UNAM), who was also the leader of the IAMCR Task Force on GAMAG—the Global Alliance on Media and Gender. The launch of the Latin-American and Caribbean chapter of GAMAG was among several events taking place at the forum. This global movement was an obvious channel for CB's multi-focal commitment to activism, research and policy intervention, and she played a key role in the Alliance since its launch in 2013. Her engagement has gone beyond regular scholarly presentations and contributions to GAMAG's publications (Byerly, 2014b, 2019b), to an involvement with its management and administration—as Chair of the GAMAG Research and Policy Committee (2016–2020) and since 2015 as a member of its International Steering Committee.

It is difficult to underestimate the importance of these contributions—voluntarily given, and undertaken alongside heavy departmental and faculty workloads—to the stability and growth of an international network such as GAMAG, whose survival depends on the regular input of ideas and expertise to resolve issues at many levels. It is a mark of the integrity of CB's commitment to the pursuit of change through a combination of activism and research that activists and academics alike have benefited from her generously given time, advice and support.

## Influence and Legacy

*The Virtual Future.* The May 2015 forum in Mexico City was to be our last "in-person" meeting. The era of letter-writing in which we first met in Paris is part of history. Now email delivers instant communication and virtual meeting platforms are commonplace, though an eight-hour time difference can complicate scheduling. But in truth, the chronology of our face-to-face meetings—just six spread over 35 years—demonstrates that connection is created through a shared worldview and cemented through empathy, rather than through regular personal contact. That said, the occasional opportunity to put the world to rights over a bottle of wine has forged good memories and a strong bond.

In July 2021 CB stepped down from her position as Professor and department Chair at Howard University. What followed could not be described as "retirement," but an extension of the research, writing, conference presentations, and community involvement that has filled her life for decades—complemented by a 3000-mile house move from the east to the west coast of the USA in 2022. We remain in close touch, whether through virtual participation in events or through writing collaborations (e.g., Byerly, 2023). CB's contribution to the field is destined to endure, not simply through her many publications but also her visible commitment to the promotion of feminist media scholarship. A highly engaged member, and one-time officer, of the ICA's Feminist Scholarship Division (FSD), she created the Byerly Award for Research in the Feminist Political Economy of Communication, to be awarded annually by the FSD for feminist research into macro-level issues in communication. The first award was made in 2023. In the same year, CB herself received the FSD's Teresa Award for the Advancement of Feminist Scholarship in recognition of her work on feminist political economy.

Throughout her career, CB has returned regularly to fundamental themes in feminist media scholarship—for example, the issue of gendered hegemonic power and its structural underpinnings; the relationship between movement-building and social change; the under-explored and under-theorized role of women's activism in advancing a democratic communication system; women's agency in the creation of a feminist public sphere. Her feminist political economy analysis of these macro-level concerns has made an indelible mark on the field, and one which will be extended not only through her own future work but that of the Byerly Award recipients. Thank you, Carolyn!

## References

Byerly, C. M. (1990) *The women's feature services and the making of world news* [Unpublished doctoral dissertation]. University of Washington.

Byerly, C. M. (1995). News, consciousness, and social participation: The role of women's feature service in world news. In A. Valdivia (Ed.), *Feminism, multiculturalism and the media* (pp. 105–120). Sage.

Byerly, C. M. (2001, August 3–4). *Inside conglomeration: Toward a feminist analytics of media mergers* [Conference presentation]. Donna Allen Memorial Symposium, Arlington, VA, United States.

Byerly, C. M. (2002). Gender and the political economy of newsmaking: A case study of human rights coverage. In E. R. Meehan & E. Riordan (Eds.), *Sex & money: Feminism and political economy in the media* (pp. 130–144). University of Minnesota Press.

Byerly, C. M. (2004a). Women and the concentration of media ownership. In R. R. Rush, C. Oukrup & P. Creedon (Eds.), *Women in journalism and mass communication: A 30-year summary* (pp. 245–262). Lawrence Erlbaum Associates.

Byerly, C. M. (2004b). Shifting sites: Feminist, gay and lesbian newsroom activism in the U.S. context. In M. de Bruin & K. Ross (Eds.), *Gender and newsroom cultures: Identities at work* (pp. 221–239). Hampton Press.

Byerly, C. M. (2004c). Feminist interventions in newsrooms. In K. Ross & C. M. Byerly (Eds.) *Women and media: International perspectives* (pp. 109–131). Blackwell.

Byerly, C. M. (2006). Feminist research in an era of globalization. *Redes.com (Revista de estudios para el desarrollo social de la comunicación*; special issue on gender and media), *3*, 39–52.

Byerly, C. M. (2011a). *Global Report on the status of women in the news media.* International Women's Media Foundation.

Byerly, C. M. (2011b). Behind the scenes of women's broadcast ownership. *Howard Journal of Communications, 22*(1), 24–42. https://doi.org/10.1080/10646175.2011.546740

Byerly, C. M. (2012). The geography of women and media scholarship. In K. Ross (Ed.), *The handbook of gender, sex, and media* (pp. 3–19). Wiley-Blackwell.

Byerly, C. M. (2013a). Women and media control: Feminist interrogations at the macro level. In C. Carter, L. Steiner, & L. McLaughlin (Eds.), *The Routledge companion to media and gender* (pp. 105–115). Routledge.

Byerly, C. M. (Ed.). (2013b). *Palgrave international handbook on women and journalism.* Palgrave Macmillan.

Byerly, C. M. (2014a). Media conglomeration and women's interests: A global concern. *Feminist Media Studies, 14*(2), 322–326. https://doi.org/10.1080/14680777.2014.909137

Byerly, C. M. (2014b). The long struggle of women and news. In A. Vega Montiel (Ed.), *Media and gender: A scholarly agenda for the Global Alliance on Media and Gender* (pp. 40–43). UNESCO/IAMCR. https://unesdoc.unesco.org/ark:/48223/pf0000228399

Byerly, C. M. (2016) Stasis and shifts in feminist media scholarship. In C. Cerqueira, R. Cabecinhas & S. I. Magalhães (Eds.), *Gender in focus: (New) trends in media* (pp. 15–27). CECS. https://core.ac.uk/download/pdf/229416126.pdf

Byerly, C. M. (2017a). Feminist activism and U.S. communications policy. In V. Pickard & G. Yang (Ed.), *Media activism: Charting an evolving field of research* (pp. 100–119). Routledge.

Byerly, C. M. (2017b). Feminist intersectionality research in communications: Origins, contributions and tensions. *Ex Aequo, 35*, 23–32. https://doi.org/10.22355/exaequo.2017.35.02

Byerly, C. M. (2019a). Neoliberalism and women's right to communicate: The politics of ownership and voice in media. In M. Meyers (Ed.), *Neoliberalism and the media* (pp. 60–74). Routledge.

Byerly, C. M. (2019b). Gender equality, policy and media structures. In A. Vega Montiel & S. Macharia (Eds.), *Setting the gender agenda for communication policy: New proposals from the Global Alliance on Media and Gender* (pp. 23–34). UNESCO/GAMAG. https://unesdoc.unesco.org/ark:/48223/pf0000368962.locale=en

Byerly, C. M. (2023). Gender dimensions of communication industries: A political economy analysis. In M. Gallagher & A. Vega Montiel (Eds.), *The handbook on gender, communication, and women's human rights.* Wiley-Blackwell.

Byerly, C. M. (2024). *Intersectionality, political economy, and media: Unifying gender, race, and class analysis* [Working title]. Routledge.

Byerly, C. M., & McGraw, K. A. (2020). Axes of power: Examining women's access to leadership positions in the news media. In M. Djerf-Pierre & M. Edström (Eds.), *Comparing gender and media equality across the globe: A cross-national study of the quality, causes and consequences of gender equality in the news media* (pp. 191–232). Nordicom. https://doi.org/10.48335/9789188855329-5

Byerly, C. M., Park, Y. J., & Miles, R. (2011). Race and gender-conscious policies: Toward a more egalitarian communications future. *Journal of Information Policy, 1*, 425–440.

Byerly, C. M., & Ross, K. (2006). *Women and media: A critical introduction*. Blackwell.
Byerly, C. M., & Valentin, A. (2016). Women's access to media: Legal dimensions of ownership and employment in the United States. In R. Lind (Ed.), *Race and gender in electronic media: Content, context, culture* (pp. 267–292). Routledge.

# 3 Optimistic Feminist Praxis: On Dr. Carolyn M. Byerly's Contributions to Transformative Feminist Activism

MEENAKSHI GIGI DURHAM

> *Feminist work in all of its forms lends itself to radical theory building because that work aims to transform society in ways that represent women's vision [and] lived experiences . . .*
>
> —Byerly and Hill (2012, p. 3)

Being a feminist is an active, not passive, identity location. It involves challenging systems of oppression, particularly in the form that bell hooks describes as "white supremacist capitalist patriarchy" (hooks, 1995, p. 29). Having a feminist conscience and consciousness —two words that are related in essence as well as form—means confronting the reality of gender and social injustices and engaging in ethical opposition to them. Carolyn Byerly's work as a scholar and teacher embodies these tenets of feminism, connecting theory and practice into praxis—that is, real-world activism informed and animated by conceptual rigor. Over the many years that I have known Carolyn, I have been struck by her steadfast commitment to this aspect of feminist epistemology.

I first heard of Carolyn's work almost three decades ago, through the Feminist Scholarship Division of the International Communication Association, when we were both starting out in faculty positions. She was a compelling presence at ICA conferences around the world, and over the years, not only did I learn about her research at paper presentations, but I gained perspective and clarity from her direct, incisive comments at divisional business meetings and through the informal gatherings where many of us exchanged ideas and talked politics deep into the evening—often with my young daughters listening in, because as an assistant professor, I often had no option but to bring them with me. (They are both strong feminist women today, thanks in part to early exposure to Carolyn's perspectives.) Later, Carolyn and I were among the small group of feminist scholars who launched the journal *Feminist Media Studies* and remain on its editorial board. And as long as I've known Carolyn, her wholehearted and steadfast embrace of praxis as a key aspect of feminist scholarship has been unwavering and inspiring.

Indeed, her first book, *The Mother's Book* (Byerly, 1985), emerged from her on-the-ground experiences working with mothers of abused children in rape crisis centers and women's shelters. Written for women whose children were sexual abuse survivors, Carolyn used feminist approaches to family structures, patriarchal power dynamics, compulsory heterosexuality, and gender violence to offer clear, accessible, and compassionate support and guidance to traumatized women and children. The book has been reprinted twice and remains a lodestone in the field of survivor advocacy, exemplifying her commitment to praxis. In this Festschrift volume, the brilliance and the practicability of Carolyn's work is addressed in many ways. She is perhaps best known for her piercing critiques of the media environment and its treatment of women and other minoritized people. Her analyses of media ownership (Byerly, 2006), newsroom cultures (Byerly & Wilson, 2009) and reporting on sexual violence (Byerly, 1994), among other topics, have highlighted ongoing patterns of exclusion, marginalization, and negligence of women and people of color. "Women are, in many ways, still 'window dressing' for industries where men continue to dominate in ownership, management, decision making roles, and content," she observes. "Even national and international communication policymaking that determines how media systems may operate are male dominated, with little or no regard for women's access or participation in them or for women's broader communication rights" (Byerly, 2023, para. 1). That point is unequivocally true. And yet, there is another aspect of Carolyn's work that has energized and sustained my personal commitment to intersectional feminist scholarship and activism and provides an important ongoing reminder of why this work continues to be vital and necessary. This aspect of her scholarship elevates and celebrates the ways in which feminist thought has wrought progressive changes in the media environment and the world.

Carolyn's focus on the gains in gender and social justice achieved through feminist activism aligns with the position taken by the feminist philosopher Sara

Ahmed in her reflections on lived feminism. Ahmed refers to the figure of the "policing feminist" or "feminist killjoy," a moralizing scold focused only on the negative, intent on "making people feel bad about their desires and investments" (Ahmed, 2017, p. 2). This figure, she writes, is a straw person invented as a way of dismissing feminism's legitimacy. By contrast, and in truth, feminist critique is valid and vibrant in its engagements with misogyny and injustices, and such critique is not self-defeating: rather, feminism is hopeful and forward-thinking, life-changing and vital force. For what is the point of critique, of revealing the ways in which injustices are perpetrated and upheld by structures as well as agents, of understanding how histories of oppression, colonization, invasion, racism, sexism, ableism, xenophobia, homo- and transphobia, have undermined particular groups and people, if not to seek redress and catalyze radical change? What is the point of speaking truth to power if not to alter corrupt power structures and make problems visible in order to solve them? Feminism is not, and never has been, about wallowing in a slough of despond. Feminism is about ethical revolution. Carolyn has made this point over and over again in her scholarship. As she writes,

> I have criticized feminist research that remains trapped in the "paradigm of the misogynist media," showing only that media representation and relations continue to stereotype, exclude or otherwise marginalize women without seeking to show how feminism has also served to imbed itself in media content, media policies, or other aspects of media industries. . . . A mature feminist media scholarship . . . is ready to consider not just women's marginalization but also the ways women have come into their own power through historical process. (Byerly, 2012, p. 15)

This is the dimension of Carolyn's work I love the most, and the dimension that I feel is the most important and game-changing principle subtending her approach to feminist media studies. She is alert and attentive to feminism as a social movement and to the ways in which feminist struggle has had material, social and affective impact. She is clear, too, that feminist theory and feminist activism are inextricably entwined. In her studies of media ownership and women journalists, she has interviewed women about their experiences, using their grounded knowledge to analyze media practice through the lens of feminist media theory. Her work is intentionally intersectional and transnational: many, if not most, of her published works address vectors of difference and foreground global dynamics. It is significant here that she spent most of her career at Howard University, a leading historically black university, and has collaborated closely with feminist scholars and activists in universities and other organizations worldwide.

The point I want to make here is that Carolyn's analyses are unique in that they confront two realities at once: on the one hand, the incontrovertible fact that the media environment is patriarchal and misogynistic, and that women and people of color face systemic barriers to both fair representation and other forms of access, such as decision-making power and ownership; on the other hand, the people who experience discrimination and bias have exceptional agency and insight, and they work tirelessly for change, in many cases effecting transformations in policy and practice to create space for new ways of making media. In this form of "double vision," making both the problems and the solutions visible, Carolyn's work exemplifies what I am calling "optimistic feminist praxis."

The notion of praxis breaks down the dichotomy and opposition of academic versus activist. In its classical Marxist definition, praxis refers to "theoretically informed and self-reflective human action devoted to the emancipation of the working class from domination by the capitalist class and the capitalist state" (Nonini, 2016, p. 242). Feminist praxis extends this definition to theoretically informed activism engaging with multiple intersecting axes of oppression and exploitation—race, class, gender, disability, sexual orientation, nation, and so on—in order to challenge and change them. The sociologist Liz Stanley argues that praxis refers to "a continuing shared feminist position in which 'knowledge' is not simply defined as 'knowledge *what*' but also as 'knowledge *for*' " (1990, p. 15). In this conjoining of knowledge and application, she writes, "the point is to change the world, not only to study it" (Stanley, 1990, p. 15). Intersectional feminist praxis is "critical of exclusionary practices in movement politics and organizations;" its goal is "to work simultaneously against capitalist globalization and patriarchal [I would add racist and other] forms of oppression, and to offer new alternatives to the dominant forms of globalization" (Naples, 2009, p. 14).

To me, feminist praxis is inherently optimistic in its focus on change. This optimism is not the same as ditzy Pollyannaism or what Teresa Ebert (1996) called "ludic" feminism. It is the kind of optimism that must undergird all emancipatory struggle. Without it, we'd lose hope; we'd give up. It is a mobilizing force, an energy, a commitment, a powerful vision of what could be. Carolyn's work has always embraced this spirit of optimistic feminist praxis. In her prolific oeuvre of books, articles, conference papers, essays, and chapters, she has shone a bright light on the ways in which feminist activism has moved the needle on institutional progress. Importantly, she substantiates this with solid evidence, using economic data, field observations, interviews with journalists, and other empirically grounded measures and methods to document the changes she theorizes. "It would be structuralist in the extreme," she wrote over 30 years ago, "to assume that change does not occur within institutions over time" (Byerly & Warren, 1996, p. 2). She's absolutely right.

For me, Carolyn's optimistic feminist praxis is much-needed corrective to the dejection I admit that I, and no doubt others who do this work, sometimes feel in a political climate in which the feminist gains of the past have been undermined and even reversed, as in the recent U.S. Supreme Court decision in *Dobbs v. Jackson Women's Health Organization*, which eliminated the abortion rights that had been guaranteed under *Roe v. Wade* for almost 50 years, as well as the mushrooming right-wing attacks on social justice and critical race studies. Worldwide, too, the picture is grim: the Taliban government has curtailed women's freedoms in Afghanistan; the COVID-19 pandemic has disproportionately affected women and children, as has the war in Ukraine; in Iran, the murder of the teenager Mahsa Amini by "morality police" have sparked protests. In the media industries, the MeToo movement has revealed media workplaces around the world to be hotbeds of sexual assault and harassment, and recent statistics show that most owners, directors, producers, editors, and executives in the media are still males, usually straight, cisgender white men.

In light of all this, I think that one of the most significant concepts Carolyn (and her co-author Marcus Hill) developed is the idea of "reformulation." In a 2012 paper where they examined the impact of feminist media activism on U.S. news of sexual and domestic violence over a period of 40 years, they found that coverage had not only increased but shifted to incorporate feminist terminology and perspectives regarding these issues. They coined the term "reformulation theory," which they define as "a way of gauging whether and to what extent feminist media activism . . . changed public discourse" (Byerly & Hill, 2012, p. 13). Though the concept is associated with the anti-rape movement, they argue that the idea is applicable "for other social movements that aim to make a fundamental shift in public discourse and institutional response" (Byerly & Hill, 2012, p. 13). Their study demonstrates the actual influence and weight of feminist media activism on journalistic practice, both with regard to content as well as reporting and writing. For me, the idea of reformulation lies at the heart of feminist praxis, especially as it plays out in feminist media scholarship and activism. Our core goal is to reformulate. We're interrogating the media—its production, its content, its reception, its encoding and decoding; its cultures and contexts—to pinpoint the ways in which patriarchal, heterosexist, racist, ableist, and other oppressive hegemonies are advanced in the mediated environment and, based on this knowledge, to radically *reinvent* this potent social force from a feminist standpoint, to *change* the way the media operate to sustain hegemonies of injustice and to *deploy* the media as a mechanism for progressive action. Sara Ahmed writes that the word feminism fills her "with hope, with energy," adding:

> It brings to mind loud acts of refusal and rebellion as well as the quiet ways we might have of not holding onto things that diminish us. It brings to mind women who have stood up, spoken back, risked lives, homes, relationships in the struggle for more bearable worlds . . . (Ahmed, 2017, p. 1)

It is precisely this hope and energy that infuses Carolyn Byerly's feminist media scholarship and makes it so compelling, so inspiring, so powerful, and so significant. For Carolyn, critical analysis is not a stopping point; rather, it is a point of departure. From her perspective, turning a feminist lens on the media must necessarily involve recognizing both "the struggle for more bearable worlds" and its outcomes: the gains, the accomplishments, the changes wrought by women and other marginalized people whose clarity and courage are driving this work. I am persuaded that Carolyn's "optimistic feminist praxis" is an indispensable restorative for feminist media scholarship, filled with the promise of gender and social justice. In conclusion, I will circle back to *The Mother's Book*, one of Carolyn's earliest published works, which begins with an epigraph that captures the spirit of her work. She quotes an old Cheyenne saying, "A nation is not conquered until the hearts of its women are on the ground. Then it is done, no matter how strong the weapons, or how brave the warriors" (Byerly, 1985). How do all of us as women ensure that our hearts do not hit the ground? What strategies might we as women use to remind us to hold our heads and hearts high?

Through her commitment to optimistic feminist praxis, Carolyn Byerly's work ensures that our hearts do not hit the ground.

## References

Ahmed, S. (2017). *Living a feminist life.* Duke University Press.

Byerly, C. M. (1985). *The mother's book: How to survive the incest of your child.* Kendall Hunt.

Byerly, C. M. (1994). An agenda for teaching news coverage of rape. *Journalism Educator, 49*(1), 59–69.

Byerly, C. M. (2006). Questioning media access: Analysis of FCC women and minority ownership data. In Benton Foundation (Ed.), *Does bigger media equal better media?* Social Science Research Council.

Byerly, C. M. (2012). The geography of women and media scholarship. In K. Ross (Ed.), *The handbook of gender, sex, and media* (pp. 3–19). Wiley-Blackwell.

Byerly, C. M. (2023). Gender dimensions of communication industries: A political economy analysis. In M. Gallagher and A. Montiel (Eds.), *The handbook of gender, communication, and women's human rights*. Wiley-Blackwell.

Byerly, C. M., & Hill, M. (2012). Reformulation theory: Gauging feminist impact on news of violence against women. *Journal of Research on Women and Gender*, *5*, 1–20. https://digital.library.txstate.edu/handle/10877/12860

Byerly, C. M., & Warren, C. A. (1996). At the margins of center: Organized protest in the newsroom. *Critical Studies in Mass Communication*, *13*(1), 1–23. https://doi.org/10.1080/15295039609366957

Byerly, C. M., & Wilson, C. C. (2009). Journalism as Kerner turns 40: Its Multicultural problems and possibilities. *The Howard Journal of Communications*, *20*(3), 209–221. https://doi.org/10.1080/10646170903069920

Ebert, T. (1996). *Ludic feminism and after: Postmodernism, desire, and labor in late capitalism*. Michigan University Press.

hooks, b. (1995). *Killing rage: Ending racism*. Holt.

Naples, N. A. (2009). Crossing borders: Community activism, globalization, and social justice. *Social Problems*, *56*(1), 2–20. https://doi.org/10.1525/sp.2009.56.1.2

Nonini, D. (2016). Praxis. *Dialectical Anthropology*, *40*(3), 241–249. https://doi.org/10.1007/s10624-016-9429-2

Stanley, L. (1990). *Feminist praxis: Research, theory and epistemology in feminist sociology*. Routledge.

4

# Dr. Carolyn M. Byerly's Media Justice Scholarship: Centering Women's Critical Information Needs in Public Interest Regulation

CATHERINE J. K. SANDOVAL

## Creating a Future Informed by Media Diversity

Dr. Carolyn M. Byerly's scholarship and advocacy highlight women's unmet critical information needs as a key deficit in American media regulation. Byerly and Valentin (2017, p. 267) observe that media access is a "condition for equality." That condition remains unrealized as women control few FCC licenses and have limited access to senior levels of media management that would enable the development and airing of content responsive to women's needs. First Amendment scholar C. Edward Baker observed that the media form the "central institution of a democratic public sphere" and media "ownership dispersal . . . is central to democracy" (Baker, 2009, p. 654).

Dr. Byerly's work raised questions that had largely been overlooked in public policy and regulation, that is, were the information needs of women, their families, and communities being met; how many Federal Communications Commission (FCC) licenses did women control; how did women-controlled media inform the public sphere and democracy; and what should the FCC do to improve its research and regulation to better serve the public interest? Her work provided an in-depth analysis of those questions, creating a roadmap for future research and regulatory innovation. Dr. Byerly's early career used her journalism training "to serve anti-violence, equal pay, and other campaigns," writing press releases and training volunteers (Byerly, 2018, p. 30). Her scholarly work draws from that experience to highlight the role of feminist organizers in convening and supporting women in shelters, church basements, and community centers. Community service in dialogue with women transformed the legal and social understanding of abusive behaviors toward women, beginning in the 1970s. Community organizing and feminist scholarship created a vocabulary that gave a name and legal cause of action to "sexual assault, acquaintance (or date) rape, marital rape, domestic violence (or abuse), sexual harassment, and others" (Byerly, 2018, p. 28). Organizing, political, and legal action recognized the violent and abusive nature of such conduct which had often been treated by courts, civic institutions, and society as private matters women should tolerate.

I had the pleasure of meeting Dr. Byerly in 2006 at a roundtable discussion with other scholars as the FCC was beginning its analysis for the quadrennial review of its media ownership rules as required by the Telecommunications Act of 1996 (Telecom Act of '96 or '96 Act). I was then an Assistant Professor of Law at Santa Clara University and Dr. Byerly was an Associate Professor in the School of Communications at Howard University. We had both come to the academy after community, government, nonprofit, and private sector work experiences. Now a tenured Professor of Law at Santa Clara University, I write this chapter (during nights and weekends) in my personal capacity as a scholar while on a leave of absence for federal service.[1] At the beginning of 2006, Dr. Byerly and I collaborated with other scholars to file comments with the FCC for its media ownership reviews, and later filed amicus briefs before the District of Columbia (D.C.) Circuit Court of Appeals and the U.S. Supreme Court (Brief, 2018, 2020; Sandoval et al., 2006, 2007). Dr. Byerly also filed FCC comments with other colleagues, contributing to the record of government proceedings while mentoring scholar-leaders. As scholars with organizing experience, we shared common goals: develop fact-based analysis of minority and female media license control (often referred to as ownership) and examine the effect of regulation on communities of color, disadvantaged communities, and women. We also share a commitment to collaboration and mentorship. Dr. Byerly was named the Chair of Howard University's Department of Communications, Culture, Media Studies beginning in 2014. In that position, she mentored PhD students, ran a world-class educational program, and developed a scholarship that informed law, public

1 This chapter reflects the author's personal views and analysis and does not reflect the views or opinions of any other entity. The author did not use government resources to research or write this chapter.

policy and the public interest. Dr. Byerly continues to contribute to scholarship through her research, writing, and inspirational example.

This essay highlights Dr. Byerly's contributions to media justice scholarship and FCC regulation. Byerly's interdisciplinary scholarship centers women's information needs in the discussion about communications regulation. Combining theory with empirical and qualitative evidence, she documented low levels of women's ownership of FCC licenses, approximately 5 percent of American television licenses and 6 percent of radio licenses in 2006 (Byerly, 2007). Those numbers inched up in 2019 to 6 percent of full-power television licenses, 9 percent of AM radio licenses, and 7 percent of FM radio licenses (FCC, 2021, pp. 13321, 13324, 13325). Her work contextualizes women's FCC license ownership and capital access barriers within gender discrimination history and law. This article concludes by highlighting the research agenda Dr. Byerly's scholarship blazed and the future informed by the media diversity that Dr. Byerly's scholarship enables.

## Socio-Legal and Historical Context of Media in the Public Interest

Byerly's scholarship examines media regulations within the socio-legal and historical context that frames media access. Media justice rests on a historical analysis that centers race, class, and gender as principal forces that shape our media system (Malkia Cyril quoted in Carlson & Baynes, 2007, p. 602). As radio was emerging as a commercial service, The Radio Act of 1927 granted insufficient authority to regulators to prevent "chaos on the airwaves," allowing broadcasters to drown each other out, creating a cacophony on the airwaves where nowhere could be heard (*Red Lion Broadcasting vs. FCC*, 1969). The Communications Act of 1934 (Communications Act or '34 Act) directed the FCC to issue broadcast licenses only if the "public convenience, interest, or necessity will be served thereby . . ."[2] The public interest standard remains the cornerstone of FCC media regulation. To promote service to local communities, conceptualized as "localism," Section 307(b) of the Communications Act of 1934 requires the FCC to "provide a fair, efficient and equitable distribution" of broadcast facilities to each of the States and communities (In re: Applications of Mid-Florida Television Corp., 1972, p. 560). The Communications Act directs the FCC to "make available, so far as possible, to all the people of the United States, a rapid, efficient, nationwide, and

2 47 U.S.C. § 307 (2000); 47 U.S.C. § 309 (2000).

world-wide wire and radio communication service with adequate facilities at reasonable charges."[3] Despite these directives, by 1971, the FCC had awarded only 10 radio licenses to minorities (*TV 9 v. FCC*, 1973).

The 1968 Kerner Commission report found that the absence of FCC license diversity contributed to riots in more than 200 cities across the United States between 1965 and 1967, most of them in poor Black and Latino neighborhoods (Boissoneault, 2018). President Johnson convened the Kerner Commission, chaired by Governor Otto Kerner of Illinois, to investigate the causes of the discontent the uprising revealed and make recommendations to improve the nation's prospects. The Kerner Commission Report faulted the media whose ownership and reporters failed to reflect America's diversity. The report noted that the public was seeing a fragmented picture of race in America, one that failed to show the everyday lives of African Americans and other communities of color (Lamb & Byerly, 2019, p. 318). The Kerner Commission highlighted the lack of diversity in newsrooms as a factor that led to distorted coverage and misunderstanding about the structural conditions that created and perpetuated racism and poverty in the years leading to the riots between 1965 and 1967 (*Id.*).

On its 50th anniversary, Lamb and Byerly (2019) observed the Kerner Report's impact as well as its oversights. For example, the section of the report on the riots' underlying causes noted that the news had failed to illuminate the sexual or racial politics of ghettoization, leaving out a critical part of the history of these events, including Black women's victimization by police (Holmes, 2016, p. 307). Sex and gender violence went unmentioned because they were not considered racial matters, according to historian Mary Frances Berry, former chair of the U.S. Civil Rights Commission (Berry, 2018, p. 16). The D.C. Circuit's 1973 decision in TV 9 (1973, p. 356) recognized the potential contributions of Black applicants to serving the public interest. Beginning in 1978–1992, the FCC credited minority participation in the ownership and management of a station (a concept called "integration") as a positive factor in determining a license award in a Comparative Hearing (WPIX, 1978, pp. 411–412). The FCC's Review Board determined in Gainesville Media (1978, pp. 149–150) that women who proposed to participate in license ownership and management were eligible for an enhancement credit in Comparative Hearings. Shortly thereafter in *Mid-Florida Television Corp.* (1978), the FCC downgraded the credit that would be given to women's ownership and management participation. The FCC Review Board

3 47 U.S.C. § 151 (2018).

concluded that although women "suffered from a discriminatory attitude in various fields of activity," by comparison, "women have not been excluded from the mainstream of society as have black people" (Ibid. at 326). Accordingly, the FCC awarded a slight credit to women and a more substantial credit to minority applicants for FCC licenses who planned to participate in station management.

The small credit given for women's proposed ownership and management in an FCC license was challenged in 1992 as violative of a male applicant's right to equal protection. In Lamprecht, the D.C. Circuit determined that the FCC had failed to present evidence to support "its predictive judgment that women owners will broadcast women's or minority or any other underrepresented type of programming at any different rate than will men" (Ibid. at 395). The FCC had presented evidence in Lamprecht that 35 percent of stations owned by women aired women's programming, a statistic the D.C. Circuit compared unfavorably to the "dramatic" evidence of a link between minority ownership and minority programming; 79 percent of Black-owned stations broadcast Black-oriented programming (Id. at 397). The D.C. Circuit did not explain why it gave less weight to women licensees' substantial contributions to women's programming, other than to emphasize that it was less than the contributions of minority owners to minority-oriented programming. In Bechtel (1992, 1993), the D.C. Circuit determined the FCC had not provided sufficient evidence to support the integration credit awarded for participation in management and daily operations. The FCC suspended integration criteria while it initially attempted to gather more record evidence, a task the FCC has since left in abeyance. After Congress authorized the FCC to auction licenses beginning in 1995, the FCC ended Comparative Hearings and turned primarily to the auction process which emphasizes access to capital. Licenses also continued to be sold on the secondary market, a process that leaves predominantly male-controlled license holders in charge of determining who will get access to those license deals.

The Supreme Court's 1995 decision in *Adarand v. Pena* shifted to strict scrutiny for the legal review standard for programs that take race into account, leading the FCC to pause consideration of race in its licensing decisions (Sandoval, 2022, pp. 466–467). Although intermediate scrutiny applies to programs that take gender into account (*Miss. Univ. for Women v. Hogan*, 1982), the FCC did not develop a record to address the concerns raised in Lamprecht or adopt gender or race-conscious programs after Adarand to promote women's or minority access to FCC licenses. In the year following the Adarand decision, the Telecommunications Act of 1996 (1996 Act) lifted the limits on the number of radio stations one entity could control nationwide and codified local market limits.[4] Television ownership was restricted to 39 percent of the national audience with local consolidation limits.[5] The Telecom Act of '96 reaffirmed Congress' decision that the radio spectrum should be regulated in the public interest.[6] The '96 Act, §202(h), directed the FCC to periodically review its media ownership regulations and broadcast rules, spawning the FCC's quadrennial media ownership proceedings. The FCC's media ownership rulemaking adopted goals of promoting competition, diversity, and localism (FCC, 2006, p. 4). The FCC adopted those goals to "serve the public interest by ensuring that multiple owners control the broadcasting outlets in any market" (FCC, 2003, p. 41). Congress adopted media ownership regulations to encourage diversity in the use of the public airwaves (*Columbia Broad. Sys., Inc. v. Democratic National Committee*, 1973). The FCC has recognized that "[t]here are five types of diversity pertinent to media ownership policy: viewpoint, outlet, program, source, and minority and female ownership diversity" (FCC, 2003, at p. 18).[7]

The '96 Act also codified the FCC's duty to promote broad access to the radio spectrum without taint of discrimination, requiring the FCC to regulate "so as to make available, so far as possible, to all people of the U.S., without discrimination on the basis of race, color, religion, national origin, or sex . . . a world-wide wire and radio communications service."[8] By counting all types of commercial broadcast stations in 2019 including Class A (i.e., full-power) television and low- power commercial television stations with a narrower market reach, the FCC concluded that women held a majority ownership interest in 8% of commercial broadcast stations. The Telecom Act of '96 went beyond non-discrimination goals to require the FCC to take steps to foster inclusion of minorities and women in the provision of spectrum-based services.[9] Despite these

4 The Telecommunications Act of 1996 eliminated the national cap on the number of AM or FM radio stations a single entity could control and established ownership limits per geographical market, based on the number of radio stations in the market, prompting a wave of consolidation. *1996 Telecom. Act*, §§ 202(a), (c)(1)(B), 110 Stat. at 110–111; §202(b)(1), 110 Stat. at 110.

5 47 C.F.R. § 73.3555(e)(1); Nexstar Media Inc. v. Spectrum Management Holding Company, LLC. 2022. (D. Del., Jan. 12, 2022, No. 1:21-CV-1358-SB) 2022 WL 610756, at *2.

6 47 U.S.C. § 303 (2000) ("Except as otherwise provided in this chapter, the Commission from time to time, as public convenience, interest, or necessity requires, shall . . . [s]tudy new uses for radio, provide for experimental uses of frequencies, and generally encourage the larger and more effective use of radio in the public interest").

7 *See also* Sinclair Broadcast Group, Inc. v. F.C.C., 284 F.3d 148, 159 (D.C. Cir. 2002); Prometheus Radio Project v. F.C.C., 373 F.3d 372, 400 (3d Cir. 2004); FCC v. Nat'l Citizens Comm. for Broad., 436 U.S. 775, 796 (U.S. 1978).

8 47 U.S.C. 151 (2000).

9 47 U.S.C. § 309(J)(3) (2000).

mandates, control of media licenses by women and minorities remains limited in 2023 (FCC, 2021, p. 13315).

## Women's Critical Information Needs

Byerly and Valentin (2016) frame their analysis of women's critical information needs in the context of women's socio-economic status. Women "continue to lag behind" in "income levels, education, access to affordable housing, and representation in political office," as well as in other measures (Byerly & Valentin, 2016, p. 65). Additionally, the authors argue that "gendered roles within families and across the broader society, with women still the primary caretakers for children and the elderly," affect women's status as well as their information needs (Id., p. 65). They also note that, as caregivers, women "assume the key roles of getting children and others to safety and caring for the injured" during disasters such as floods, and they are generally at greater risk than men during and after disasters (Ibid., p. 70). Lower incomes, caretaking roles, and the legacies of sexism, racism, and ableism add to the challenges of daily life and pose additional risks to women during disasters. Women with disabilities may face difficulties in finding and using news due to accessibility issues (such as lack of screen readers) and lack of coverage of issues facing women with disabilities. Women also make up a higher proportion of the elderly, one of the groups with the highest mortality rates during disasters (Byerly & Valentin, 2016, p. 71). The "interaction of gender, race, and economics has serious implications for government policy in managing disasters (Adrian, 2006), as well as ensuring that people receive the information they need to respond and survive" (Byerly & Valentin, 2016, p. 71). Fulfilling the information needs of women, the majority of the American and the world's population, is critical to society, to those who women care for and serve, and to women's work, contributions, and well-being.

Byerly and Valentin (2016, p. 73) question whether the internet can fill this information gap, a concern that remains as of this writing in 2023. Internet access, computer, smartphone, and training gaps frustrate internet use, especially for those in rural areas, in poverty, the elderly, and people with disabilities (Perrin & Atske, 2021; Vogels, 2021a, 2021b). Byerly and Valentin ask, do women "have control over what kinds of information is organized and posted?" (p. 73). Kostovska et al. (2021, p. 13) emphasize that the media ecosystem, including broadcasters, internet sources, newspapers and others, are increasingly interdependent, forming a multi-layered, dynamic structure where media outlets feed each other in a cycle. The paucity of women broadcast owners tilts the media ecosystem's control and content. "The paradox of the information revolution of the 21st century is the simultaneous abundance of information availability for some groups and in the midst of information poverty for others" (Byerly & Valentin, 2016, p. 74). Byerly's ethnographic and survey research conducted in 2006, with co-investigators Kehbuma Langmia and Jamila A. Cupid, surveyed 196 people, two-thirds of whom were African American, the rest comprising Latino, African or other ethnicities, in three diverse neighborhoods, Columbia Heights and Mt. Pleasant, in Washington, DC, and nearby Hyattsville in Maryland. Their survey, supplemented by in-person interviews, sought opinions about whether residents' information needs were met by the media they consume. Their research began by understanding the neighborhoods' histories and local challenges including gentrification, rising rents, lack of job and training opportunities, and concerns about crime (Byerly et al., 2006).

Residents surveyed cited local television as their most frequent source of local information, followed by newspapers (p. 23). Those who relied on radio for local news preferred African American-owned (and/or operated) radio stations. In the Washington, DC market, Radio One, owned by African American female entrepreneur Cathy Hughes, operates several radio stations, while Howard University, a historically Black University, controls an FCC radio and television license. Both offer programming from an African American perspective. Survey respondents "who emphasized the localism aspect of news referred specifically to stories with a minority angle, e.g., 'they tell you what is going on in African-American communities,' or, as one Hispanic participant said, 'I like to get local news in Spanish'" (p. 26). Survey respondents wished that a broader range of minority problems than crime and criminality be covered; they listed the need for health care, problems of illiteracy and widespread poverty as things they wanted to see on the news. Byerly et al. (2006) concluded, much as the Kerner Commission did four decades earlier, that the mainstream news should be doing more to serve the interests and needs of minority communities and expand opportunities for minority media ownership (p. 33). Their study, now nearly two decades old, should be replicated to understand the information needs of other communities and whether the media ecosystem and regulatory environment are meeting them. Funding and training are needed for this labor-intensive research grounded in community dialogue methodology to understand local information gaps in America's multicultural communities.

Byerly and Valentin (2016, p. 65) insist that a feminist perspective on critical information is also needed to consider the paltry amount of information available in the media about women's well-being and participation in society, and to analyze who produces information. Two related studies (Byerly & Valentin, 2016; Byerly et al., 2006) link access to communication and information relevant to women and racial minorities with control over publication and editorial decisions.

## Persistently Low Levels of Women's Ownership of FCC Licenses

### *A. Women Control Few FCC Licenses*

Byerly engaged in quantitative and critical research of FCC forms that disclose license ownership information (form 323s), making suggestions to identify and rectify information gaps created by the FCC's data-gathering and reporting mechanisms (Byerly, 2007, p. 28). She confirmed the persistently low levels of broadcast ownership by women from the FCC's founding in 1934 through the first decades of the twenty-first century (p. 25). Although designated as a "public resource" since the Radio Act of 1927, the airwaves in 2006–2007 were 95 percent under the control of male owners (Byerly, 2007, also noted in related research by Turner & Cooper, 2006; U.S. GAO, 2008). Byerly (2007) found that in 2006 women in the United States owned only 5 percent of the 2,388 television and 6 percent of the 10,506 full-power commercial broadcast radio stations. Most of the women-owned broadcast stations were in small towns and rural areas, markets that reach smaller audiences and yield lower advertising revenues to support operations.

A related study found that non-White women comprised approximately 0.1% of stations with no controlling interest with ownership dispersed among several shareholders (Turner, 2007, p. 19). By counting all types of commercial broadcast stations in 2019 including Class A (i.e., full-power) television and low-power commercial television stations with a narrower market reach, the FCC concluded that women held a majority ownership interest in 8 percent of commercial broadcast stations (FCC, 2020, p. 13315). In 2019, persons belonging to racial minority groups held a majority ownership interest in 4 percent of commercial broadcast stations, and Hispanic/Latino persons held a majority ownership interest in 6 percent of commercial broadcast stations (Turner, 2007). Broadcast stations similarly have had few females in top management, for example, only 1 percent in radio (Turner, 2007, p. 5), and equally low numbers on boards of directors (Byerly, 2011, p. 25). Byerly observed that as a result of the low level of media control by women, fulfilment of the public interest requirement is heavily tilted toward men's interests, both in relation to ownership and to management (Byerly, 2011).

Media license ownership matters as to the content the public hears and sees. The D.C. Circuit Court of Appeals in *TV9* (D.C. Circuit, 1973, p. 938) stated it is "upon ownership that public policy places primary reliance with respect to diversification of content, and that has historically proven to be significantly influential with respect to editorial comment and the presentation of news." Broadcast license "owners decide what programs to air, which commercials to accept, which editorials to broadcast, and who to hire" (Sandoval, 2020, p. 5). Byerly (2014) defines women's media access as "women's ability to own or hold [or achieve] positions of decision-making authority in media companies" that confers upon them the power to "determine the direction and content of information disseminated by media companies." A Congressional staff memorandum to support the 2020 legislative hearing titled "Lifting Voices: Legislation to Promote Media Marketplace Diversity" recognized Dr. Byerly's scholarly insights into the nexus between FCC license ownership and access to content in the public interest: "Media outlets provide viewers with educational, political, entertainment, and news programming. Diversity helps to ensure that programming offers different perspectives and that viewers have access to programming that is relevant to them" (Byerly, 2011). Byerly observed that as a consequence of skewed broadcast license ownership, "women's concerns are either missing or under-reported in mainstream (i.e., the large, corporate-owned) news media within the United States, particularly in the serious news of politics and economy" (Byerly, 2011, p. 26).

Byerly's research also contributed a geographic focus on the smaller markets and predominantly rural areas women licensees serve, factors that affect their ability to gain market share necessary to access capital and grow their reach. Access to capital is a barrier for minorities and women seeking to enter or expand broadcast license ownership (GAO, 2008; Byerly, 2011). Byerly's research harnessed methodologies developed in the anthropology field to interview women about the barriers they faced in trying to serve the public interest. Women media owners interviewed said that "they find broadcasting as a masculine environment in which women are unwelcome and systematically squeezed out" (Byerly, 2011, p. 35). One network executive in sales said, "Broadcasting is still an old boys' network. The top positions go to White men who then make decisions about who moves up next" (*Ibid.*). Their work highlighted six barriers that block women's broadcast media ownership: "Exclusion from places where decisions are made . . . circumstances where women are not invited—on the golf course, at dinner, over drinks, and at other professional and social occasions" (*Ibid.*). Denial of promotion, lack of mentorship, dismissal of women's skills and differences, rejection by investors, and a "hostile regulatory apparatus" that "has allowed consolidation and conglomeration throughout the industry since the mid-1990s" created layers of impediments to women's broadcast ownership (Ibid. at 35–38). Byerly's research characterizes capital access barriers as a form of gender discrimination that limits women's ability to provide, maintain, or grow broadcast or other media services.

Byerly's (2014) qualitative study of 40 women FCC television and radio licensees found that they "operate in a hostile regulatory environment and in an industry that blocks women from gaining experience and access to capital to prepare and successfully compete for station ownership" (Byerly 2017, p. 272). Title VII of the Civil Rights Act of 1964 bars discrimination on the basis of sex, race, color, national origin, and religion. A 1972 sex discrimination lawsuit against WRC-TV (an NBC affiliate) challenged unequal pay and limited opportunities given to women as sex discrimination under Title VII, resulting in a victory for the plaintiffs that required the station to alter its hiring and promotion practices (Byerly & Valentin, 2017, p. 273). Similarly, a scholarship and sabbatical program to support female journalists was established to settle a 1972 Equal Employment Opportunities Commission (EEOC) complaint against the *Washington Post* which alleged that the newspaper restricted the upward mobility of female employees and gave preferences to males (Id.). Women have had mixed success in using the courts to address sexual harassment and other forms of treatment that limited women's job opportunities and career advancement. Many legal settlements keep the terms private, limiting public access to information about the patterns of conduct that supported gender discrimination and sexual harassment suits against several media outlets. Legal, scholarly, and organizing work remains necessary to support women's employment opportunities and to meet women's information needs.

## The Path Forward

Limited data on FCC licensing decisions in the twentieth and early twenty-first centuries confound research and initiatives to increase broadcast license access. In 2011, the Third Circuit Court of Appeals in Prometheus v. FCC observed that the FCC's quadrennial review of its broadcast ownership rules "referenced *no* data on television ownership by minorities or women and *no* data regarding commercial radio ownership by women. This is because, as the Commission has since conceded, it has no accurate data to cite" (*Prometheus v. FCC*, 2011, emphasis in original).[10] The Supreme Court's 2021 *FCC v. Prometheus Radio Project* decision determined that the FCC is not required to conduct studies for its rulemaking and may rely on admittedly incomplete data to inform its decisions.[11] The FCC retains discretion to determine how to gather and report data in what it considers to be consistent with its public interest obligations. Sandoval (2022, p. 417) contends that the FCC's poor data management and analysis created "data darkness" that thwarts sound regulatory decision-making and disserves the public interest. Making FCC data accessible and committing resources to studies about women's critical information needs and media ownership remain crucial to sound media regulation, and to serving democracy, public safety, public well-being and the public interest. Byerly and Valentin (2016, p. 75) contend that "structural problems require structural solutions." They argue that women's lack of access to and control over communications processes requires laws and policies that will enable women to be better represented at the ownership levels in media industries, as well as in positions of decision-making in both traditional and online news organizations.

Byerly's scholarly leadership creates a path forward that centers women's information needs in the public interest, research, and media justice.

## References

Adrian, L. M. (2006). Definitions and disasters: What hurricane Katrina revealed about women's rights. *Urbana: Forum on Public Policy*. https://www.thefreelibrary.com/Definitions+and+-disasters%3A+what+Hurricane+Katrina+revealed+about. . .-a0180163929

Baker, C. E. (2009). Viewpoint diversity and media ownership. *Federal Communications Law Journal*, *60*, 651–671.

Berry, M. F. (2018). Still separate & unequal: Fifty years after the Kerner Commission report, is our nation still moving toward two societies—one White and one other? *The Crisis*, *125*, 12–17. https://maryfrancesberry.wordpress.com/2018/03/19/50-years-after-kerner-report-the-crisi/

10 Prometheus Radio Project v. Federal Communications Commission (3d Cir. 2016) 824 F.3d 33, 44 (citing *Prometheus Radio Project v. FCC*, 652 F.3d 431, 438–444 (3d Cir. 2011) [*Prometheus II*]).

11 *FCC v. Prometheus Radio Project*, 141 S. Ct. 1150, 1152 (U.S. 2021).

Boissoneault, L. (2018, April 4). Martin Luther King Jr.'s assassination sparked uprisings in cities across America. *Smithsonian Magazine*. https://www.smithsonianmag.com/history/martin-luther-king-jrs-assassination-sparked-uprisings-cities-across-america-180968665/

Brief, A. (2018). Professors of Administrative, Communications, Energy, Antitrust, and Contract Law and Policy as Amicus Curiae Supporting Petitioner, Mozilla v. FCC, (2018, D.C. Cir.), 940 F.3d 1 (No. 18-1051).

Brief, A. (2018). Professors of Administrative, Communications, Energy, Antitrust, and Contract Law and Policy as Amicus Curiae Supporting Petitioner, Mozilla v. FCC, (2018, D.C. Cir.), 940 F.3d 1 (No. 18-1051).

Byerly, C. M. (2004). Women and the concentration of media ownership. In R. R. Rush, C. E. Oukrop, & P. Creedon (Eds.), *Seeking equity for women in journalism and mass communication education: A 30-year update* (pp. 245–263). Lawrence Erlbaum Associates.

Byerly, C. M. (2007). Questioning media access: Analysis of FCC women & minority ownership data. In *Does bigger media equal better media? Four academic studies of media ownership in the United States* (pp. 27–37). Benton Foundation and Social Science Research Council (SSRC).

Byerly, C. M. (2011). Behind the scenes of women's broadcast ownership. *Howard Journal of Communication*, *29*(3), 24–42.

Byerly, C. M. (2014). Women and media control: Feminist interrogations at the macro-level. In C. Carter, L. Steiner, & L. McLaughlin (Eds.), *The Routledge companion to media and gender* (pp. 105–115). Routledge.

Byerly, C. M. (2017). Feminist activism and U.S. communications policy. In V. Pickard & G. Yang (Ed.), *Media activism: Charting an evolving field of research*. Routledge.

Byerly, C. M. (2018). Feminism, theory, and communication: Progress, debates, and challenges ahead. In D. Harp, J. Loke, & I. Bachmann (Eds.), *Feminist approaches to media theory and research* (pp. 19–35). Palgrave McMillian.

Byerly, C. M., & Valentin, A. (2016). Feminist perspectives on critical information needs. In M. Lloyd & L. Friedlander (Eds.), *Communication policy and how to fix it* (pp. 65–79). Palgrave Macmillan.

Byerly, C. M., & Valentin, A. (2017). Women's access to media: Legal dimensions of ownership and employment in the United States. In R. Lind (Ed.), *Race and gender in electronic media: Challenges and opportunities*. Routledge.

Byerly, C. M., Langmia, K., & Cupid, J. A. (2006, October). Media ownership matters: Localism, the ethnic minority audience and community participation. In *Does bigger media equal better media? Four academic studies of media ownership in the United States* (pp. 4–26). Benton Foundation and Social Science Research Council (SSRC).

Carlson, N. F., & Baynes, L. M. (2007). Rethinking the discourse on race: A symposium on how the lack of racial diversity in the media affects social justice and policy. *St. John's J. Legal Comment*, *21*, 575–614.

Folkerts, J., & Teeter, D. L., Jr. (1998). *Voices of a nation: A history of mass media in the United States* (3rd ed.). Allyn and Bacon.

Holmes, K. (2016). Beyond the flames: Queering the history of the 1968 DC Riot. In E. P. Johnson (Ed.), *No tea, no shade: New writings in Black queer studies* (pp. 304–320). Duke University Press.

Kostovska, I., Raats, T., Donders, K., & Ballon, P. (2021). Going beyond the hype: conceptualising "media ecosystem" for media management research. *Journal of Media Business Studies, 18*(1), 6–26. https://doi.org/10.1080/16522354.2020.1765668

Lamb, Y. R., & Byerly, C. M. (2019). Kerner @ 50: Looking forward, looking back. *Howard Journal of Communication, 30*(4), 317–331.

Perrin, A., & Atske, S. (2021, September 10). *Americans with disabilities less likely than those without to own some digital devices.* Pew Research Center. https://www.pewresearch.org/short-reads/2021/09/10/americans-with-disabilities-less-likely-than-those-without-to-own-some-digital-devices/

Sandoval, C. J. K. (2020, January 15). *Media diversity protects democracy and the public interest.* United States Congress, House Energy & Commerce Committee, Communications and Technology Subcommittee, Testimony, Hearing, Lifting Voices: Legislation to Promote Media Marketplace Diversity. https://docs.house.gov/meetings/IF/IF16/20200115/110373/HHRG-116-IF16-Wstate-SandovalC-20200115.pdf

Sandoval, C. J. K. (2022). Prometheus serving: Incubating diverse and inclusive media in the public interest through data democracy. *Berkeley Technology Law Journal, 37,* 413–487. https://lawcat.berkeley.edu/record/1257868

Sandoval, C. J. K., Baynes, L. M., Hammond, I. V., Allen, S., Byerly, C. M., & Subvervi, F. (2006, October 23). *Comments filed in the 2006 quadrennial review of the Commission's broad. ownership rules and other rules adopted pursuant to section 202 of the Telecommunication Act of 1996* (MB Dockets No. 06-121, 02-277, 01-235, 01-317, 00-244). https://www.fcc.gov/ecfs/document/5513684641/1

Sandoval, C. J. K., Byerly, C. M., & Folami, A. (2007, October 19). *Comments in FCC media ownership proceeding, 2006, Regarding the FCC-commissioned study, minority and female ownership in media enterprises* (MB Dockets No. 06-121, 02-277, 01-235, 07, 00-244). ). https://www.fcc.gov/ecfs/document/5514894650/1

Turner, D. (2007). Off the dial: Female and minority radio ownership in the United States, How FCC Policy and Media Consolidation Diminished Diversity on the Public Airwaves, Review of Current Status and Comparative Statistical Analysis, FreePress (2007), https://www.freepress.net/sites/default/files/legacy-policy/off_the_dial.pdf

Turner, S. D., & Cooper, M. (2006). *Out of the picture: Minority & women's TV ownership in the United States* (Report). https://mediajustice.org/wp-content/uploads/2014/04/out_of_the_picture.pdf

Vogels, E. A. (2021a, September 10). *Some digital divides persist between rural, urban and suburban America.* Pew Research Center. https://www.pewresearch.org/short-reads/2021/08/19/some-digital-divides-persist-between-rural-urban-and-suburban-america/

Vogels, E. A. (2021b, June 22). *Digital divide persists even as Americans with lower incomes make gains in tech adoption.* Pew Research Center. https://www.pewresearch.org/short-reads/2021/06/22/digital-divide-persists-even-as-americans-with-lower-incomes-make-gains-in-tech-adoption/

## *Legal Cases and Materials*

*Adarand v. Pena* (U.S. 1995) 515 U.S. 200.
Bechtel v. FCC (1992, D.C. Cir.) 957 F.2d 873.
Bechtel v. FCC (1993, D.C. Cir.), 10 F.3d 875.
Brief for Professors of Administrative, Communications, Energy, Antitrust, and Contract Law and Policy as Amicus Curiae Supporting Petitioner, Mozilla v. FCC (2018, D.C. Cir.), 940 F.3d 1 (No. 18-1051).
Brief for Professors of Communications Law and Policy, Administrative Law, and Drs. of Economics and Social Science as Amicus Curiae Supporting Respondent, FCC v. Prometheus Radio Project v. FCC (2020), 141 S.Ct. 1150 (Nos. 19-1231 and 19-1241).
Columbia Broad. Sys., Inc. v. Democratic Nat'l Comm. (1973) 412 U.S. 94.
FCC v. Prometheus Radio Project (2021) 141 S. Ct. 1150.
Gainesville Media, In Re Applications of Gainesville Media, Inc. for Constr. Permits (1978), 70 F.C.C.2d 143.
Lamprecht v. FCC (1992, D.C. Cir.), 958 F.2d 382.
Mid-Florida, *In re:* Applications of Mid-Florida Television Corp. (1972), 37 F.C.C. 2d 559.
Mid-Florida, *In re:* Applications of Mid-Florida Television Corp. (1978), 70 F.C.C. 2d 281.
Miss. Univ. for Women v. Hogan (1978), 458 U.S. 718.
Nexstar Media Inc. v. Spectrum Management Holding Company, LLC. (2022, D. Del.), 2022 WL 610756 (No. 1:21-CV-1358-SB) (D. Del., 2022).
Prometheus Radio Project v. Federal Communications Commission (2016, 3d Cir.), 824 F.3d 33 [*Prometheus III*].
Prometheus Radio Project v. FCC (2011, 3d Cir.) 652 F.3d 431 [*Prometheus II*].
Red Lion Broadcasting Co. v. FCC (1969), 395 U.S. 367.
TV 9, Inc. v. FCC (1973, D.C. Cir.), 495 F.2d 929.
WPIX, In Re Applications of WPIX, Inc. for Constr. Permit for New Television Broad. Station (1978), 68 F.C.C. 2d 381.

## *Statutes*

47 C.F.R. § 73.3555(e)(1).
Communications Act of 1934 ('34 Act), 47 U.S.C. §151, 303, 307, 309 (1934).
Telecommunications Act of 1996, 47 U.S.C. §§ 202(a), (c)(1)(B), §202(b)(1), 309(J)(3) §202(h) (1996).

## *Government Documents*

Committee on Energy and Commerce Staff. (2020, January). *Memorandum to Subcommittee on Communications and Technology Members and Staff re: Legislative hearing on "Lifting Voices: Legislation to Promote Media Marketplace Diversity," January 9, 2020.* https://docs.house.gov/meetings/IF/IF16/20200115/110373/HHRG-116-IF16-20200115-SD002.pdf

FCC. (1978, May). Statement of policy on minority ownership of broad. Facilities, 68 F.C.C.2d 979.

Federal Communications Commission (FCC) (2003, July). In Re 2002 Biennial Regulatory Review-Review of the Commission's Broad. Ownership Rules & Other Rules Adopted Pursuant to Section 202 of the Telecommunications Act of 1996, 18 F.C.C. Rcd. 13620.

FCC. (2006, July). In the matter of 2006 quadrennial regulatory review—Review of the commissions broad. Ownership rules & other rules adopted pursuant to section 202 of the Telecommunications Act of 1996, 21 F.C.C. Rcd. 8834.

FCC. (2021, September). *Fifth Report on broadcast stations, FCC Form 323 and Form 323-E Ownership Data as of October 1, 2017.* https://docs.fcc.gov/public/attachments/DA-21-1101A1_Rcd.pdf

Government Accountability Office (GAO). (2008, March). *Media ownership, economic factors influence the number of media outlets in local markets, while ownership by Minorities and Women Appears Limited and Is Difficult to Assess* (GAO 08-383). https://www.gao.gov/assets/gao-08-383.pdf

Kerner Commission Report. (1968). *Report of the National Advisory Commission on Civil Disorders.* U.S. Government Printing Office. https://www.hsdl.org/?abstract&did=35837

5

# In Honor of Dr. Carolyn M. Byerly: Contributions from Her Feminist Scholarship

ELIZABETH L. TOTH

After passing each other in numerous Association of Education in Journalism and Mass Communication (AEJMC) national conference hallways, Carolyn M. Byerly and I connected. In those hallways, we said we should "get together," but our conferences were always full of presentations, meetings and prior commitments. Back home and working at universities only a few miles from each other, we did find the time, at least once a semester over breakfast, to become fast friends, until she moved in 2022 to Washington State. It was an entirely organic thing. Frequently, two University of Maryland colleagues, Linda Steiner and Linda Aldoory, joined us. Over the years, I learned so much just by talking about our work. We shared career advice and experiences. Hearing of Carolyn's professional journey, my feminist thinking was sharpened immeasurably. To me, Carolyn is fearless in the face of discrimination and oppression. She has inspired me many times to be much bolder about my own research on women and public relations.

I am a feminist public relations scholar who does research on how masculinity dictates the practice of public relations. I have worked and taught for over 50 years in the field of public relations. So, it might be odd to include me in this festschrift. In contrast to Byerly's feminist scholarship on women and media that renders women invisible or in gendered ways, my feminist work on the field of public relations looks at the oppressions and lack of influence by a female-intensive field. In public relations, women comprise 70 percent of public relations practitioners (Meng & Neill, 2021, p. 4). However, despite their numbers, women working in public relations are constrained by societal, media, organizational, professional, and individual beliefs and values to follow masculine norms (Aldoory & Toth, 2021). Even with their record numbers in both technical and managerial public relations positions, women public relations practitioners are not known to improve women's equality, whether in salary disparities or influencing the marketplace of ideas. However, despite what would seem to be our different feminist interests, Byerly's research contributions have important overlap in the area of mediated communication theory that has helped theorize from a feminist perspective about the effect of media relations on public relations practice (Aldoory & Toth, 2021).

## Feminist Contributions to Global Media Studies and Political Economy Research

Byerly's impact on feminist studies in mass communication is prodigious and impossible to do justice to in this book chapter. Over a lifetime academic career, she has published widely in books, academic refereed and non-refereed journals, book chapters, and conference presentations. Her scholarship has influenced many important research issues that affect women's lives. I have chosen to write about three—her global research on women and media; her theoretical advancement on the impact of the media's political economy on women; and her efforts to advance feminist communication theory for media studies, the latter to be discussed in a separate section. Byerly's global leadership for women scholars is an indelible contribution (Byerly, 2011a, 2013a; Ross & Byerly, 2004). She edited *The Palgrave International Handbook of Women and Journalism*, a 29-chapter anthology on the status of women in media organizations across the world. The handbook was inspired by the *Global Report on the Status of Women in the News Media*, a 59-nation study for which Byerly was the principal investigator (Greenwald, 2015, p. 523). These two projects encouraged and supported women media scholars' voices from all over the world by publishing their work and connecting them with one another.

Byerly's political economy research agenda has called attention to how the media hold economic power and can create rules and laws, determining how resources are allocated; thereby, disadvantaging women's representation in media and women who work in media (Byerly, 2011b, 2013b, 2014, 2016). To encourage research on political economy theory, Byerly created the Byerly Award for Research in Feminist Political Economy of Communication, in the International Communication Association, to help fund research on macro-level issues in communication within a feminist analytical framework. Launched in 2023, the award call defines feminist political economy thusly:

> Concerned with ways that male privilege and domination are institutionalized within communication organizations and other social institutions, with a focus on the economic and policy arrangements that give men greater power. Feminist political economy research is also concerned with the impact of institutional bias related to women and communication, as well as how women's activism has challenged it. Women may be interpreted broadly to include all who are woman-identified.

## Byerly's Contributions to Feminist Communication Theory Building, Naming and Intersectionality

I highlight Byerly's research agenda advocating for more feminist communication theory because of her call to move beyond the study of women's representation in media, "examinations of content as disembodied phenomena" (2014, p. 14). Although her essay urged scholars to examine the structures that determine content, this quote resonated with my observations of the many public relations studies describing media content, such as Twitter messages, with few substantive interpretations or theory building on if and how these messages communicated meanings that influenced public's perceptions, opinions or behavior, let along gendered perceptions. Communication is an overused and overly looked-after term that has all but receded into the background of scholarly studies. Yet, communication as a concept is not neutral. It carries with it presuppositions, such as whether it is studied as a product or a process. Nastasia and Rakow (2006) classified communication as *a priori* or essentializing and fixed in meaning, the product view, and *a posteriori* or the process view. The *a posteriori* view assumes that the meanings in communication, whether through speech, visuals, sound, etc., are socially constructed; therefore, meanings change through an exchange process, meant to persuade, reinforce or potentially aid in dialogue. By consciously acknowledging the *a posteriori* view, feminist communication scholarship is helped in its efforts to understand how women's lives are disadvantaged or possibly improved.

Byerly has urged feminist scholars to strive for improving their communication theory building—to be intentional, specific to a field and a phenomenon, and to address the challenges women face because of the communication processes in media. Feminist communication theory, Byerly wrote (2018), should be defined as "a coherent set of propositions that together provide an overarching explanation for phenomena associated with women and communication that is observed, researched, and analyzed" (p. 22). Feminist communication theory should be rigorous with a specific purpose. It "serves to make up our debate and discourse about how gender constitutes society and how it is used for power" (Linda Aldoory, personal communication, in Byerly, 2018, p. 22). Feminist communication theory helps to explain how media content reinforces organizational and social values. Feminist communication theory should be used for women's progress in advancing women's equality. Theories after all begin with ideas articulated and over time these words are refined, taken-up by others, and some become consensus ways of expressing concepts among the general public.

Byerly reinforces that the way important theory building process begins is with the articulation through words that can have profound consequences: "feminist communication theory begins with language and the speech acts that bring it into the public discourse" (2018, p. 28). Feminist communication scholars should strive to understand the specific concepts and constructs of communication, as for example "difference, voice and representation" (Rakow & Wackwitz, 2004). Byerly adds to the list that additional concepts of communication should include not only women's representation in media but also the misrepresentation, silence, and invisibility of women (Byerly, 2018, p. 26). Byerly (2021) also called attention to other missing concepts that should be studied in feminist communication work, such as women's rights, civil rights and human rights concerns missing because of the lack of women and people of color on major TV news programming who could give voice to their meanings.

Illustrating how feminist communication theory is built, Byerly and Hill (2012; see also Byerly, 2020) proposed reformulation theory, a means and analytical framework for explaining how feminist political activity reframes (reformulates) the social meaning of women's experiences in women's own terminology (p. 17). Their research found that between the years 1960 and 2000, the *New York Times* made adjustments to its language choices covering violence against women, over time adopting terms published by feminists working in the battered women's and the anti-rape movements (p. 12). Byerly and Hill called their reformulation theory an example of radical theory building because it sought to explain social changes that are transformative. Two additional feminist communication theory concepts that gained specificity through Byerly's writing are naming and intersectionality.

Naming ideas is a human enterprise. Even with established rules and best practices in scholarship for developing theories, we are challenged to see the potential biases of words we use that reinforce social inequities. Naming in journalism was theorized by Byerly in her essay on the use of names of victims of sexual assault. Byerly (1996) wrote about the disagreements in newsrooms about naming victims; some arguing that naming destigmatizes female victimization, and others arguing that the naming is not enough to overcome social rape narratives that find some victims worthy of sympathy and others not, depending on race, class, marital status. Byerly contributed a feminist communication analysis of rape and battering language used in media that showed overtime the media adopting new narratives, "e.g., sexual harassment, acquaintance rape and martial rape" that agenda-setting social movements have advanced (p. 57). Byerly has continued to argue for the importance of naming choices. In her planned but undelivered remarks for a 2022 ICA conference panel, she makes us reconsider how the naming choice of "gender" erases "woman/women" because the word "gender" is more acceptable. She wrote:

> The word gender is a bit like the word diversity—everyone likes it because its meaning is harmless, non threatening and never raises the REAL specter of discrimination, marginalization, secondary status, hatred, or harm that women and other marginalized groups experience. (C. M. Byerly, personal communication, June 7, 2022)

Byerly advanced feminist communication theory by calling attention to the scholarly responsibility to use intersectionality to make sure our feminist theorizing is valid:

> Intersectionality theory in communication studies has grown through the diverse work of feminist scholars who insist on broadening the analytical terrain to encompass power relations associated with gender *and* nationality, race, ethnicity, textuality, and processes of globalization. (Byerly, 2018, p. 24)

This point has become very apparent to me in my own work that reinforced unconsciously over several years with what has become known as "the standard White woman in public relations." Examinations of public relations women's roles done quantitatively consistently have reported samples that were almost all White females because so few women of color practice public relations. However, rather than seeking out women of color to bring their voices into public relations and gender analyses, there has been an unspoken, unacknowledged generalization that White female practitioners stood in for all females (see Aldoory & Toth, 2021). Byerly tells of her own intersectionality consciousness developing because of her work in an anti-violence center in the 1970s and 1980s. A center advocate brought a Latina woman to the police after she had been beaten and raped by a boyfriend. Because of her accent and physical appearance of poverty, the police officer directed his questions not to the victim but to the advocate who was white, middle-class, and educated, making the victim demeaned and invisible. As a result of such stories, it became clear to Byerly that to understand situations of violence against women:

> We had to factor in racism, classism, ethnocentrism, national origin and homophobia that we saw in institutional practices that surrounded and enabled the violence to exist. In the process, we also had to call out the demons in our own lives, in our family and in personal relationships, and in communities that had shaped us. (2017, p. 25)

Intersectionality, attributed to Crenshaw's work in the late 1970s (1993) on the institutional biases of discrimination along more than one axis of oppression, was developed by Byerly (2017) in her essay on feminist intersectional research by including the voices of intersectional feminist scholars. Among them was Cucklanz's assertion that:

> Feminist theory on communication should account for not only the interplay of gender and power but also the relevance of other textual elements including race, sexuality and class. Power imbalances of gender are understood as intersecting with power relations of class, race, sexuality and other categories including religion and ethnicity. (Cucklanz, 2016, p. 1)

While transparency as a goal in feminist communication research is generally accepted, Byerly (2017) took the next step in theory building by confronting the challenge of how to learn through research the ways that multiple identities with their oppressions intersect. Bringing us the work of Wallis (2015), Byerly emphasizes Wallis' point that "to identify the conditions or practices that cut across all of the oppressions, thereby uniting them to an intersection, we must target the structural underpinning of the practices that have to be ended" (Wallis, 2015, p. 605). For Wallis, the structural underpinning was class. For Byerly, the underpinning is the agency exercised in capital:

> Intersectionality scholars cannot investigate or address the under-representation of women or people of color in media without considering who owns the media, and this takes us headlong down a linear path of media ownership, communication policies, and structures of capitalism that allow discriminatory practices. (Byerly, 2017, p. 31)

## Conclusion

Byerly's body of scholarship shares with us a wonderfully multidisciplinary knowledge and intellect. Her essays have been extremely welcome to this reader, giving historical context for understanding her arguments and advancements for feminist theory. Her published research expands the feminist media agenda by making it possible through her editing leadership the voices of global feminist scholars; and, by introducing and advancing knowledge on political economy; women's activism; and, theorizing on the transformation of media to achieve women's social equity. Byerly's call (2018) to give more rigor and depth to feminist communication theory's body of knowledge in an important message for feminist media scholars. Byerly's work on feminist communication theory provides a middle-range level of analysis that also helps explain the communication processes of naming and intersectionality—providing more specificity to revealing the impact of media content on women's lives. Her writings on feminist communication theory have led to an increased understanding of feminist activist strategies.

Byerly's research has enriched my feminist research on public relations. Her scholarship on feminist communication studies of media overlaps and contributes to understanding the gendered media relations found in public relations practice. Public relations practitioners are almost two-thirds women who create messages for organizations that stand to reinforce organizational and socially gendered norms. Public relations women are message makers and disseminators. It is very likely that they reinforce masculine norms through their language, voice and representation choices and subsidize the news-gathering process rather than attempting to reformulate societal meanings leading to improved women's equity. Byerly's writings on the communication concepts of naming and intersectionality are especially important because of the bias toward fixed and oversimplified meanings endemic in communication research, especially the academic quantitative striving toward generalization. Overall, Carolyn M. Byerly's contributions have led immeasurably to the advancement of women throughout the world by exposing inequities but also in providing a path forward to alleviate them.

## References

Aldoory, L., & Toth, E. L. (2021). *The future of feminism in public relations and strategic communication.* Rowman & Littlefield.

Byerly, C. M. (1996). Beyond the question of naming: Ethical dimensions of sex-crime reporting: An essay review. *Journal of Mass Media Ethics, 11*(1), 53–57.

Byerly, C. M. (2011a, March). *Global report on status of women in news media* (Technical report). International Women's Media Foundation.

Byerly, C. M. (2011b). Behind the scenes of women's broadcast ownership. *Howard Journal of Communications, 29*, 24–42.

Byerly, C. M. (Ed.). (2013a). *Palgrave international handbook on women and* journalism. Palgrave Macmillan.

Byerly, C. M. (2013b). Factors affecting the status of women journalists: A structural analysis. In C. Byerly (Ed.), *Palgrave international handbook on women and journalism* (pp. 11–23). Palgrave Macmillan.

Byerly, C. M. (2014). The geography of women and media scholarship. In K. Ross (Ed.), *The handbook of gender, sex, and media.* John Wiley & Sons. https://doi.org/10.1002/97811181425.chi

Byerly, C. M. (2016). Stasis and shifts in feminist media scholarship. In C. Cerqueira; R. Cabecinhas & S. I. Magalhaes (Eds.), *Gender in focus: (New) trends in media* (pp. 15–27). CECS. https://repositorio-aberto.up.pt/bitstream/10216/107734/2/218923.pdf#page=15

Byerly, C. M. (2017). Feminist intersectionality research in communications: Origins, contributions and tensions. *Ex Aequo, 35*, 23–32. http://exaequo.apem-estudos.org/artigo/35-feminist-intersectionality-research-in-communications-origins-contributions-and-tensions

Byerly, C. M. (2018). Feminism, theory, and communication: Progress, debates, and challenges ahead. In D. Harp, J. Loke, & I. Bachmann (Eds.), *Feminist approaches to media theory and research* (pp. 19–35). Palgrave Macmillan.

Byerly, C. M. (2020). Incels online: Reframing sexual violence. *Communication Review, 23*, 290–308. https://doi.org/10.1080/10714421.2020.1829305

Byerly, C. M. (2021). *Why white male dominance of news media is so persistent.* Women's Media Center. https://womensmediacenter.com/news-features/why-white-male-dominance-of-news-media-is-so-persistent

Byerly, C. M., & Hill, M. (2012, December). Reformulation theory: Gauging feminist impact on news of violence against women. *Journal of Women and Gender (Symposium Issue).* https://www.academia.edu/2247510/Reformulation_Theory_Gauging_Feminist_Impact_on_News_of_Violence_Against_Women

Crenshaw, K. (1993). Mapping the margins: Intersectionality, identity, politics, and violence against women of color. *Stanford Law Review, 43*(6), 1241–1299.

Cucklanz, L. (2016). Feminist theory in communication. In *The international encyclopedia of communication theory and philosophy* (pp. 1–10). John Wiley & Sons.
Greenwald, M. (2015). The Palgrave international handbook of women and journalism. *Journalism and Mass Communication Quarterly, 92*(2). https://www.proquest.com/openview/2b5b977b67b639498a379930ee49a3f0/1?pq-origsite=gscholar&cbl=15546
Meng, J., & Neill, M. S. (2021). *PR women with influence: Breaking through the ethical and leadership challenges.* Peter Lang.
Nastasia, D., & Rakow, L. (2006). *What is communication? Unsettling a priori and a posteriori approaches.* Paper presented to the International Communication Association Annual Conference.
Rakow, L. F., & Wackwitz, L. (Eds.). (2004). *Feminist communication theory: Selections in context.* Sage.
Ross, K., & Byerly, C. M. (Eds.). (2004). *Women and media: International perspectives.* Blackwell.
Wallis, V. (2015). Intersectionality's binding agent. *New Political Science, 37*(4), 604–619.

# 6

# Carolyn the Brave: Five Lessons from a Trailblazer

DAFNA LEMISH

Carolyn and I met for the first time in Miami in 1992, during a retreat sponsored by what was then the Feminist Scholarship Interest Group, preceding the International Communication Association (ICA) annual conference. I had traveled from Israel, scouting my way for the first time, and very unsure about the feminist scholarship community. At a certain point, I decided to just jump straight into the heart of this new world. My life has never been the same since. I cannot recall how and why we started to speak—knowing Carolyn the way I know her now. I am guessing she could sense my wonder and discomfort and initiated a conversation to help me feel at ease. The next thing I knew Kay, Carolyn's loving partner, was teaching me self-defense, as I became aware that my LGBTQ colleagues were vulnerable to harassment and violence. As a heterosexual married woman from across the ocean, I had no idea: I was that naive and ignorant.

So, what shall I write about? What lessons learned from Carolyn since that day do I treasure most? It is not about feminist theory and scholarship (although this became critical knowledge!). It is not about political economy and gender inequalities worldwide (although these were life-changing lessons!). It is not even about the professional world of journalism and the role that gender plays in the stories we are told and how they matter in our lives (although these have changed how I consume news in fundamental ways!). I am sure others in this collection will do a much better job writing about these topics, and more. I want to write about what I have learned from Carolyn regarding the qualities of an engaged feminist scholar-activist. I titled this piece—Carolyn The Brave. BRAVE is also an acronym, with each letter representing a quality of Carolyn's that impacted so many of us.

## B

B in BRAVE stands for Lesson No. 1—BE A ROLE MODEL. "Be the change you want to see" is clearly a guiding light for Carolyn, as she demonstrates in her behavior—both through action and speech—the values she preaches. A new feminist initiative? She will take charge. Support the vulnerable? Stand up for your principles? She will be out there demonstrating, gathering, signing petitions, and motivating others. Volunteering time and resources for a just cause? She will find the energy, the money, the capacity, and the time. Mentor younger colleagues? She will spend endless hours of quality time with students through face-to-face, emails, reviews, and Zoom—seemingly in any form of communication known to humans.

As a role model, Carolyn leads fearlessly. In my School of Communication and Information at Rutgers, there is an old-and-torn poster hanging next to one of the offices with an image of Roxane Gay. The best-selling author, commentator, feminist, and social justice activist is currently our Gloria Steinem Endowed Chair in Media, Culture, and Feminist Studies. The poster reads: "When you can't find someone to follow, you have to find a way to lead by example" (Gay, 2014, p. 7). I am guessing Carolyn would have happily hung that poster, too.

## R

R in BRAVE is for RESEARCH that can make a difference. Much of Carolyn's scholarship was engaged in research, grounded in political economy, and focused on journalism and women's experiences. She often wrote about how her scholarship is grounded in her activism: "My understanding of journalism's role in shifting public discourse and creating better awareness of women's problems—which I would carry with me into research and teaching—dated from those experiences in grassroots activism. [. . .] it was feminist activism that shaped what would become my academic path" (Byerly, 2012, pp. 42–43). She validates what a colleague, Angharad (Anghy) Valdivia, offered in the adaptation of the feminist statement "the personal is political" into "the intellectual is the personal is the political" (Valdivia, 1999, p. 159). I have quoted this saying in my writing several times, but none is more fitting than in this context.

Carolyn's interest in women's activism (Byerly, 1995), cross-cultural studies of women's work inside and outside mainstream media organizations (Byerly & Ross, 2006), and on situating women and their interests within the policy, finances, and ownership of media industries (Byerly, 2014) are just a few examples of a scholarly trajectory deeply grounded in research that is relevant, actionable, and impactful. The women in her research whose voices she brought to the pages of her publications were not only the marginalized or victimized but also agents of change, actively intervening and pursuing equality, and societal transformation. Her scholarship documents how women have organized to improve working conditions, media content and establish women-owned media to gain and protect a public voice.

We have had multiple conversations over the years when Carolyn was lamenting the overemphasis in feminist media studies and publications on gender representations that are devoid of analyses of the institutions that produce them and the structural constraints of the media industry. She expressed the strong view that representation studies alone do not provoke the much-needed change of women's status in the media. She always strongly advocated for research that makes a significant difference in the lives of women and marginalized communities.

## A

A in BRAVE stands for ALIGNING feminism against all forms of injustice and discrimination. Carolyn, working within a framework of intersectional feminism, aligned her feminism with gender, LGTBQ, racial, social, and other forms of injustice. It is evident in her cross-cultural writing, in her leadership as the chair of the Feminist Scholarship Division of the ICA, in her interpersonal relationships, and perhaps more than anything else—in her deep commitment to her career leadership and mentorship at Howard University, a historically black institution, where she represented a very negligible minority of white faculty.

What is also unique about Carolyn's commitment to social justice is that her mentorship flows in all directions, not only to young and inexperienced students. For example, her impressive scholarship is internationally recognized and models the same principles of accessibility, diversity, and collaboration. I have followed her work on an enormous project, the *Global Report on the Status of Women in the News Media* (Byerly, 2011; also as an academic edited book, Byerly, 2013) where she managed as the principal investigator and editor to assemble a very large international group of 170 diverse researchers from 59 countries. She trained and coordinated the supervision of these participants over three years. The result was not only this highly valuable project on the state of women in journalism worldwide—something no one had attempted to accomplish before—but also a ripple effect of creating a large cadre of new researchers working around the world, including in many marginalized and disadvantaged societies. In itself, this has been a monumental and exemplary task of mentorship of women of all human demographics and characteristics.

## V

V in BRAVE stands for VOICING one's opinions and speaking up to power.

Carolyn's career is marked by risk-taking: courageously expressing her views in the pursuit of social justice, sometimes at great risk. Her experience of being unjustly denied tenure and promotion was the price paid for a clear, outspoken feminist agenda in teaching and research, openly supporting gay rights, and engaging in critical curriculum activist interventions for a progressive social justice agenda. The loss of the subsequent lawsuit to reverse the decision could have been detrimental to anyone. But not to Carolyn The Brave. She turned this traumatic experience into the fire that fed her revolutionary spirit. As she reflected on this and other experiences, she wrote: "Generally speaking, activist academics walk an uncertain path. It has never been easy for those of us on the political left to survive in the essentially conservative environment of higher education—particularly when we raise challenges to that system. The classroom curricula we teach, the kind of research we undertake, the kinds of questions we raise about the world, and the academic processes we enter into will probably always put us at risk—even if we are nice people who work hard, do our jobs well and are meaningful contributors to our fields" (Byerly, 2012, p. 43).

Over the years she used her unique voice to mentor her peers, including myself, by constantly challenging assumptions about our discipline as well as our teaching and advising. She set herself a goal that underscores everything she has been doing: "Helping women's voices to be heard, both among each other and in the general population" (Byerly, 1995, p. 120). Throughout her career, she has consistently "mentored up" the ICA board and leadership, for example, in advocating for feminist and international scholars and scholarship, as well as introducing critical thinking about taken-for-granted blind spots in understanding our discipline's power structures. As the chair of the Feminist Scholarship Division, she challenged the ICA Publications Committee to expand contributions by women and international scholars and supported Marian Meyers' initiative to establish the *Journal of Communication, Culture & Critique*, ICA's flagship that "publishes critical, interpretive, and qualitative research examining the role of communication and cultural criticism in today's world." She also led the Feminist Scholarship Division in requesting that the ICA board place its funds in Socially Responsible Investments (SRIs), a practice that was adopted. It was often a difficult path, with a personal price (one wonders why her accomplishments were not recognized by any of ICA's awards, for example). I am reminded by the quote attributed to the U.S. Congresswoman and activist Shirley Chisholm: "If they don't give you a seat at the table, bring a folding chair." Carolyn carried around so many folding chairs to so many boardrooms and executive offices of people with the power to make change.

## E

E in BRAVE stands for ELEVATE others, a key characteristic of Carolyn's conduct in the world that should have already become evident from the lines so far. At every step of the way, she engaged in promoting colleagues and students. During more than a decade and a half at Howard University, she mentored dozens of graduate students from across the globe, many of whom returned to their home countries as change agents. Her devotion to young scholars and their ability to conduct research in the service of social change expanded beyond her academic institutions to leadership in mentorship for the Commission on the Status of Women of the Association for Education in Journalism and Mass Communication (AEJMC).

Furthermore, taking the broad view of mentorship that Carolyn holds, she advises young scholars on every aspect of their work: reviewing articles and conference papers; engaging in her research in a collaborative and supportive manner; developing networking skills at conferences; and completing tenure reviews. Indeed, in every encounter she looks to guide her mentees by materializing their potential while contributing to the better good of society. First-hand stories from former students about the role and impact she has had in their lives illustrate it best. I was introduced at an ICA conference to one female student from Africa, who was a part of Carolyn's ceaseless efforts to help young scholars network. She told me how Carolyn spent endless hours in conversations with her, providing opportunities, offering enthusiastic encouragement to attend the event, and assisting her in developing networking skills at conferences. Similarly, a male student from India who continued his graduate degree at my previous institution, told me that he owes his desire to remain in the academic world to Carolyn; she modeled for him what a professor at a university can do to elevate students and make a difference. Through such encounters, I have seen and heard about Carolyn guiding her students through doors she opened for them to find their own voices, challenging them to think for themselves and to commit to making a difference in the world.

The Teresa Award for the Advancement of Feminist Scholarship at ICA, which Carolyn was key to establishing and stewarding (with Marian Meyers, and recently with Natalia Rybas) from its inception in 2009, is one of the jewels of her efforts to elevate other women. In an introduction to a book featuring essays by the first decade of awardees, she and her colleagues explain: "The award is important in reaffirming the Division's commitment to theory, research, and activism in the international arena and to establish what it means to give priority to feminism as a global concern" (Byerly et al., 2022, pp. xi–xii). But Carolyn did not rest on her laurels with this successful endeavor. She was one of the organizers of the Helen award to recognize and support emerging feminist scholars who are bound to be the next movers and shakers (named after Professor Linda Steiner's mother). As I write these lines, I just learned that she has established the Byerly Award for Research in Feminist Political Economy of Communication to encourage and support research on macro-level issues in communication within a feminist analytical framework.

## BRAVE

So, what have I learned from Carolyn The Brave more than 30 years since our first encounter in Miami in May of 1992? I have learned how a feminist approach to life is all-encompassing—in activism, scholarship, teaching, politics, and relationships—as one moves through the world. I learned that the values of being a role model, such as doing research that matters, aligning feminism with all forms of discrimination and injustice, voicing one's opinions fearlessly, and elevating others are the true hallmarks of her legacy to feminist media scholarship and to our disciplines more generally. I have learned that her pedagogical practices in and out of class follow, according to her own testament, Henry Giroux's argument that critical pedagogy is "deeply civic, political and moral practice" (Byerly, 2012, p. 54). I have learned that having someone like Carolyn Byerly in your life as a colleague, a leader, and a role model serves as a guiding lighthouse and a beacon of hope. I learned that I am so very fortunate to call her also—my friend.

## References

Byerly, C. M. (1995). News, consciousness, and social participation: The role of women's feature service in world news. In A. N. Valdivia (Ed.), *Feminism, multiculturalism, and the media: Global diversities* (pp. 105–122). Sage.

Byerly, C. M. (2011). *Global report on the status of women in the news media.* International Women's Media Foundation. https://www.iwmf.org/resources/global-report-on-the-status-of-women-in-the-news-media/

Byerly, C. M. (2012). Gender, critical scholarship, and the politics of tenure and promotion. In M. Meyers (Ed.), *Women in higher education: The fight for equity* (pp. 41–56). Hampton Press.

Byerly, C. M. (Ed.). (2013). *The Palgrave international handbook of women and journalism.* Palgrave Macmillan.

Byerly, C. M. (2014). Women and media control: Feminist interrogations at the macro-level. In C. Carter, L. Steiner, & L. McLaughlin (Eds.), The Routledge companion to media and gender (pp. 105–115). Routledge.

Byerly, C. M., & Ross, K. (2006). *Women & media: A critical introduction.* Blackwell.

Byerly, C. M., Rybas, N., & Meyers, M. (2022). Foreword. In S. Eckert & I. Bachmann (Eds.), *Reflections on feminist communication and media scholarship: Theory, method, impact* (pp. x–xii). Routledge.

Chisholm, S. *Seat at the table* (original quote source unknown). https://nam02.safelinks.protection.outlook.com/?url=https%3A%2F%2Fwww.bringyourownchair.org%2Fabout-shirley-chisholm%2F&data=05%7C01%7Cdafna.lemish%40rutgers.edu%7C84b524b880c8405b518a08da56ea7540%7Cb92d2b234d35447093ff69aca6632ffe%7C1%7C0%7C637917862235011812%7CUnknown%7CTWFpbGZsb3d8eyJWIjoiMC4wLjAwMDAiLCJQIjoiV2luMzIiLCJBTiI6Ik1haWwiLCJXVCI6Mn0%3D%7C3000%7C%7C%7C&sdata=k%2FOiYbn8orSxL0MIIAhG%2BIaHvWN1Jnyu3RUeX75nrNI%3D&reserved=0

Gay, R. (2014). *Bad feminist: Essays.* HarperCollins.

*Journal of Communication, Culture & Critique.* https://www.icahdq.org/page/Journals

Valdivia, A. (1999). A guided tour through one adolescent girl's culture. In S. R. Mazzarella & N. O. Pecora (Eds.), *Growing up girls: Popular culture and the construction of identity* (pp. 159–171). Peter Lang.

# 7

# From the Local to the Global: Dr. Carolyn M. Byerly's Praxis and Theory

LANA F. RAKOW

The year was 1986. The place was Chicago, Illinois, at the International Communication Association annual conference. Feminist scholars from across the country and some from other parts of the world gathered in multiple sessions for the first time in that organization to hear each other present their feminist work. The excitement was palpable. The energy was contagious. Only a year before at the association's Hawaii conference, a group of feminists, frustrated at the lack of venues for feminist work in ICA, had started a petition to form the Feminist Scholarship Interest Group. Within a few years the group would grow so rapidly it would be granted division status. Those of us who gathered then could not foresee what the next 40 years would bring as a result of that Chicago conference. Careers of new scholars would be launched. Work that would reshape the field of communication was propelled forward. The lifelong friendships of women would be started. Networks that would span the globe began.

Carolyn Byerly was in that group that gathered in Chicago. She would prove to be an exemplar of what that moment in time foretold. After her feminist anti-violence activism in the 1970s and 1980s and an initial career in journalism, she was a graduate student then at the University of Washington, where she focused on women and news. It didn't take long for her to establish what would be a decades-long career as a feminist scholar and to help carry forward the commitment to making feminist change in academic organizations and institutions. She also reflected the zeitgeist of the movement of feminist scholars at the time, combining research with activism, pushing for change in media organizations, and networking with feminists across the globe.

While feminist activists have long repeated the social change mantra to think global and act local, Byerly demonstrated that the reverse is equally important. Our local experiences are the fodder for what makes us feminists. Byerly points to her own consciousness-raising from lived experience as the basis for her understanding of complex power relations (Byerly, 2017b, pp. 26–27). By collecting and connecting our personal knowledge to that of others, regional and global patterns that shape our lives become apparent. The need for making those connections at an international level and incorporating them into her publications came early in Byerly's academic career, marking the productive next decades of her work. This essay's reflection on Carolyn Byerly's career will point out briefly two of the most significant contributions made by Byerly. The first is found in her own praxis and her research on feminist praxis. The second is her attention to political economy and policy. These are interrelated themes that tie together the need for change from injustice experienced at the local level but derived from larger forces that stratify and oppress people on the basis of class, gender, and race. She at one point recently summed up the relations between the themes in her work, saying they provided her an analytical framework. With a commitment to women's media activism through her own praxis, she explained that her research used feminist political economy to describe how media policy has reinforced male dominance through ownership and control (Byerly, 2017a, pp. 108–109).

## Praxis and Feminist Change

The feminist activism that Carolyn Byerly engaged in prior to her doctoral work clearly provided the basis for her organizing and networking initiatives as a feminist scholar. She not only made a bridge between her own activism and research but also she would herself become a bridge between activists and scholars. She would serve as a steadfast mentor and colleague to other women. It began with her leadership of the Feminist Scholarship Division, serving as chair and vice-chair early on, and continuing with a lifetime of steadfast support for the Division and the cause of feminist work. She was instrumental in establishing the ICA Teresa Award for the Advancement of Feminist Scholarship and recently created the Byerly Award for Research in Feminist Political Economy in Communication.

In the Association for Education in Journalism and Mass Communication, she would serve on the Commission on the Status of Women as its research chair and as co-chair of its mentoring program, as well as serve as chair of the Ethical Standards Committee of the Minority and Communication Division. Reflective of her international work, she was a member of the Steering Committee for the Global Alliance on Media and Gender and chair of its Research & Policy Committee, a cooperative program of the International Association for Media & Communication Research and UNESCO (Byerly, 2016, p. 25).

Byerly's own research was punctuated by several large-scale global projects. One example of this feminist praxis was her study for the International Women's Media Foundation, in which women's status in 522 news companies in 59 countries was investigated looking at the relationship between to explain the advancement or lag in women's status in relation to their media (Byerly, 2016, p. 21). Throughout her commitment to making feminist change in and through professional associations and global networks, Byerly didn't leave behind her commitment to ending rape, harassment, and violence against women, using research to aid our understanding of how it was manifesting in a new era of communication. Through recent research she conducted on the incel movement (Byerly, 2011; Byerly, 2020), for example, she demonstrated the potential long-term consequences of feminist praxis. She explained that traditional and internet news sources provide the public most of its information about incels, which she defined as "involuntary celibates with misogynistic and often violent tendencies" (p. 1). Her study demonstrated that social media helped incels find each other and organize. On the other hand, most news stories about incels provided thoughtful explorations of their misogyny, stories influenced, she concluded, by the feminist movement (p. 17). Thus, feminist research can help us understand the consequences of feminist activist strategies.

This looks at the consequences of feminist activism had precursors in Byerly's work. Her commitment to praxis and social change was evident in the model of women's media activism that she and co-author Karen Ross laid out in 2006. Because feminist activism has had to address women's invisibility and lack of access to public spaces, Byerly and Ross described how women's media activism seeks access and alternatives to the dominant public sphere (Byerly & Ross, 2006, p. 100). They explained that the first of four paths used by activists leads them to produce media products as part of their political work. The second leads women media professionals to work within industries to change practices. The third leads feminists outside media industries to use strategies applying pressure to media to expand women's available means of communication through, for example, policy. The final path leads women to create their own media, gaining control over messages and distribution (pp. 125–127). This model would be extended with Byerly and Marcus Hill's reformulation theory in 2012. Looking at coverage by the New York Times over a 40-year period, they traced changes in language about rape, incest, wife battering, and other gender violence (Byerly & Hill, 2012). They credited the feminist activism that began around the beginning of that 40-year period with shifts over time in reporter language to more feminist terms and with increased coverage using feminist frames (see the discussion in Byerly, 2018, pp. 30–31). As a contribution to radical feminist theory, the authors suggested that it was an example of research that can demonstrate feminist media activism's impact on news. Identifying and naming the phenomenon of reformation theory responded to Byerly's own call for feminist communication scholars to build on our work by giving names to our theories (Byerly, 2018, pp. 27, 30).

## Policy, Political Economy and Macro-Level Analysis

Byerly's concerns with media, policy, and the economy have had a long history in her career but are found with increasing frequency in the titles of her work in the last decade, as she urged her feminist communication colleagues to attend to the macro level. She expressed concern about the overemphasis of feminist communication research on women's representations in media content rather than on the structural causes for those representations, which result in women's underrepresentation in media decision-making and news programming (Byerly, 2016, p. 1). She argued that a macro-level analysis was least developed in feminist scholarship, such that the institutional and financial arrangements of media industries have been ignored or overlooked (p. 23).

Her work on policy has consistently described the low rate of women's ownership and control of media as the result of economic and policy barriers. Three publications in the past decade provide examples of her approach, also demonstrating the problem of policy and media as a fast-moving target, as political players and the technology landscape change at a dizzying pace. In 2011, she and her co-authors from Howard University could afford some optimism that the rise of media mergers and acquisitions during the 1980s and 1990s and the concentration of media power and ownership in the hands of a few mega-corporations under neoliberalism had been countered by the U.S. 3rd Circuit Courts of Appeal's decision in 2011 to deny more media cross-ownership (Byerly et al.,

2011, p. 425). They were hopeful that the case would finally make it possible to develop race- and gender-conscious communication policies that would increase media ownership by women and racial minorities. At the same time, they also urged anti-trust actions to break up the current media oligopoly. By 2017, it was clear such progress would not be made. In a publication that year, Byerly (2017a) provided details about one important aspect of feminist media policy activism in which the FCC was challenged, a partial history of feminist activism that has been neglected by both critical and feminist communication scholars. In 2019, responding to UNESCO's goal of empowerment of women. She set out to show the structural obstacles preventing women from exercising their right to communicate (Byerly, 2019). The obstacles are financial-, policy- and governance-related, she concluded (p. 24). Noteworthy in the publication is a table of women's global underrepresentation on boards of major digital companies, including, for example, Alphabet Google (owner then of Google, YouTube, and many others) at a shocking eight percent (p. 25). In the short period of time from 2011 to 2019, Byerly's work showed that the policy landscape had changed, new media concentrations had developed, media barons of the twenty-first century (wealthy white men) were buying and selling media technology "real estate" and making fortunes, and regulation on behalf of women and racial minorities was more and more difficult to mount.

The part played by capitalism in these struggles over ownership and control has been first and foremost the explanation reached for by Byerly. The importance Byerly places on the economy in systems of oppression can't be overstated. In recent years, she has made her position clear: "In my own research, I typically adopt a feminist critical economy theory of media, which is grounded in Marxist assumptions but which also factors in intersectionality concerns of gender and race relations" (Byerly, 2018, p. 26). White men's wealth enables them to own media and control media law and policies because of their ability to control Congress and the Federal Communications Commission, she said (p 26). The role of class in producing these outcomes therefore assumes center stage in her understanding of intersectionality, a key theory of feminist scholarship.

Calling herself a proponent of intersectionality, Byerly explained she came to intersectionality through her early feminist anti-violence work in the 1970s and 1980s, where she and others in the movement realized they "also had to factor in racism, classism, ethnocentrism, national origin and homophobia that we saw in the institutional practices that surrounded and enabled the violence to exist" (Byerly, 2017b, p. 25). She credits early critical scholars, citing histories by Victor Wallis (2015) and Eve Mitchell (2013) rather than Kimberle Crenshaw (1993), for recognizing intersectionality, defining intersectionality as "the complex intersection of identities that produces discrimination and marginalization" (Byerly, 2017b, p. 24). "The matter of the hierarchy of concerns in intersectionality has been raised most clearly by Marxist feminists like Eve Mitchell (2013) . . ." she argued (Byerly, 2017b, p. 28). Capitalism has been the "key determinant of power in men's and women's relationships," and in the same way, shaped race relations, Byerly concluded in Mitchell's argument (Byerly, 2017b, p. 28). The need to navigate "multiple oppressions" leads Byerly to side with Mitchell's conclusion that gender or sexuality or race relations should be considered within class (p. 29). She notes that Wallis concludes "that the original goal of intersectionality theory—that of binding the oppressed constituencies together into a coherent political force—has not been realized" (Byerly, 2017b, p. 29; Wallis, 2015, p. 607).

Byerly summarized her position on the economic determinants of power the next year by saying, "In the wider society, those who hold class power are able to make decisions that create the rules and laws and determine how resources are to be allocated" (Byerly, 2018, p. 26). Byerly's criticism that the economy is seriously overlooked in most feminist communication scholarship is accurate. Even so, her Marxist analysis is controversial, even among materialist feminists. It cannot explain why it is white men who overwhelmingly have class power. It cannot explain racism and misogyny before capitalism and in locations around the globe with different economies or how race and gender interact. It does not take into account the sustained rebuke by women of color, who reject white women's notion of solidarity around a false universal "woman," which enables white women to ignore their own privileged identities and marginalizes the experiences of other women.

Intersectionality as theorized by Crenshaw (1989) and others after her rejects a view of gender, race and class as simply additive identities rather than particular configurations of privilege and oppression in conflict with each other. In contrast to Byerly, materialist feminist Victoria Basham (2021) adds the historical role of patriarchy back into consideration alongside the rise of capitalism. She advocates "analyzing class as co-constitutive of race, gender and other social categories—and not race, gender and other social categories as constitutive of class," in order "to understand and challenge how capitalism is organized in different settings, and how it interacts with other social relations. There is not one struggle but many," Basham concludes (p. 181).

## Implications for the Future

Carolyn Byerly, through her career as a feminist scholar, has advocated that we recognize and engage in feminist media activism. She has insisted that we account for the role of capitalism if we are to understand media policy, ownership, and control. As a member of a cohort of feminist scholars who found companionship and support 40 years ago through the Feminist Scholarship Division of the International Communication Association, she has made her own mark on the field, on the development of feminist communication scholarship, and on changes of benefit to women. She made her mark by extending her early concerns about violence and harassment of women and the part played by news media to an awareness of the international prevalence of women's exclusion from media systems. She undertook her own scholarly praxis, putting research to the cause of feminist media activism, at the same time insisting that macro-levels of policy and the economy require our attention.

Despite her efforts and so many others, we are left with so much more work to do. Feminist scholars coming behind Byerly would do well to heed her advice. At a time when feminist advances are being overturned in the United States and across the world, we must pay attention to what changes have staying power and why, what feminist strategies worked, and how social change was undone. We must pay attention to the ownership and control of media and communication systems and who decides. We need more attention to how the internet should be designed and governed. We must continue to work on creating alliances across conflicts arising from various forms of privilege and marginalization.

One piece of work that remains almost untouched in the work of feminist communication scholars is designing and planning for the communication we need, civic and social communication systems of benefit to all, enabling participation and agency. We cannot advocate for change without knowing what we want and need, what these systems will look like, how they will be financed, how they will be regulated and by whom, how news could be defined and shared, what spaces for public discourse must be created, what processes for effecting democratic participation will make a difference. In a recent argument responding to UNESCO's goal for the empowerment of women, Byerly noted the lag in significant progress across the world in women's relationship to media ownership and decision-making. She succinctly captured the work ahead:

> The salient question to pose with this realization is how will women become full participants in their societies if they cannot affect the telling of their own

stories, if society does not see the wide array of images and roles they occupy, and people cannot obtain the information they need for society's advancement by addressing gender inequality? (Byerly, 2019, p. 29)

## References


Basham, V. M. (2021). A necessarily historical materialist moment? Feminist reflections on the need for grounded critique in an age of crises. *International Relations, 35*(1), 178–182. https://doi.org/10.1177/0047117821992408

Byerly, C. M. (2011). *Global report on the status of women in news media.* International Women's Media Foundation.

Byerly, C. M. (2016). Stasis and shifts in feminist media scholarship. In C. Cerqueira, R. Cabecinhas, & S. I. Magalhães (Eds.), *Gender in focus: (New) trends in media* (pp. 15–27). CECS.

Byerly, C. M. (2017a). Feminist activism and U.S. communications policy. In V. Pickard & G. Yang (Eds.), *Media activism in the digital age* (pp. 100–119). Routledge. https://doi.org/10.4324/9781315393940

Byerly, C. M. (2017b). Feminist intersectionality research in communications: Origins, contributions and tensions. *Ex Aequo, 35*, 23–32. http://exaequo.apem-estudos.org/artigo/35-feminist-intersectionality-research-in-communications-origins-contributions-and-tensions

Byerly, C. M. (2018). Feminism, theory, and communication: Progress, debates, and challenges ahead. In D. Harp, J. Loke, & I. Bachmann (Eds.), *Feminist approaches to media theory and research* (pp. 19–35). Palgrave Macmillan. https://doi.org/10.1007/978-3-319-90838-0

Byerly, C. M. (2019). Gender equality and media structures. In A. Vega Montiel & S. Macharia (Eds.), *Setting the gender agenda for communication policy.* United Nations Educational, Scientific & Cultural Organization. https://en.unesco.org/gamagandunitwin

Byerly, C. M. (2020). Incels online: Reframing sexual violence. *Communication Review, 23*(4), 1–19. https://doi.org/10.1080/10714421.2020.1829305.

Byerly, C. M., & Hill, M. (2012). Reformulation theory: Gauging feminist impact on news of violence against women. *Journal of Women and Gender, 5*, 1–20. https://www.academia.edu/2247510/Reformulation_Theory_Gauging_Feminist_Impact_on_News_of_Violence_Against_Women

Byerly, C. M., & Ross, K. (2006). *Women and media: A critical introduction.* Blackwell. https://doi.org/10.1002/9780470774908

Byerly, C. M., Park, Y. J., & R. Miles. (2011). Race and gender-conscious policies: Toward a more egalitarian communications future. *Journal of Information Policy, 1*, 425–440. https://doi.org/10.5325/jinfopoli.1.2011.0425

Crenshaw, K. (1989). Demarginalizing the intersection of race and sex: A Black feminist critique of antidiscrimination doctrine, feminist theory and antiracist politics. *University of Chicago Legal Forum, 1*, 139–167. https://chicagounbound.uchicago.edu/uclf/vol1989/iss1/8

Crenshaw, K. (1993). Mapping the margins: Intersectionality, identity politics, and violence against women of color. *Stanford Law Review, 43*(6), 1241–1299. https://doi.org/10.2307/1229039

Mitchell, E. (2013, September). *I am a woman and a human: A Marxist-feminist critique of intersectionality theory*. Unity and Struggle. https://unityandstruggle.org

Wallis, V. (2015). Intersectionality's binding agent. *New Political Science, 37*(4), 604–619. https://doi.org/10.1080/07393148.2015.1089032

# 8

# An Interview with Dr. Carolyn M. Byerly: Feminist, Scholar, Activist and "Partner in Crime"

MARIAN MEYERS

I have known Carolyn Byerly for more than 35 years. And she has been my friend and "partner in crime"[12] for the duration. We met as doctoral students at the annual conference of the International Communication Association, where we both contributed to shepherding the Feminist Scholarship Interest Group into a division within the organization. We came to academia as feminists and activists, and we had much else in common: we both came from working-class families, were first-generation college students, had backgrounds working in what, in the 1970s, was called the "battered women's movement" (me as a volunteer; Carolyn was staff); had worked as journalists; and began our academic careers in 1990, retiring a month apart in 2021. Our personal and professional lives would continue to track: we at different times served as chair of ICA's Feminist Scholarship Division, we are both married to women (and attended each other's weddings), and we would spend most of our academic careers insisting that women be included, in our research and elsewhere.

Our collaborative efforts, like our friendship, also have spanned the decades. Within ICA alone, they include, but certainly are not limited to: working to

12 The term is commonly used in the United States not to connote actual criminal activity but to indicate mutual friendship and collaboration to attain specific goals.

establish ICA's first and only critical journal, *Communication, Culture & Critique*[13]; getting ICA to move its funds into socially responsible investments; and establishing the Teresa Award for the Advancement of Feminist Scholarship,[14] which was endowed with a generous donation by Yoo Jae Song of Ewha Women's University in Korea. The annual Teresa Award was first presented by the Feminist Scholarship Division in 2007 and has since become one of the most prestigious honors for feminist scholars in the field of communication. Most recently, Carolyn has endowed a new FSD award—the Byerly Research Award in Feminist Political Economy of Communication. I have served as chair of the award's selection committee. In addition, Carolyn has consistently "had my back" in ways large and small—from offering feedback on my early research articles prior to submission, to providing me with the names of potential external reviewers when I was going up for promotion, to introducing me to the literature of critical scholars whose writings would influence my own.

This chapter is my attempt to shed light on Carolyn as a scholar, activist and feminist, on the events, challenges and opportunities that have shaped her, and her views and hopes for the future. What follows is a gently edited transcript of my interview with her. It is my hope that it will provide guidance and inspiration to future feminist scholars—as Carolyn has guided and inspired countless students and colleagues over the years. At the time of this interview, Carolyn was 77 years old and had recently moved back to Olympia, Washington, from the Washington, DC, area, where she had taught at Howard University for 17 years.

## The Interview

**MM:**

There are a lot of incidents that led to your becoming the person you are—the researcher and the feminist. One of the things that I wanted to explore was the idea of social location, particularly in terms of your working-class background, and how that might have influenced you, or the lessons learned.

13 The idea for a critical ICA journal that would include qualitative, feminist and other critical scholarship was born out of the rejection of an article I had submitted to ICA's flagship publication, *The Journal of Communication*. My article used narrative analysis which, according to the rejection letter, was not an acceptable methodology.

14 Over the years, our work for the Teresa Award evolved so that I acted as chair of the award selection committee while Carolyn was primarily responsible for organizing the reception. Carolyn continued to serve as a trustee of the award until 2021. I had stepped down a few years prior.

**CB:**

For years, I had no consciousness that I had a working-class background because I saw myself moving into a professional life. I always wanted to be where other people were, or where I thought they were, and I didn't know that I had other people in my sphere who also had working-class families. It was really the women's movement, when people started talking about working-class backgrounds, that I began to think about my own. In Olympia, in the Rape Relief collective, I was often the oldest person in the group. Some were still college students, and they were all emulating working classness, for lack of a better word. Everything had to have a class analysis and so forth. And then after a while, I began to realize that a lot of times I was the only one with a real working-class background in the group. Most had come from professional families. Some of them had trust funds. Their fathers and mothers were doctors and lawyers. And the lights began to go on in my head. Why was it so uncomfortable for me to talk about my own background? Well, it's because I didn't have a family that could give me the same advantages. In fact, I was on my own financially from the time I was about 19 because my parents got a divorce that year, and the family finances fell apart.And I think the second part of your question was, "How did that influence me?" I've been able to factor that into how I saw the world since then. I mean, that has been 40, 50 years ago. It really made me begin to look at life from a different angle. I owned my family and upbringing as my personal base.

**MM:**

So you really weren't aware of your class background until after you were in college?

**CB:**

Right. When I began to embrace it, I began to look for other people—writers, particularly, who were writing from a working-class perspective and could reflect on their lives and how they struggled. And I think I've always been aware of it professionally in the academy. All of my education, from kindergarten through PhD level, has all been in public schools and universities. I know a lot of people who had more elite credentials and have been able to go much farther than I have in terms of the kind of jobs that they got. And so the class reality has followed me around, but it hasn't held me back in what I wanted to do. In fact, it has driven my perspectives and the kind of things I chose to examine and the way I teach.

**MM:**
Would you say more about its influence on the kind of work that you do?
**CB:**
Well, journalism has been the thread that has held many of my interests together. I wanted to pursue journalism professionally, but for one reason and another—and that's a whole discussion unto itself—I've pursued journalism in other ways. But it's been part of my life. I've also been a critic of journalism, mainstream journalism, or corporate journalism as it's known by those of us on the Left, because it doesn't bring in working-class or social movement perspectives. It's really elitist in its sourcing. I think that's why I appreciate [the radio news program] Democracy Now so much. It's one of the few journalism companies or news groups that really does ensure the coverage of social movements and those on the margins.

**MM:**
You mentioned in your chapter [for this festschrift] that you were in semi-rural Colorado, and a lot of your classmates were Mexican American. I'm assuming that most of them were probably also working class.

**CB:**
Yes, many—maybe almost everybody. When my dad retired, in the late fifties, we were living in the Colorado Springs area, where there are five military bases. And so I grew up essentially in an all-military environment, until I went to college. And we lived in a lower middle-class community, like one of those that [folk singer] Malvina Reynolds sang about—little houses all in a row, looking alike. I mean, the houses were moderately well-built, but they looked mostly alike. You could pick a color—white, tan or green—but they were pretty much all the same. And we were all pretty much the same in terms of social class. Most of our parents, our fathers, were, or had been, mostly non-commissioned officers, you know, lower ranks. My dad retired as a captain, but he had had to work hard for that. And then they forced him out—as they did many, many in the military—after the war. After these men retired, they had to get civilian jobs to support their families. My dad sold cars for a while, then moved into insurance. Many of my classmates did not go to college. The girls started getting pregnant when they were in their teens, and the boys got into trouble of some kind. At one time, three of my neighbors were either in prison or reform school. It was that kind of a community. But it was also very eclectic. The ethnic group that was most dominant was Mexican American. But the kind of classmates and friends that

I had were of all sorts of different ethnicities, religions and backgrounds—Asian, Jewish, Catholic, Protestant.

**MM:**

One of the reasons I wanted to pursue this line of discussion is because I was interested in how your ideas and worldview were shaped by your social location along the lines of standpoint theory—the idea that who we are in terms of gender, race and class shapes our worldview. But we don't really develop a standpoint until we can look at our lives critically. And, so what I saw your chapter doing is talking about the ways that you got to that place of looking critically and to really developing your standpoint.

**CB:**

Yes. What I've had to do also is to look at the time period that I've lived in. I remember going to one of my high school reunions—this would have been the twentieth, I guess—and I wanted to talk to everybody about what an amazing history we'd lived through. And they still wanted to tell the same stupid jokes they were telling in school, or to remember all the stupid things we did. And I thought, I'm really different now, you know? I'm always constantly evaluating where my situatedness is, you know, within the historical moment. History has always meant a lot to me in terms of what's going on now. And I think this is where Marx comes into this. I know that history continues to change things. Nothing stays the same. And to keep track of the evolution, you know, the process, the historical process that's going on at any given time—it's not just political, it's not just economic, it's also cultural, right? And these days, it's also environmental.

**MM:**

So, what do you see about this particular historical moment—where are we as a culture socially, economically and politically? How do you see from where we got here, and where do we go?

**CB:**

We have upheavals, cycles of events. I'm not a pessimist, and, in fact, I don't accept pessimism as a perspective because I think once you adopt pessimism, it lets you out of having to do anything. You know, it lets us just say nothing can be done. We're beyond the turning point. I mean, I know people who look at the environmental situation, or who look at even the political situation, and say that.

But what I see is reform, a kind of re-emergence of social processes and social movements. They don't look the same as they did in the 1960s and seventies. We don't have the same kind of leaders. We don't have the same kind of music—which, by the way, I really miss a lot. We don't have, you know, the same kinds of many things. But what we have are the same issues—sexism, racism, inequality, and war, right? And so people are coming at those things in different ways. The environmental problems are factored into that. Because look at what's happening. Every time there's a tornado coming through Mississippi, guess who it's going to wipe out? The poorest of the poor, and most of them are usually African American. And so I think that it's hard to tell where or how some of this is going to come together. There needs to be a lot more coalition work across issues and across the movements. And, speaking of coalitions, I think my African American students at Howard were completely amazed at how many white people joined them in the Black Lives Matter marches after the George Floyd murder. That's become a black-led multicultural movement, right? One of the students in my methods class at Howard made her semester project interviewing white people to find out why they participated because she was really curious about their positionality and motivation. And look at the reproductive rights movement. It's a multicultural movement across class lines. So, should I not take heart and hope in these things? When I see people out in the streets or writing petitions and all of the new media that's coming out—you know, the various blogs and things, I think something is happening.

**MM:**

You know, there are so many times that I think we need to get out and take to the streets, like in France [where they've been protesting cuts to benefits]. We just need to in massive numbers, but we don't. So why do you think that is the case?

**CB:**

Right now, there are protests going on. Yesterday there were big protests in Seattle and Washington, DC, that Planned Parenthood organized around reproductive rights. But also I think a lot of us who have come through movements in earlier times have shifted our thinking about political work. We come at it from other ways. We give money, we meet with representatives. Some of us have already run for office and are in office. It's a different kind of participation. But in some ways, we're all so weary. I mean, I just moved from Washington, DC, where I lived for more than 20 years. In the early years of the Iraq and Afghanistan wars that the

U.S. government perpetrated on Middle Eastern countries, poor countries, there were hundreds of thousands of people in the streets. And I was with them. Kay and I and people we knew, we went to every single anti-war march. I missed one march. Our house was jammed with people coming from out of town, and they brought their kids. We had 13 people at our house, our little house, for one of those marches. And it was a couple of times a year we would have those marches. And I think when the risk is bad enough, the challenge is big enough, people get into the streets. But right now, this week, I've been signing petitions for (the removal of Supreme Court Justice) Clarence Thomas. Each month, you know, it's reproductive rights and other things. I'm old enough now that I can't walk in the marches so easily, so I find other ways to stand up and be counted.

**MM:**
Your commitment to both the Democratic Socialists of America and the Feminist Scholarship Division of the International Communication Association has been really significant. I wanted to ask you about that commitment.

**CB:**
I joined Democratic Socialists of America (DSA) in the late 1980s, when I wanted a more formal association with and commitment to socialist causes and socialism as a political process. And I have been active in DSA for all of the years since, in every city I've lived in, actually. What's been really encouraging to me is that DSA went from a membership of fewer than 4,000 to its recent of almost 100,000. The surge happened within two years after democratic socialist Bernie Sanders ran for president, but when Trump became president instead. Almost all those new members are under 35 – they were inspired by these and other political shifts. It gives me great hope for the new generation that they're not afraid of democratic socialism. Many young people today identify as socialists. And they're not just socialist by identity. They're out there doing things. They've got projects, they're working in the communities. They're volunteering for things. They're helping elect progressive people to office. I don't think most Americans are aware of how many people in Congress are DSA members, and also in local offices. And the man who was just elected mayor of Chicago – DSA helped elect him, just as other local chapters helped put AOC (Alexandria Ocasio-Cortez), Jamal Bowman and others into Congress, and into state legislatures. DSA works in coalition with other groups. It's been a really important affiliation for me, because it gave me a socialist context, and I was able to meet and talk with other people on the same wavelength politically.The Feminist Scholarship Division has

been another really important association for me, an academic one. I came in, as you did, right around the time it was forming within ICA, and have been part of its growth and institutionalization of feminism in our field. I'm an organization person. I think that we can do very little by ourselves. We really have to work together in strong, visible groups. Part of what I've tried to do, as an academic, is to help build those and make them viable financially, and also to develop rituals, you know, things we do routinely to celebrate and reaffirm the importance of our scholarship and leadership.

**MM:**
You mentioned elsewhere that you learned about navigating organizations while at an educational think tank prior to entering academia. What are some of the lessons you learned? And how did you apply them to your academic career?

**CB:**
For three or four years, I worked at the Western Interstate Commission for Higher Education—it's an agency of the 13 Western states. Quasi-governmental. We had a lot of different programs. Some were promoting the use of technology in academic administration, others were in mental health, nursing, criminal justice, etc. I worked in the new program development office. I got to work on some great things. For instance, I staffed a committee of deans of graduate schools in Western universities who were trying to increase minority enrollment. That was in the early seventies. And feminism was just coming into universities. Women's studies was emerging. So, I proposed to my director, "Why don't we do a study to find out what kind of programs the colleges in our 13 states offer for women—child care, special accommodation, women's studies programs?" I edited three books while I was there on different things, in addition to that study on services and programs for women. It's outdated, of course, but it's a historical piece.One thing I learned in that organization was how to get things done on a larger scale. I think that was useful to me about ten years ago when I was the principal investigator for the research for the *Global Report on the Status of Women in News* study, which included 59 countries, 522 news organizations, and a 170-member research team under my supervision. At WICHE, I also learned how to participate in professional meetings with civility, how to write memos, how to create paper trails, how important documentation is, how important reports are. So those were just really practical things about functioning professionally.

**MM:**
What are some of the things that you learned about teaching as a student at the University of Colorado that you've used in your teaching, things that were modeled for you or that you developed on your own?

**CB:**
I loved the University of Colorado, and I was there at a special time. It was the late sixties. Everybody was excited about something. The students were always worked up. Some had to make a speech or argue. It was such a stimulating environment. I had some really gifted professors, too. I took a class in intellectual history from Dr. Robert Skotheim, who went on to be a college president. I had never thought of there being such a thing as a history of ideas. We looked at the expatriate movement of the "Lost Generation," and the counterculture movement that was happening at the time. I took Dr. Matthew Downey's U.S. history class, and Dr. Jane Martin's biology class. She was an ecologist and very energetic. There must have been 500 people in the auditorium, and she had three blackboards and would march back and forth writing on those blackboards. She made science come alive by tying it into what was going on in the environment. And there was, of course, a budding environmental movement with the first Earth Day that year. You know, she tied all that stuff together. So, what I learned at CU was how to be intellectually excited and to listen to people in class. And I learned the importance of textbooks in class. Because all of my teachers made us read, and that was the basis for whatever happened in class that day. They were really academically thorough—there was a pedagogy in place that I looked back to when I started teaching. My own students were quite amazed how I made them responsible for doing their readings, and they had to write every single week. And it had to be a valid piece of writing, based on the texts for the day. Many of the students have said that that was the best part of the whole course, having to read and write each week.

**MM:**
What were some of your early lessons about finding allies and creating networks in terms of your learning how to function within an organization?

**CB:**
I credit that to feminism, where I learned that you could only challenge the system through networks. In the case of working on violence against women, we challenged male violence through our system of local rape crisis centers,

and through our national counterpart, the National Coalition Against Sexual Assault. We were sharing analyses, and shaping ideas, building strategies. I mean, in the late seventies and early eighties, with the grassroots work we were doing in violence against women in Washington state, where I lived, we got all sorts of legislation passed, such as allowing child victim's testimonies to be videotaped, for the courts. We had the marital exclusion removed from the rape laws. We established a state-level program to fund domestic and sexual violence organizations and services. All of this happened because we collaborated and acted together through networks.When I got into graduate school, I realized that the graduate program I was in didn't align with the experiences I had had. For one thing, I didn't feel like the social movements of the sixties and seventies had touched the department. I really felt like I was the only lesbian, I was the only radical within the department at the time. It turned out neither of those were true. But that's how I felt because nobody seemed to talk about issues we were studying in a political way. I began to go to conferences like ICA. I began to meet people like you, Joy Morrison, Lana Rakow, Linda Steiner, and all these other people who would become such important colleagues. Then I began to feel like I had a network of personal support and for my intellectual work.

**MM:**

In many ways, you have developed a far more extensive network than a lot of people, and certainly myself, so that you know who does what in ways that I don't.

**CB:**

Part of it is that I'm kind of a busybody by nature. Kay [my spouse] claims that I'm not in a room with somebody for 3 minutes before I learn their life histories. Maybe it's my training as a reporter. But I also just like people. I like to interact with people. So it's just a quirk of personality, I guess. I told my students that I've had to overcome early life shyness and self-esteem problems, and that's true. Even after all these years, I suppose I still carry an impostor syndrome within me. It doesn't make any sense, but it's sort of there. It definitely came up during my tenure denial at Ithaca College.

**MM:**

Discussing your tenure denial at Ithaca brings up the dominant ideology within academia, you know. And it's like, nobody talks about that because it's the dominant one and you can't see it. If you want to do anything else, it looks like you've got an agenda. So, what I want to ask you about is what do you see as the dominant ideology and the agenda in higher education? Because you've fought it, you know.

**CB:**

We've all fought it in our own ways, if we're feminists, if we're critical theorists. The dominant ideology is strongly Eurocentric and strongly male and definitely boring. It reinforces the status quo in every possible way. You know, right now, the book I'm writing, *Intersectionality, Political Economy and the Media*, I can't get away from all of the people who have really defined that strand of research, of political economy research in communication, because I'm drawing on their work. But I'm also quite critical of it. I mean, they're wonderful writers, and reading them, I've had a lot of "aha" moments. But at the same time, they say nothing about women or people of color to speak of. And yet their work seems so authoritative, who would question them? They're almost all white men, either British or American, a couple of Canadians, a German. They're very white, they're very male, and they're very exclusionary in considering how gender and race enter into structures of power where the media are concerned.I mean, a lot of the pushback I got at Ithaca College around tenure was from a small, vocal and very influential group of students who were friendly with the dean. And the dean encouraged what they did, which was to write anonymous nasty comments on my course evaluations every semester, things like, "She has an agenda. She supports feminism. She supports gay rights." I had one news reporting class read your book, *News Coverage of Violence against Women*, because I thought journalism students ought to be able to go out and report on any issue, and they ought to understand what made it an issue. I also had them read things on gay rights, which was bubbling up in the news all over the place in those days, and about racism and how to cover it in the news. I thought those things mattered. And the students, some of them anyway, saw that the teacher had an agenda. Well, yes, I did, of course. But you know, here's the thing. After I moved to the D.C. area, I began to hear from some of the students I had had at Ithaca College, and also at Radford University before that. I had brought Salim Muwakkil, who is one of my favorite black writers, to Radford and he lectured on the black experience and how to cover news in the black community. Some years later, a student wrote to me and said, "I just got a job at such-and-such newspaper because I was the only one in the newsroom who had any idea about how to develop sources in the black community." He said, "Thank you, Dr. Byerly." I had another student write and say, "Remember that information you had us read on gay rights?" He said,

"I never thought it made any difference at the time." This former student lived in and worked at a newspaper in Massachusetts, where they had just approved same-sex marriage. And he said, "I was the only one who knew how to cover the story. Thank you, Dr. Byerly." So those are the kind of reinforcements that you get, but I had to wait for them.

**MM:**
What was the most gratifying thing about your career in academia?

**CB:**
Well, I love the classroom experience, which I had to grow into. I was, as I said, a shy person who had to learn to teach and not to be afraid. At some point I recognized that there's a certain performance element in teaching. And once I learned how to be on stage and to crack jokes and to challenge students and to let them talk, and to facilitate a dynamic in the classroom, I really began to feel like I'd found my ground, that I was going to hit my stride as a teacher. And, really, that was very gratifying. I'm a writer by nature, but it has been even more gratifying, I think, to teach. And the other thing is, I'm a learner, open to other people's ideas and new information. I was very straightforward with my students about how to do research from start to finish. And I learned a lot from them. I mean, they did dissertations on things that I didn't know anything about. I was their technical and logistical guide and, in the process, I learned a lot of things I would never have known. And particularly being at a historically black university like Howard, I confronted my whiteness on a regular basis. You know, I just let myself be a white person who was learning on their turf. And I wasn't afraid of that. I was really open to my students' and colleagues' experiences. And I like them so much, and the chance to interact daily. I miss them. That's the hard piece of being retired and living in a new community away from DC.

**MM:**
So what do you see as the future of higher education? I mean, higher education is under attack in many ways, particularly in red states dominated by Republican legislatures. Where do you think the struggles are, and what needs to happen?

**CB:**
I am very worried about it. For one thing, more and more colleges and universities are closing. Community college enrollment is down, and we know that

low-income and non-white students make up the majority of the community college population. So that means that we're looking at a whole cohort of people who are not going to get an education. And then there's the backlash problem—you know, the rejection of critical race theory and critical theory—in the disciplines. And the erosion of tenure. All of these things together suggest that we are going to fall onto pretty hard times in higher education in this country. Neoliberalism is killing our educational system, both public schools and universities. We're moving toward a social class gap. And for those who do go, the student debt is crippling, and it's going to be years before they dig out. I'm not quite as optimistic about where higher education is going as I am a few other things.

**MM:**
We've looked at things in different ways in terms of our research. I've looked at content for the most part, and you've looked at structure. We've taken different perspectives. But in both cases, we're saying, "Hey, women matter. You can't keep producing research that excludes women, because it's not complete, it's not accurate."

**CB:**
When I started doing political economy work, it was pretty early in my academic career. I began to recognize that studying representation alone didn't explain how representation came to be. I mean, I've always been a big picture person. When I read *Capital* and the *German Ideology* and some of Marx's other work, there was an overarching logic there that I couldn't refute, and I didn't know how anybody could refute it. It was so clear to me how capitalism worked. And I recognize that Marx and Engels wrote 200 years ago. But the nuts and bolts are still useful, and they help to explain so much in terms of power. So interrogating power became central to everything I would be concerned about. Who has it, how did they get it, how is it constructed, and how can someone change the power dynamics and structural relations? I also understood that capitalism was from the beginning androcentric and Eurocentric. Women's free labor at home and in the reproduction of the species took place in patriarchal households and contributed to the political economy of capitalism. But when I began to read black Marxists like Paul Gilroy and some of the postcolonial scholars, I saw more clearly how capitalism also incorporated racism. Capitalism expanded as a world system through slavery after the 1600s, as well as through brutality against indigenous people in the Americas, Africa and Far East, and then the taking of their resources for production.So, when I began to look at the political economy of the media, I was

initially concerned with where women fit into the whole structural landscape of the media. And then I realized that, you know, you look at who's employed, look at who has power within these organizations and who doesn't. And with news, it's often whose stories are published, who gets to speak. It always came down to white powerful men. For my dissertation, one of the things I examined in the Women's Feature Service stories was the difference between elite sources and not elite sources. Well, the Women's Feature Service agencies were all in the Global South, not affiliated with mainstream news—they lay outside that dominant news-making structure, and their stories were all by women writers. Those stories quoted many non-elite sources, mostly women. But you look at the news sources in the mainstream U.S. news—they're white, they're typically males in positions of authority. This pattern was pointed out in Gaye Tuchman's (1978) study, *Making News*. You could be reading that book today, and it makes just as much sense as it did 40 years ago, because the structures and news-gathering standards that she talked about are still intact. So, I had to begin to really look at the nuts and bolts of news under capitalism and to begin to make sense of how the industries were organized, financed, where media policy fit in, employment patterns, and, of course, ownership and control. It's not just women who are marginalized in news—people of color, LGBTQ, low-income, immigrants, are also too often the missing perspectives. These are the things I've been concerned with for the last 30-some years. And those are the big picture things. Those are the kind of macro-level concerns that have driven my work.I had this one brilliant student, an undergraduate in a journalism class years ago. She finished her B.A., and she went off and got a job at one of the big newspaper chains. She did an investigative series on a toxic waste site near a minority community where she lived and worked. She identified the polluting industry. And the editors got very nervous, so they toned down her stories, reduced them from like five to four. She said she barely recognized some of them. They published those stories. She won a regional Pulitzer. Not long afterward, she came back to the college where I was teaching, took me out to lunch and told me that she was quitting the journalism business. She said she was so disheartened by winning a prize for something that was so badly done, so watered down. And she said that there's no way you can report honestly about power. She was completely discouraged. She went into another field. I mean, this is the kind of thing that really troubles me. You have brilliant journalists who really know what they're doing, they're savvy, and they're taking the risks. But the corporate powers won't let them perform because they don't want to lose advertisers or alienate powerful companies. I saw this myself when I was finishing my PhD program. I worked at a daily newspaper in the Seattle area. We were having a mild recession then nationally. And the publisher met with those of us on the copy desk where I was working, and he said "It's going to be a problem, all these national stories coming through about the recession. Be sure to always add a little language in the story that says Seattle isn't experiencing these." We were told to add that language, right? Well, it was dishonest and all of us copy editors agreed among ourselves not to do it—we just quietly didn't change the stories. And the publisher never brought it up again. There's a certain level of cow-towing to the powerful by journalists, but some will refuse, the way my colleagues and I did at that paper. And then we're not even talking about outlets like Fox News, which is pure propaganda and lies.

**MM:**
Do you hold out much hope for change, or what do you see that could challenge that dynamic, if anything?

**CB:**
Well, the death of corporate daily newspapers is on our doorstep. And digital news is coming into its own. In my community, Olympia, there's a small group of people who got a nonprofit newspaper together, which I subscribe to. It's online, and it puts out news every day. It's called the *JOLT*, which stands for *Journal of Olympia, Lacey and Tumwater*. It doesn't have the whole newspaper, but it has a lot of things and it's good. It's properly written and vetted. So that's one possibility—nonprofit news. But obviously the days of two-newspaper towns are over. And broadcast news—you know, when Amy Goodman is too old to report, what's going to happen to *Democracy Now*? That really is the best broadcast news that you can hope for. There are alternative news magazines like *In These Times*, also a lot of blogs that are progressive, and I'm a fan of web news like Truthout, the Intercept, and others. ProPublica is doing good reporting. Almost all my discretionary funds these days go into supporting alternative media. And I think that's where the future for progressive news is.

**MM:**
What advice do you have for grad students in communication or those contemplating life in higher education?

**CB:**
Well, they should be aware that they're on shifting ground, that the changes that are happening on campuses now will continue. There will be fewer tenure-track

positions. I also would tell them that you don't have to be at a big research university to be happy and to do meaningful work. You can do your research and write, and you can teach meaningfully at smaller schools. I am in favor of public universities and colleges, more than private ones, but some private schools are progressive. Actually, I talk to students about this all the time, even now. When you get into your faculty role, make some friends outside the department, get acquainted with people in your own field and in your department and school, of course, but make a bigger network for yourself and get off your campus once in a while and have a personal life.You know, there are also some practical things, like don't buy a house in your first year. If you don't feel comfortable and are not feeling supported by your administration by the second year, get out on the job market. Don't look for it to get better. Listen to your heart. If you don't feel like you're in the right place, it's not a fit for you, start looking around. And if you're in your own neighborhood, where you grew up and have lived most of your life, get the hell out of there. See the world, explore who you are, see and learn some new things. This [staying put in your own community] is very common on the East Coast, by the way. It's not so common out West. I grew up out West, and I guess I have a Westerner sensibility. Spread your wings, get out of the country, travel, learn another language.

**MM:**
Is there anything else that you would like to add?

**CB:**
I think it's important for people who want an academic life to really enjoy it, to really take advantage of everything that's there—everything. Be part of campus life, be part of the fiber, the politics and the intellectual culture of the campus and participate, and learn. And contribute. Don't take a job and stop doing scholarship once you get tenure. Continue to do your part. And the other thing is—I'm a strong believer in the (academic) organizations, sharing your work. Your responsibility is to participate in the community of scholars.

9

# Three as for Carolyn: Affection, Appreciation and Admiration

AMMU JOSEPH

Carolyn Byerly and I have been fellow travelers for two decades on the long and winding road toward equal representation of women—and other underrepresented sections of society—in media workplaces, content and policy. We first met in the spring of 2003, when I was in the Washington DC area after attending the 47th Session of the U.N. Commission on the Status of Women (CSW) in New York in March 2003. I had been invited to represent the U.N. Expert Group on "Participation and access of women to the media and its impact on and use as an instrument for the advancement and empowerment of women," which had met in Beirut in November 2002, and to present our findings and recommendations to the CSW. That was around the time Carolyn and Karen Ross were beginning work on their book, *Women and Media: A Critical Introduction*. I think Carolyn was already aware of the media-related books I had worked on up to then: *Whose News? The Media and Women's Issues*, focusing on the coverage of women's issues in the Indian media, which I co edited and authored with Kalpana Sharma, and *Making News: Women in Journalism*, my book on women working in the Indian media (the former first published in 1994 and the latter in 2000).

We met over lunch and talked about our shared interest in various issues relating to gender and media. I was fascinated to hear about her work on media conglomeration, an idea I had first been exposed to many years earlier thanks to Ben Bagdikian's 1983 book, *The Media Monopoly.* It was interesting—and alarming—to be updated on the continuing and increasingly rapid concentration of media ownership across the world, and to also learn about the implications of the ongoing process for women. Although Carolyn was by then an academic, I think her background in journalism and our common involvement in media activism enabled us to quickly and easily establish a rapport. That was the beginning of our 20-year-long relationship, which evolved beyond professional association into a personal friendship.

By the time we met, the Network of Women in Media, India (NWMI) was a little over a year old, having been formally launched at the first national gathering of Indian media women in New Delhi in January 2002. That historic meeting took place at the end of a bottom-up network-building process I anchored from November 2000 onwards. The second national meeting was scheduled to be held in Mumbai in January 2004, just before the Fourth World Social Forum (WSF) was to open on the outskirts of the city, so that interested network members from around the country could attend both events if they wished to. We agreed that it would be a good idea for Carolyn to try and make it to India at that time, using the opportunity to interview Indian women in the media. She managed to secure a small travel grant that enabled her to conduct interviews in Delhi, Bangalore and Mumbai, and to also attend the NWMI meeting and interview participating members from across the country. She was able to attend some sessions at the WSF as well.

At the network meeting Carolyn presented a paper titled "A Feminist Analysis of Media Conglomeration," drawing from her chapter, "Women and Media Concentration," in a book titled *Seeking Equity for Women in Journalism and Mass Communication: A 30-Year Update* (Byerly, 2014). She pointed out that while there was no shortage of critiques of media conglomeration, feminist analysis of the phenomenon was still lacking, despite the fact that gender is deeply embedded in it. "It is essential for women to develop a solid cross-cultural gender analysis of media conglomeration if we are to find a way out of the present deadlock," she said (Byerly, 2004). Fast-forward to 2022, when the NWMI celebrated its 20th anniversary with a virtual event (thanks to the lingering effects of the Covid pandemic). Carolyn sent a warm message of solidarity and support, highlighting the network's role in challenging sexism and discrimination in newsrooms across India and appreciating the fact that all its work is done on a volunteer basis.

One of the first international publications to which I have contributed was the 2004 book, *Women and Media: International Perspectives*, edited by Karen

Ross and Carolyn. Almost a decade later I again wrote for a volume edited by Carolyn: *The Palgrave International Handbook of Women and Journalism* (2013). In between, I was South Asia Coordinator for the 2011 *Global Report on the Status of Women in the News Media* initiated by the International Women's Media Foundation (IWMF), for which Carolyn was the principal investigator.

We were, of course, in regular touch in between and even met a few times in different parts of the world—across four continents!—over the years. We were together at two events in 2006—the Women, Action and the Media conference held in Boston that year and the 56th Annual Conference of the International Communication Association (ICA) in Dresden. Besides speaking during a symposium on women and news at the ICA conference, I participated in a roundtable discussion on the "globalisation syndrome," organized by Carolyn. The next time we met was in Johannesburg in 2008, during the third Gender and Media (GEM) Summit, hosted by Gender Links, the Media Institute of Southern Africa (MISA) and the Gender and Media Southern Africa (GEMSA) Network. We were also together in Paris in 2013 for a meeting convened by UNESCO to begin work on a report on *World Trends in Freedom of Expression and Media Development*, which was eventually published in 2014. Carolyn, Margaret Gallagher and I were members of the Advisory Group set up to contribute to the report; we were each tasked with examining the gender aspects of media freedom, pluralism, independence and safety, and required to submit papers that were subsequently summarized in the respective sections of the publication. We also managed to squeeze in a dinner in Baltimore with family when I was in the United States on a personal visit in 2013. Carolyn and I met again at the annual conference of the International Association for Mass Communication Research (IAMCR) in Hyderabad in 2014. We were both among the speakers during the launch of the e-publication, *Media and Gender: A Scholarly Agenda for the Global Alliance on Media and Gender*, and the regional launch of *World Trends on Freedom of Expression and Media Development* (both published under the auspices of UNESCO). Our last meeting to date was in New York in 2016, when we attended a workshop on "Gender Equality Assessment Standards for Media: Potential and Possibilities," jointly organized by UN Women and the Global Alliance on Gender and Media (GAMAG), as well as the strategy meeting of GAMAG's International Steering Committee (ISC) that followed.

We were often room-mates at these locations; not only did our relationship survive the close encounters but we got to know each other all the better as a result. Whenever possible, we also stayed on an extra day or two to jointly explore the interesting cities we found ourselves in. Of course, we have additionally spent many hours in several of these places—and, more recently, on Zoom—discussing issues, planning activities and developing documents. Since both she and I are in the habit of writing annual letters updating relatives and friends about our lives, we have managed to stay in touch at the personal level, too, even when we have not been able to meet as regularly as before.

I do not have academic qualifications as a media educator or a media researcher, although I have taught in journalism schools in India and done some amount of research on different aspects of the Indian news media—relying mainly on my knowledge and experience as a journalist. I am, therefore, not in a position to comment authoritatively on Carolyn's academic work as a professor or scholar. I would, however, like to record here that my longtime interest in broader media-related concerns—such as media policy, ownership and concentration/conglomeration—were very much influenced by Carolyn's pioneering work in these areas. Her early focus on women's access to media ownership and the impact on them of the ongoing process of concentration and conglomeration of ownership was eye-opening. I remember in particular her 2011 article in the Howard Journal of Communication, "Behind the Scenes of Women's Broadcast Ownership," based on a qualitative study that examined how female owners of radio and television companies enter the U.S. broadcast market, stay in the market and contribute to their communities, while also looking into the ways in which communication policy, economics and sexual politics tend to exclude women from ownership. It was startling to learn that at that time women in the United States owned fewer than 6 percent of radio and television stations.

I would also like to register my deep appreciation of her consistent and passionate advocacy of diversity in the media, paying special attention to gender and race—not only in terms of representation in media content and personnel but also, significantly, in ownership. This aspect of her work particularly resonated with me because in India, too, the impact of caste-based exclusion and discrimination had not been taken into account in studies and commentary on gender-based exclusion and discrimination in the initial years of activism and research on gender and the media; the double whammy of caste plus gender on women from the so-called "lower" castes, especially Dalits, was acknowledged and highlighted only much later.

Carolyn's statement on "Gender-and-Race-Conscious Research Toward Egalitarian Broadcast Ownership Regulation" at the Media Ownership Workshop on Diversity Issues of the Federal Communications Commission (FCC) in January 2010 was remarkable in this context. By then, she had been concerned about the relationship of women and people of color with the news and other media for over two decades. Speaking on behalf of the Howard Media Group, a research collaborative within Howard University, she said her comments represented their "shared concern, hope, and suggestions for how the Commission might proceed toward its quadrennial review of women's and minorities' media ownership" (Byerly, 2010). Focusing specifically on ownership of broadcast stations, she said, "Media ownership in the United States today divides along the historical fault lines of gender and race. The low single-digit ownership rates for women and people of color in broadcasts say quite loudly that the nation is faced with both a women's rights and civil rights crisis in policy . . . The media today do not and cannot serve the public interest as long as this skewed media ownership pattern continues, and the situation could actually worsen without policy changes" (Byerly, 2010). Carolyn's contribution to this aspect of media policy is evidently still remembered. It was, for example, mentioned in a *2021 article* on the U.S. Supreme Court's consideration of two consolidated cases, *FCC v. Prometheus Radio Project* and *National Association of Broadcasters v. Prometheus Radio Project*, which raised the question of whether the FCC had adequately considered the effects on minority and female broadcast media ownership of certain regulatory changes that it had adopted. Acknowledging that "experts have been ringing the alarm about the effects of lackluster media diversity for years" (Constitutional Accountability Center, 2023), the piece mentioned that Carolyn had highlighted the issue during the FCC's own 2010 workshop.

I also appreciate the fact that, despite her long years in academia, Carolyn continues to be an activist who champions the causes highlighted by her research. An article about the FCC's 2016 launch of an auction that would allow broadcasters to sell all or parts of their broadcast spectrum, which could then be purchased by wireless carriers looking to expand their reach, mentioned that WHUT, Howard University's public TV station, was among those that could be up for auction. The piece reported that the Howard Media Group, which is part of the School of Communications, had published a position paper outlining its objections to participating in the auction. According to the paper, the WHUT television station on campus was the only black-owned public television outlet in the country and the importance of diversity in public media needed to be kept in mind. The university decided to proceed with participation in the auction despite the objections. Carolyn was quoted in the Nieman Lab report saying that she found the institutional response to be "really discouraging," and pointing out that the university was "just looking at the station as a cash cow." She also noted that not only did WHUT provide a public service, but students gained invaluable experience working at the station.

Apart from all this I owe Carolyn a debt of gratitude for helping me to get over my diffidence around academics and my reluctance to contribute to academic publications. She convinced me that the kind of work I had done and was doing in the area of gender and media—including writing on the subject—was valuable even though it was not based on any established scholarly theory or research methodology. I still remember her saying, during the early days of our acquaintance, something along the lines of: don't underestimate the importance of your work—we use it to build theory. In my experience not many scholars are so respectful of and gracious toward those whose work contributes to knowledge and understanding about a subject area even if it does not fit into any recognized academic doctrine. And, of course, I would be remiss if I did not acknowledge and appreciate the fact that it was thanks to Carolyn's nomination that in 2003 that I received the Donna Allen Award for Feminist Advocacy instituted by the Commission on the Status of Women of the Association for Education in Journalism and Mass Communication. I see this as yet another example of her open-mindedness and magnanimity.

I am happy to have been given this opportunity to recall some details of the convivial, collegial relationship Carolyn and I have shared over many years and to place on record some aspects of her personality and work that I have discovered and benefited from during this period. I wish Carolyn many more years of a happy, healthy, productive and fulfilling life.

## References

Byerly, C. M. (2004). Women and media concentration. In R. R. Rush, E. C. Oukrup, & P. J. Creedon (Eds.), *Seeking Equity for women in journalism and mass communication: A 30-year update*. Lawrence Erlbaum Associates.

Byerly, C. M. (2010). *Gender-and-race-conscious research toward egalitarian broadcast ownership regulation*. A paper presented at the Media Ownership Workshop on Diversity Issues Federal Communications Commission, Washington, DC.

Byerly, C. M. (2014). *A feminist analysis of media conglomeration*. NWMI website. https://nwmindia.org/at-work/a-feminist-analysis-of-media-conglomeration/

Constitutional Accountability Center. (2023). *Diversity of media ownership matters*. https://www.theusconstitution.org/blog/scotus-weighs-in-on-the-diversity-of-media-ownership/

# 10

# Never Losing Sight of the Bigger Picture with Persistence

STINE ECKERT

I first met Carolyn M. Byerly at the annual conference of the International Communication Association (ICA) about ten years ago. While I do not remember the exact year, I clearly recall the first conversation I had with her. I was a Ph.D. candidate at the University of Maryland at the time. It must have been after a business meeting or during a social at ICA. She came up to me, and she had an idea: a candidacy! She introduced herself and asked if I would like to run for the position of vice-chair for the Feminist Scholarship Division of ICA as she had noticed that I was regularly attending the business meetings of the division and many of its paper sessions. I was a bit surprised that someone had noticed my consistent presence, perhaps because I was a new person coming to these sessions. I was still getting oriented on what different divisions were doing and how ICA was working in general. At that point, I had not held office for a division as I was focusing on my dissertation. But I was motivated after Carolyn's kind remarks and her strong suggestion that I should run for the position. So I did. Little did I know the long, joyful, and productive journey within ICA, that awaited me after my first conversation with Carolyn.

Almost 10 years later, I look back on my experiences as an officer for the Feminist Scholarship Division of ICA thus far: I ran and was elected as vice-chair and subsequent chair followed by immediate-past chair and treasurer, a total of six years.[15] It was in great part a result of Carolyn's first time approaching me that I got started on this track quite early when I was still a graduate student. I am very grateful that she pulled me into the division leadership and that she has been a thoughtful mentor to help navigate the division's business and ICA structures. Her tales of how to get things done and her energy to be persistent were part of every meeting I have had with her since. Hence, my involvement did not stop at the end of these six years, and neither did Carolyn's ideas for boosting feminist communication and media scholarship.

During my time as division chair, the Feminist Scholarship Division was giving out its Teresa Award for the Advancement of Feminist Scholarship to honor renowned communication and media studies scholars for the tenth time. By now the award has gained an international reputation as prestigious, coveted and very competitive. Perhaps not surprisingly, Carolyn was involved in its beginnings: as former chair of the Feminist Scholarship Division, she and Marian Meyers were approached by Korean feminist scholar Yoo Jae Song around 2007 to oversee a new award for feminist scholars as Yoo Jae had observed that the ICA organization had been overlooking "gender-oriented research" (Byerly et al., 2022, p. xi). The award was created with Carolyn serving as one of its two trustees, a position she held until recently (Elizabeth Toth replaced her in 2021 to join Natalia Rybas, the other trustee who had replaced Marian Meyers).

But this is just the background story for the next project that Carolyn pulled me into. In 2019, when the tenth award winner was announced, Carolyn approached me with another idea: a book! This publication was meant to make the feminist scholarship achievements in communication and media studies more visible, to build a written monument to its scholars, and to provide younger generations with a record and lessons learned. Each of the first 10 winners of the Teresa Award would write a chapter reflecting their contributions for feminist communication and media scholarship, in terms of theory, method or other insights, including personal ones into their own professional journey as feminist and/or women scholars. Ingrid Bachmann, then vice-chair of the Feminist Scholarship Division, and I set to work, and quickly had all award winners on board and a book contract with Routledge.

Despite the COVID-19 pandemic shaping the months when we all worked on the book, it was published in what felt like record time. It featured ten beautiful

15 These positions go together in a set sequence: vice-chairs serve for two years and then automatically become chair for another two years, followed automatically by another two years of serving as treasurers in the role of immediate-past chair.

chapters by the award winners: some looking back on past projects and following up on them, some self-critically admitting oversights in past scholarship, and some demanding better scholarship and structures for the future, especially in the ICA context with its emphasis on being *international*. The book also provided a first cut of a feminist communication and media analysis of what happened during the COVID-19 pandemic in regard to women. This special chapter was based on the transcript of a recorded ICA panel with all Teresa award winners and Carolyn in conversation with each other, a live take on our volatile contemporary times (Eckert & Bachmann, 2022). Without Carolyn, and everyone in the team for what we fondly only referred to for short as the "Teresa book," this edited volume and the feminist comradery it brought during difficult times, would not have happened. A second success story, thanks to Carolyn and her nudges, advice and organizing.

The book safely launched; it was already tied to Carolyn's next idea: another award! A brand-new prize that the Feminist Scholarship Division would give to emerging feminist scholars. The proceeds from the "Teresa book" would flow into financing the new award. Of course, that would not be enough, also given the book needed to be in the market for a long time to generate any money. Hence, Carolyn and I approached colleagues and launched a fundraising campaign. It was greatly boosted by the idea that Carolyn suggested the Teresa Award fund provide seed money of $10,000 to start a new award in the Feminist Scholarship division to honor emerging scholars in communication. With the leadership and members of the division voting in favor of this support, we raised enough funds to start a new award account at ICA. Subsequently, we built a selection committee and gave out the first Helen Award for Emerging Feminist Scholarship in 2022. The selection for the 2023 award winner for presentation at ICA in Toronto has also been made as of this writing. Making feminist scholarship visible this way was again in huge part an accomplishment through Carolyn's initiative. For me, it was another fun and rewarding collaboration with her and our co-fighters for elevating the contributions of feminist scholarship to communication and media studies.

Of course, this has not been the ending by far. Soon Carolyn emailed me to ask for feedback for a new idea she had: a third award! This time her energy was focused on feminist political economy research, which she had observed was gaining little traction and perhaps needed an incentive to be taken up by established and emerging scholars. Working with ICA, she turned her vision into an actual award in no time with a personal endowment of $50,000 and hopes for additional donations. The first call went out in late 2022 "to encourage and support research on macro-level issues in communication within a feminist analytical framework" and to fund studies that analyze how men's privilege and domination are institutionalized within communication organizations, in policy, ownership, labor and technology. Her initiative is a much-needed reminder to link the currently seemingly predominant research on the coverage of women in news media and other media and the representation of women in newsrooms with the overarching structures of journalism and media landscapes in terms of ownership and leadership. The Byerly Award for Research in Feminist Political Economy of Communication was given out for the first time at the annual conference of ICA 2023, in Toronto, Canada.

These are just the projects that I had the honor to work on after Carolyn and co-fighters for the visibility and recognition of feminist communication and media scholarship got me involved. Carolyn was ready to give advice at each turn, fueled by her wealth of experience and practical insight over decades. She has been a moderator, respondent, panelist, presenter, speaker, and/or keynote speaker as well as organizer and leader of workshops, panels and roundtables since 1988 for well over a hundred times, at times having six, seven, or even nine such engagements per year. She participated this way and in other leadership capacities at ICA, the International Association for Media and Communication Research (IAMCR) and the Association for Education in Journalism and Mass Communication (AEJMC) or other conferences every single year—with the only exception being during the COVID-19 pandemic in 2021 which affected all of us—while climbing the ladder at Howard University in Washington, DC to become chair of her department. At the same time, she has also been a member of the International Steering Committee of the Global Alliance on Media and Gender (GAMAG), an initiative of the United Nations Educational, Scientific and Cultural Organization (UNESCO).

More importantly, her persistence not only in this leadership position but also in her scholarship has centered around issues that are salient to and affecting women, for instance, in terms of coverage: the quality of news media reporting on rape and sexual violence, the rights of rape victims in journalistic coverage, the need for journalism education that teaches how to cover rape, and the underrepresentation of lesbian, gay, bisexual and trans people among others. And keeping an eye on the political economy perspective, she also consistently analyzed how women are, or not, represented in news media ownership and production, including their intersections with issues of race and class in the United States and worldwide. The *Global Report on Status of Women in News Media* (Byerly, 2011), for which she was the principal investigator and which was published by the

International Women's Media Foundation with UN and other funding, provides detailed summaries on the situation of women journalists in 59 countries in the Mideast and North Africa, Sub Saharan Africa, the Americas, Asia and Oceana, as well as Eastern, Nordic, and Western Europe, based on the data-gathering of more than 160 researchers and interviews with 522 media company executives. Part of that work flowed into her editing the *Palgrave International Handbook of Women and Journalism* (Byerly, 2016), in which she assembled detailed studies on 29 different countries across all continents, ranging from Australia to Bangladesh, Chile, Estonia, Mexico, Lebanon, Poland, and Namibia to Uganda. Inspired by the *Global Report*, the book's chapter authors go in-depth about these countries' contexts and *how* women journalists are helped or hindered to fully participate in journalism at all levels. It combined quantitative and qualitative methods, in many cases providing the most comprehensive summary of the status of women journalists in a country that is available in English or overall. Her work and collaborations on original systematic data generation and interpretation across the globe that puts women front and center of the analysis has become a tremendous resource to journalism and media scholars, although journalism studies as a whole still need to pick up this invaluable work much more. Especially country-specific intersectional approaches in regard to which women journalists can work where and under which conditions as voices in the public sphere remain a lacuna in journalism studies.

Carolyn Byerly's ideas, enthusiasm, and persistence have hugely contributed to feminist scholarship in terms of the studies she produced, panels she organized, keynotes she held, awards she initiated, and books she wrote and edited. Her insistence and creativity have also touched the lives of many scholars, including me, through her thoughtful, kind, and consistent mentorship. The networks that she has charged with her energy and their future possibilities and projects are difficult to assess—so much more positive impact is still in the making of the herstory that Carolyn created. I was lucky to have been approached by her about a decade ago to get invited to join this ongoing joy ride to help build more visibility and recognition for feminist communication and media scholarship alongside Carolyn. In turn, here is an idea that I have for her. For all her tireless efforts, a special award for her should be created on the spot: The Carolyn Award for Persistence for Feminist Media Scholarship! I ran the funding (privately provided), built an award committee of one (me), and selected the winner: Carolyn M. Byerly, professor emerita of Howard University. To be given at ICA 2023 in Toronto. Let's celebrate Carolyn!

## References

Byerly, C. M. (2011). *Global report on status of women in news media*. International Women's Media Foundation. https://www.iwmf.org/resources/global-report-on-the-status-of-women-in-the-news-media/

Byerly, C. M. (Ed.). (2016). *The Palgrave international handbook of women and journalism*. Palgrave Macmillan.

Byerly, C. M., Rybas, N., & Meyer, M. (2022). Foreword. In S. Eckert & I. Bachmann (Eds.), *Reflections on feminist communication and media scholarship: Theory, method, impact* (pp. x–xii). Routledge.

Eckert, S., & Bachmann, I. (Eds.). (2022). *Reflections on feminist communication and media scholarship: Theory, method, impact*. Routledge.

Section III

# Pedagogy and Leadership

11

# Dr. Carolyn M. Byerly: The Perfect Combination of a Sound Researcher and a Feminist Activist

AIMÉE VEGA MONTIEL

My relationship with Carolyn Byerly goes from the scholarly field of feminist communication studies to activism for the improvement of women's communication rights. Personally, I have been honored by her friendship. She is such an inspiration for countless feminists all around the world. I would like to start by saying that it is difficult to focus on only one specific aspect of Carolyn Byerly's leadership, as the complexity of her work—a mix of sound research with committed activism in favor of women's rights invites a holistic view of her contributions. In my trajectory as a Latin-American researcher and activist, my first encounter with Carolyn Byerly was with her co-authored (with Karen Ross) book *Women and Media: A Critical Introduction* (2006). That work is not just a comprehensive outline of feminist communication scholarship, but of women's activism in the media. It resulted in an inspiration for me as a young scholar, as it made me realize that feminist theory makes sense only if it is devoted to social change. In some way, the book shows the equilibrium between being a consistent researcher and a committed activist.

The way Carolyn Byerly has approached the analysis of media corporations has been highly influenced by the feminist political economy framework. This interdisciplinary field, which looks at the political and economic structures and their influence in cultural practices, has helped Byerly to understand how male domination is institutionalized in media business and how it affects gender equality in the media. Based on the assumption that equality between women and men is determined by who owns, leads and controls media companies and production processes, and most of her research has demonstrated the relationship between the structural dynamics among these sectors and contents, as well as their impact on women's status within media and even on women's activism.

One of the most brilliant examples of how to take the feminist political economy approach to the empirical field is Byerly's *Global Report on the Status of Women in the News Media* (Byerly, 2011). This study, supported by the International Women's Media Foundation, demonstrated the male dominance in all levels of news media and women's marginalization from ownership, decision-making, reporting, editing, and other media positions. Thanks to this research in 59 nations, we also have a better understanding about women's underrepresentation as subjects in news media, as it was demonstrated with sound data the gender gap in decision-making roles of the 522 news corporations surveyed. In particular, the methodology proposed by Carolyn Byerly became a roadmap for research at the national level in my own nation, Mexico (Vega Montiel, 2010).

By putting into practice the feminist principle of sorority, the next step followed by Carolyn Byerly was the editor of *The Palgrave International Handbook of Women and Journalism* (Byerly, 2013), with the chapter contributions of feminist scholars from 29 countries. Most of them were the original researchers for the *Global Report* study. This time, and following the common goal of giving a more academic approach to the data contained in the *Global Report*, authors analyzed women's relationship to journalism in neoliberal contexts, where the rise of political and economic policies produced gender gaps. Each chapter of the book is a complete picture about women journalists in their respective nations, with a historical view of the cultural, political and economic factors that define women's situation in their newsrooms. Personally, for Carolyn Byerly, this book is a milestone achievement of her own research on women journalists' struggles within the news sector.

Carolyn Byerly's leadership in the field has extended from the Howard University space. During her career, she also played an active role in the improvement of feminist research in communication within the International Association for Media and Communication Research (IAMCR) and the International Communication Association (ICA), composed of scholars from around the world. These organizations have provided the framework for Byerly to generously disseminate her research, form groups with scholars from all over the world, and contribute to the training of new generations of feminist scholars. These organizations have also provided the framework in which Carolyn has led groundbreaking initiatives for global activism in feminism and communication. As a member of the IAMCR, for example, her wisdom was instrumental in the creation of the Global Alliance on Media and Gender (GAMAG) in 2013. This alliance, supported by the U.N. Educational, Scientific, and Cultural Organization (UNESCO) and over 600 organizations, aims to promote gender equality in and through media. As a representative of the IAMCR Task Force for GAMAG, Carolyn has been involved in initiatives aimed at influencing gender and communication policies globally, within the framework of the United Nations.

Alongside other feminist scholars, representatives of civil society organizations, and women journalists, she participated in various meetings of the United Nations Commission on the Status of Women (CSW) and influenced its Agreed Conclusions in 2018, which focused on "Gender and Communication" as the review theme. She also contributed to the development of gender equality indicators in media, in collaboration with GAMAG and U.N. Women, in 2016. Just recently, in 2022, she participated in the consultation on the *UN Plan of Action for the Safety of Journalists and the Issue of Impunity* on its 10th anniversary. Throughout these years, Carolyn has played a decisive role in keeping the feminist agenda in communication at the center of the IAMCR through her involvement in a GAMAG Special Session at the IAMCR annual Conference.

In collaboration with scholars from 19 countries across the five regions, Carolyn also participated in the establishment of the UNESCO-UniTWIN project on Gender, Media, and Information Communication Technology (ICT). UniTWIN is an international network of universities composed of specialists in feminism and communication, with the aim of promoting research, teaching, and dissemination activities at the global, regional and national levels. A milestone of this network has been the publication of the syllabus *Gender, Media & ICTs: New Approaches for Research, Education and Training* (French, Vega Montiel & Padovani, 2019). This initiative responds to a need identified by UNESCO and university partners in the UniTWIN, which is to equip a new generation of journalists and media practitioners to be fully gender-sensitive, both in their workplaces and in their work products. In preparing the syllabus, members of the network did research to map gender mainstreaming in the curriculum in order to identify relevant courses and other institutional resources in journalism and communication programs at universities.

In summary, during her career Carolyn Byerly developed a strong expertise in feminist scholarship, activism, gender and communication policy and advocacy, gender mainstreaming in education and feminist leadership, at national, regional and international levels. Her potential for providing intellectual, strategic and operational initiatives for the promotion of gender equality in and through the media, with positive impact in gender transformative policies and programs and in the strengthening of the field of gender and communication at the overall international arena, has made her an exceptional feminist. The agenda for her academic work has been driven by her desire to better understand how to improve gender equality in and through communication and information systems, in fields such as education, media, legislation and policy. This has strengthened her ability to exercise intellectual authority.

Historical circumstances gave her a combination of different skills: doing and publishing research, training, understanding of international standards on gender equality and women's human rights, influencing legislation and policy, leading global initiatives, building bridges with and between different actors (e.g., scholars, U.N. agencies, civil society activists, unions, governments and regulatory bodies and mainstreaming gender in education).

I also want to mention her high sense of professional integrity. In every field where Carolyn entered, she showed what it is to be an exemplary scholar. Finally, I want to emphasize Carolyn Byerly's outstanding character. Throughout all these years, I have been fortunate enough to have her friendship. In both professional and personal circumstances where I have needed her advice, she has always responded with sisterhood, offering wisdom and warmth. And that is priceless. I have so much to be grateful to Carolyn Byerly for. My own academic and activist life, as well as my personal life, are better today because of her.

## References

Byerly, C. M. (2011). *Global report on the status of women in the news Media*. International Women's Media Foundation.

Byerly, C. M. (2013). *The Palgrave international handbook of women and journalism*. Palgrave Macmillan.

French, L., Montiel, A. V., & Padovani, C. (2019). *Gender, media & ICTs: New approaches for research, education and training*. UNESCO.

Vega Montiel, A. (2010). Las mujeres y el derecho humano a la comunicación: Su suceso y participación en la industria mediática. *Revista Mexicana de Ciencias Políticas y Sociales, 208*, 81–96. UNAM.

12

# Mentor or Other Mother? Byerly Feminism Meets Black Feminist Thought at a Historically Black College and University

ASHLA C. HILL ROSEBORO

Dr. Carolyn Byerly, former professor and chair of the Communication, Culture and Media Studies Department at Howard University, mentored countless students across decades, particularly supporting Black women doctoral students in navigating research and careers in academia. As described by Patricia Hill Collins's (2005) Black feminist thought (BFT), Dr. Byerly emphasized empowered voices of racial and gender minorities in her graduate courses, where we discussed strategies that Black women often must adopt to think and speak for themselves. Legislative efforts today have threatened changes in curricula to exclude the teaching of marginalized stories, histories and culture of Black, indigenous and people of color (BIPOC) in higher education. This political climate emphasizes a need for increased mentoring by faculty who study and practice in spaces that focus on marginalized populations (Mata et al., 2022). As a Black woman who fits into the BFT construct who has experienced motherhood and mentorship, the author is interpreting these ideas as a participant. The immersive mentoring with Dr. Byerly as my dissertation advisor and ongoing academic mentor offers first-hand knowledge of her leadership, scholarship, advocacy and activism in struggles for freedom to liberate those who are on the margins.

Organizing has been an approach that Dr. Byerly leaned into consistently across time and spaces in the struggle for civil rights, women's liberation and, in more recent years, Black Lives Matter and #MeToo movements. She has been a force speaking truth to power, while teaching students at a historically Black university (HBCU) to own their voices in bringing about action for social justice. Media policies were research interests of Dr. Byerly to which she devoted a great deal of energy in scholarship and activism, especially in the latter years as a professor on the faculty at Howard University. Dr. Byerly has studied the intersection of feminism and political economy that interpreted systems that distribute wealth and power to a small group, while the masses struggled to survive and maintain their positions in society.

## Intersectionality at HBCUs

The matrix of domination that women face, specifically Black women, occurs when women's ideas are critiqued, taken from them by others and silenced (Collins, 2005). During my defense of my dissertation proposal, Dr. Byerly would not allow the committee to proceed without addressing the matrix of domination, which some had questioned. Those specific words "matrix of domination" needed to be stated, she said. At the time, it seemed like a preference, but now, with my own experience as a professor navigating academia, it has become clearer as to the reason my study on Black college women had to address these intersectional barriers alluded to in "matrix of domination." Acknowledging that Black, Brown and Indigenous women are the lowest earners of all other groups in the United States is evidence of how this matrix appears in everyday life for women, particularly women of color.

Activists in the 1960s and 1970s were involved in civil rights, feminism and union movements that prioritized one category of focus as either race, gender or class, rather than combined efforts (Collins & Bilge, 2016). Dr. Byerly often reminisced on the years of her early activism for women's liberation in the 1970s. She would tell her students they needed to get angry about what was happening in the world that was unjust to prompt them to move to action. During the early 2000s, a rise in student activism on college campuses reemerged with protests for Black Lives Matter. Howard University had student sit-ins and "teach-in" forums as ways to unite students, faculty and administration. Dr. Byerly unofficially mentored students by sharing advice on how to organize effectively to bring about change, especially on the campus and in the community. This approach opened the door to conversations between Howard administration and students. Though all demands from students were rarely accepted, the environment of having experienced activist-scholars mentoring students has far-reaching effects in teaching how to voice concerns and take action for change.

Black women used intersectionality to address limitations of movements having a singular focus that omitted aspects of the interconnected social struggles that minority women faced. When Dr. Byerly advised graduate students on dissertations, she was eager to take on feminist topics that illuminated Black women in media who had little or no scholarly research previously conducted on these individuals and the organizations in which they were contributors. These studies were frequently original research that used qualitative methods to collect archival data, interviews and observations to study a phenomenon. Double jeopardy combined both gender and racial bias in laws, institutional policies and practices, and within social environments that favored capitalism (Collins & Bilge, 2016). Dr. Byerly reminded students that what was being studied had a political angle, and she encouraged budding researchers to uncover the political issues. Historically Black Colleges and Universities (HBCUs) have been celebrated for their elevation of Black progress in society. W. E. B. DuBois critiqued Booker T. Washington's position:

> Black people give up, at least for the present, three things—First, political power, Second, insistence on civil rights, Third, higher education of Negro youth—and concentrate all their energies on industrial education, the accumulation of wealth, and the conciliation of the South. (DuBois, 1994, pp. 30–31)

Washington (1986) was taught at Hampton Institute, then went to Tuskegee, Alabama, to establish a school for minority students with the Alabama legislature covering only the salaries of the instructors, no expenses for buildings and upkeep. Washington traveled mostly on a mule across the countryside of Alabama and lodged in cabins with the people whom he recruited to his school (Washington, 1986). These experiences shaped how he advocated for career readiness training at HBCUs that were overwhelmingly located in the U.S. South to prepare students to enter careers that were available to Blacks, especially during the height of Jim Crow. As a feminist activist, Dr. Byerly would more closely fit into the DuBois's thinking of developing intellectuals who would have an equal standing in society, while at the same time she embodies the characteristics of Washington by being united with people in the struggle. This festschrift honors Dr. Byerly's work to move the marginalized to the center through economic justice and reconciliation. This is a reminder of an indigenous people's reconciliation program at Dr. Byerly's church in Maryland that she invited me to attend, because of my ancestral Native American lineage. The ceremony was memorable in that there were spoken acknowledgments of past harms and reaffirmations to heal. The exercise demonstrated community activism that embraced everyone for their humanity. For her, activism was not what Dr. Byerly did, but who she was in running toward the fires when equity, justice and equality were in peril.

In a world where people are marginalized for being part of a certain race, ethnicity, class, gender, or color, heroes and heroines are needed. Discrimination and criminalization of select groups have a sordid history in U.S. systems, including law enforcement, housing, employment and public spaces. Injustices should sound alarms, be called out and investigated. This may point to Booker T. Washington having an immediate solution that would allow Blacks to be employed (Washington, 1986). Though the work was often in subordinate roles with lower pay, this suggests that Washington understood that progress toward an equitable world would be slow.

Discussions in graduate classes taught by Dr. Byerly often came back to power and class. She seemed to understand the economic and political forces that prevented certain groups from excelling beyond the glass ceiling, whether they were women, racial minorities or working-class people. Her focus was on using strategies that could effect change, whether large or small, such as speaking truth to power. Where do African Americans stand economically in the twenty-first century, particularly women who are earning college degrees in high numbers? Social and political life often are shaped by many diverse factors that result in social divisions, such as race, gender or class. Collins and Bilge (2016) described intersectionality as an approach used to understand and analyze societal and human complexities in the world. As a mentor to graduate students, Dr. Byerly emphasized the ongoing struggle for equality.

## Byerly Feminist Mentorship

The most competitive HBCUs, such as Howard University, often attract and accept the highest achieving students, most of whom are Black or other minorities. Faculty mentors and advisors at HBCUs teach students to meet academic expectations, while also holistically adapting when other needs arise, whether those be financial, mental, emotional or social challenges. Living in a world where minority students may have fewer safe spaces to belong, faculty advisors can fill some of these gaps. Numerous students encountered challenges with funding their studies and housing in D.C., where the cost of living and tuition are high. Many semesters, stipends were released after the semester began, so students had to wait for disbursements, and that created a greater challenge for some than others. Dr. Byerly was an advocate for students, while navigating the layers of bureaucracy in the academy, demonstrating her ability to lead at a HBCU. Her instruction of HBCU doctoral students helped them to identify power differences and find the emancipatory potential in any problem they investigated. She trained scholars to problematize issues through the use of critical theories, such as feminism, Afrocentricity and cultural studies, to develop a complex analysis through their scholarship. Newspaper and magazine content analysis studies that Dr. Byerly had published where assigned readings that students had to analyze in her classes. For example, one of the first courses that Communication, Culture and Media Studies graduate students had to take was a theory class taught by Dr. Byerly that required weekly readings and a one-page analytical summary.

One Byerly (2012) article defined the international geography of women and media studies by using a four-part critique: (1) absence, (2) representation, (3) employment/production and (4) consumption. Alternative presses were the voice of people who were on the margins and overlooked, or frequently written about negatively, in mainstream papers. Subsequently, the absence of women in major news stories led to silencing or reducing them into support roles. A history of women being ignored, most notably in radio and television, elevated the status of mothers, wives and females who were associated with male achievers (Byerly, 2012). Feminist activism movements that seemed to be newsworthy were often overlooked in mass media (Byerly, 2012). Media representations, especially of women whose bodies were objectified through over-sexualization and depicted in powerless roles where they were abused, commonly negatively labeled women (Byerly, 2012). Stereotypical ideologies privileged masculine dominance. Historical patriarchy has been critiqued because of the progress that came from feminist movements. However, images of sexualized Black and Latina women continue to be prevalent in the media. Pay inequities, harassment and glass ceilings demonstrate a lack of access to managerial and production positions for women media employees. Consumption of new digital media in the public and private have opened paths for women to engage in, control and benefit in more ways than they had from traditional legacy media.

## Black Feminist Thought Translates to Other Mothers' Empowerment

Motherhood has been widely studied; however, little if any scholarship has investigated where women, regardless of race, may fit into Black feminist thought, particularly if they mentor Black students in higher education institutions. My dissertation, *National Association of University Women: Advocacy in the Black Press for an Organization of African American Intellectual Women, 1910–1980*, was supervised by Dr. Byerly, who was my advisor. I found that the "other mother" phenomenon of college-educated women nurturing and mentoring youth in the community appeared in Black newspapers that wrote about a familial dichotomy of like-minded women who shared a sisterhood as community other mothers. These women were often educators by profession in the early to mid-1900s who invested time and resources to raise the status of people of their race and improve interracial relationships (Roseboro, 2019). Dr. Byerly displayed a great deal of empathy and compassion as my dissertation advisor, while finding ways to push me to excellence.

Collins (1990) reconceived motherhood by highlighting "other mothers" and the important status of being a mom, differently than being cast into the role as subordinate to men. Collins' (2005) Black feminist thought (BFT) was defined as empowering Black women's ideas and intellectual production as legitimate. Dr. Byerly advised graduate student dissertations that used feminism to study Black women who were written about in presses around the world. Black women who thought and spoke for themselves demonstrated Black feminism in how they used their empowered voices (Collins, 2005). Dr. Byerly, now professor emerita, trained a cadre of feminist scholars to continue this important work of feminist scholarship and advocacy. BFT endeavors to correct social injustices to fully empower Black women whose ideas were frequently diminished, taken from them or silenced. Consequently, the suppression or censoring of intersectional studies in the academy today continues to be met with challenges. Community "other mothers" embraced Afrocentric ideals of working collectively as a group (Collins, 1990).

"Other mothers" became political advocates concerned with raising the status of the Black race through community work. Collins (1990) characterized educated Black women as community "other mothers" who were a source of strength and support for Black women who were social justice reformers in their communities. The activism of Dr. Byerly is interwoven into her being. For example, her leadership of the Howard Media Group at Howard University facilitated the writing of numerous statements to the Federal Communications Commission (FCC) regarding media ownership equality. One such statement was on "Gender-and-Race Conscious Research Toward Egalitarian Broadcast Ownership Regulation." In this statement, Dr. Byerly addressed the low occurrence of women and people of color as broadcast media owners (Byerly, 2010). She further asserted that there was a racial and gender crisis in U.S. communication policy.

College women like Dr. Byerly are an example of community "other mothers" who tried to advocate for vulnerable people by using their status as public figures to ensure everyone had equal rights as citizens and access to leadership. Collins (1990) conceptualized a "mothering the mind" relationship, similar to a mother-daughter dyad, except this was between a teacher and Black women students who connected as Black women in a community. In Black culture, whether a blood mother, "other mother" or community "other mother," motherhood was considered a symbol of power and status (Collins, 1990). This suggests that women teachers whose pupils are Black take on the image of other mothers, gaining respect and high esteem of their students. The transformative power women scholars possessed to influence young people and vulnerable communities has been a source of liberation. These college women wanted to improve the community by developing self-reliant and independent individuals who could join the movement for equality. College women were often leaders in the community, because they were teachers in majority Black schools and respected as role models. Many of these teachers wanted to reach back to their communities to inspire and support youth who had the ability to attend college (Miller & Pruitt-Logan, 2012). Black higher educational institutions, such as Howard University, emphasized the importance of community outreach to elevate others in the race (Shaw, 1996). Many faculty members at HBCUs are non-Black crusaders for justice and equality. They are committed to educating students to be culturally competent, inclusive and change-agent leaders in their local communities and the world.

## Reflections

Dr. Byerly has the attributes of a community mother as demonstrated in her ability to offer sound advice, share personal experiences and strategies to excel as a researcher and academic. I view Dr. Byerly as a mentor, advocate and "other mother" who I am grateful to have in my life. In my opinion, Dr. Byerly meets the criteria for an "other mother" according to Collins BFT, if the color of her skin were not a factor. Her determination and character uniquely make her who she is and this inspires others, including myself to continue the struggle for equal rights for all people. Women who have been marginalized, silenced or excluded are still asking the question "am I a woman"? Whether a single mother, part of the LGBTQ community, working class, Black, Latina, Indigenous, disabled, incarcerated or other minority group, today the plight of all women being treated justly, equally and fairly still is a struggle that must be addressed.

The reality is that at the intersection of motherhood is class, gender and race. Dr. Byerly identifies as a feminist political economist with a keen eye on media ownership that underrepresents women and people of color. Solutions that she recommended in the FCC report were:

1. research to establish (a) impact of deregulation on loss of minority-related public affairs programming and (b) impact of such loss on minority communities;
2. research to establish clear criteria for determining public interest in relation to minority communities;
3. research to determine (a) market-entry barriers to women's ownership and (b) ways that gender enters into programming for local community needs and interests (Byerly, 2010).

As Dr. Byerly often stated to her students, research begins with a problem, and there are no shortage of issues to be investigated beginning with approaches for the FCC to open more opportunities for women and minorities in media. There are consequences of regulation and deregulation for media policies, from broadband access, net neutrality and social media, in this age of new technologies. Likewise, the number of women and minority media owners still is low, but with the advent of digital media there are hopes for strides forward in greater equity for the voices of all people to be represented. In academia, women are still making progress in leadership that recognizes their abilities to contribute as administrators. Realistically, there still are significantly fewer women HBCU presidents and administrators, though women often comprise a larger population of enrolled students, as well as shifts in the alumni class composition that reflects higher percentages of women graduates, particularly at HBCUs (Hill Roseboro, 2020). Though BFT focused specifically on African American women, this theory has not been explored beyond the social construct of race to include women who immerse themselves in HBCU culture as non-Black women faculty committed to justice and equality for all people.

**Author Note**

*In my experience when Dr. Byerly was chairperson and professor of the Communication, Culture and Media Studies graduate department at Howard University, I grew beyond my wildest imagination into an inquisitive researcher who learned to ask questions and see beyond what appeared on the surface. Dr. Byerly encouraged me to become a member of the Howard Media Group, an organization that wrote statements and responded to FCC policies and decisions. She believed in my research interests and the significance of the original study I conducted for my dissertation. When I was recruited for a tenure-track position in academia, Dr. Byerly spoke on my behalf and used her influence to support me in successfully securing the role. Dr. Byerly describes what she sees of my future in academia. She is a gift and bright light. I am grateful to have been mentored, nurtured and enlightened as her student, graduate assistant, and now a faculty member by this distinguished, international scholar. Thank you, Dr. Byerly, for all you have done and for who you are.*

## References

Byerly, C. M. (2010). *Gender-and-race-conscious research toward egalitarian broadcast ownership regulation.* Federal Communications Commission. https://transition.fcc.gov/ownership/workshop-012710/byerly.pdf

Byerly, C. M. (2012). The geography of women and media scholarship. In K. Ross (Ed.), *The handbook of gender, sex, and media* (1st ed., pp. 3–19). John Wiley & Sons.

Collins, P. H. (1990). *Black feminist thought.* Routledge, Chapman and Hall.

Collins, P. H. (2005). *Black sexual politics: African Americans, gender and the new racism.* Routledge.

Collins, P. H., & Bilge, S. (2016). *Intersectionality.* Polity Press.

DuBois, W. E. B. (1994). *The souls of Black folk.* Dover.

Hill Roseboro, A. C. (2020). Historically Black colleges and universities access to digital media: An intersectional content analysis of Black women social entrepreneurs. In L. S. Byrd (Ed.), *Cultivating entrepreneurial changemakers through digital media education* (p. 19). IGI Global. https://doi.org/10.4018/978-1-7998-5808-9.ch012

Mata, I., Trevino, M., & Torres, M. G. (2022). *The change higher education needs today: As attacks on critical race theory accelerate, colleges must create more mentoring environments designed by BIPOC faculty themselves, write Irene Mata, Melva Trevino and M. Gabriela Torres.* Inside Higher Ed.

Miller, C. L. L., & Pruitt-Logan, A. S. (2012). *Faithful to the task at hand: The life of Lucy Diggs Slowe.* State University of New York Press.

Roseboro, A. H. (2019). *National Association of University Women: Advocacy in the Black press for an organization of African American intellectual women, 1910–1980* [Manuscript in

preparation]. Department of Communication, Culture and Media Studies, Graduate School, Howard University.
Shaw, S. J. (1996). *What a woman ought to be and to do: Black professional women workers during the Jim Crow era.* The University of Chicago Press.
Washington, B. T. (1986). *Up from slavery.* Penguin Books.

13

# Finding My Voice: Dr. Carolyn M. Byerly's Impact on My Academic Journey

SHOAA ALMAKI

When I started my doctoral program at Howard University, I had too many questions about the value of critical research. The thought of continuing in the program was one I seriously pondered. It was an intimidating realization: critical thinking implied challenging everything, be it religion, politics, culture, or societal power dynamics. In my first class with Dr. Carolyn Byerly, I saw passion and dedication to social justice and critical research that made me rethink my decision. It felt overwhelming to grapple with such critical concepts; however, having an activist scholar like Dr. Byerly has made my doctoral journey a remarkable one. Her presence in my life as a professor and a mentor was transformative, altering the course of my academic journey and life overall.

In writing this essay, I remind myself of what it means to be a true mentor. Dr. Byerly is an example of an activist scholar whose research and work have a real-world impact. Her contributions to the field of communication are invaluable. She is one of the few scholars who advanced the scholarship on feminist political economy in the media as a distinct area of study. Dr. Byerly's research showcases her commitment to interrogating patriarchal media structures that obstruct women's participation in policymaking, media ownership, and representation. Beyond her noteworthy and enduring scholarly contribution, Dr. Byerly has been a beacon for the feminist community through her activism and mentorship, advocating for their presence locally and globally.

When considering the many facets of her remarkable career, one aspect stands out: her unwavering dedication to the empowerment of women and marginalized groups. Her life's work is evidence of her steadfast belief that all voices, especially those of women and marginalized groups, deserve to be heard. Faced with a system that often silences these voices, Dr. Byerly has demonstrated great perseverance in her advocacy, fighting tirelessly to confront and change the status quo. Her commitment to those values has inspired countless students, colleagues, and activists and sparked a passion for social justice in a new generation of academics and activists. Dr. Byerly's legacy, therefore, is not only one of personal achievement but also of systemic change.

## Dr. Byerly as a Teacher and a Mentor

As a mentor, Dr. Byerly was able to bring out the best in her students, encouraging us to reach our full potential while offering unwavering support and guidance. Her dedication to social justice inspires a new generation of activists and academics to confront systemic inequality and fight for a more equitable world. Working with Dr. Byerly taught me three things: one is to speak truth to power, the second is to build scientific research that challenges the status quo, and the third is to advocate for those marginalized and amplify their voices.

Speaking truth to power was the first important lesson I learned from Dr. Byerly. This idea was more than just a mantra; it was a way of life for her. She insisted that academics should act as society's watchdogs, uncovering uncomfortable truths and holding those in power accountable. When I came up with ideas for my class papers, she always challenged me to address the real problem head-on instead of dancing around it. I remind myself of this every time I write a new paper. Always asking myself, what would Dr. Byerly say? To this day, Dr. Byerly continues to be my sounding board and my mentor who challenges me to speak my truth and advocate for the less fortunate.

The second lesson I learned from Dr. Byerly is that research is not only about accumulating knowledge; it is also about shaking the very foundation of the status quo and provoking intellectual debates. She introduced us to the critical role of research, emphasizing its potential to promote policy change and challenge the status quo. She encouraged us to think of research as a tool for societal change. I vividly recall a classroom discussion in which I questioned the practical value of social justice research. Dr. Byerly's response was enlightening. She introduced us to Diana Russell, a researcher whose work radically changed the laws around marital rape. In a time when the idea of marital rape was not recognized by the law, Russell and her students undertook an in-depth investigation. They secured a federal grant, went door to door, and conducted interviews with hundreds of married women (1990). Their findings were staggering: 10–14 percent of these women were frequently forced into non-consensual sex by their husbands.

This study was a catalyst for change rather than merely an intellectual exercise. Hearing about the impact of Dr. Russell's research on policy change, Dr. Byerly and other women raised funds to bring Dr. Russell to Washington State in the early 1980s so she could present her findings to legislators. The impact was immediate. That same year, the state passed legislation designating marital rape as a crime. As a result of the evidence provided by Dr. Russell's study, other states enacted similar policies. This single research project drastically altered the law around marital rape across the United States. Dr. Byerly used this example to illustrate the profound potential of social justice research. She explained that our work as researchers could extend far beyond academia and have a real impact on social and policy change. It was an invaluable lesson in the power of research and an enduring testament to the potential of critical, justice-oriented inquiry.

Lastly, at the heart of Dr. Byerly's critical approach to research is her commitment to amplifying marginalized voices. I had the pleasure to co-author a chapter titled, "The Other," in which we examined the concept from a global perspective. We explain,

> To grasp the serious and measurable global consequences it has had in both oppression and liberation requires an exploration of the Other concept in different intellectual traditions, as well as varied political applications and liberation movements for equality and justice (e.g., racial, feminist, and lesbian, gay, bisexual, transgender, and queer [LGBTQ]). (Byerly & Almalki, 2022, p. 40)

Working with Dr. Byerly on this project has taught me to see my own identity within the context of local and global history. I came to explore my intersectional identity and understand the concept of the other and apply it to my culture and society. This was a project that I learned the most from as I worked closely with her to build my narrative.

## Dr. Byerly's Influence on My Scholarship

My academic journey has been greatly influenced by Dr. Byerly's scholarship. Although my primary areas of study—gender and culture, technology and research methods, and strategic communication—may appear to be unrelated to her areas of expertise which include feminist political economy, her feminist and critical approach, mainly her focus on marginalized voices and her global research, has had a significant impact on my research. When I think about her research influence on my scholarship, four things come to mind: her invaluable mentorship, her approach to academic writing, her emphasis on reflexivity and the researchers' connection to their study, and her dedication to empirical and ethical research.

I had the privilege to be Dr. Byerly's last advisee before her retirement. Her mentorship and guidance helped me throughout the process. Writing my dissertation was not an easy task. I started working during the pandemic which made it difficult to communicate with my other professors, but not with Dr. Byerly who was always on top of everything. I remember working with her on the topic of my paper and how she challenged me to bring something original, something of value. We had many conversations where we both would push back to convince each other. What I learned from Dr. Byerly during this process is that no matter how much you believe in your argument you must back it up with research and stand by it. Every time we had a meeting, and she pushed back on something I would go back and work on my proposal again. I did my research and constructed a narrative that would help me win her approval. I appreciated that process greatly. It ingrained in me how to accept feedback and learn, and to work on making my arguments clearer and more persuasive. I gained so many skills from my time working with her on my dissertation.

Another thing that influenced my scholarship is Dr. Byerly's academic writing style. I became fond of writing in an easy language keeping in mind that my audience can be anyone interested in my research. In most of her work, Dr. Byerly effectively expresses complicated intellectual ideas through her clear, insightful, and elegantly simple writing style without falling victim to the obscurity that frequently afflicts academic writing. Her writing style is a product of her experience as a journalist who was entrusted with presenting the world in understandable words, and she applied the same idea to her academic writing. She taught me that academic knowledge should not be elitist but should be accessible to people from all backgrounds.

Dr. Byerly's influence extended far beyond writing style, shaping the very essence of my research and the way I view my role as a scholar. I learned the value of reflexivity in research from her emphasis on addressing the researcher's thoughts and biases toward the studied issue. In her paper titled, "Feminist

Intersectionality Research in Communications: Origins, Contributions and Tensions," she explains how this principle is at the heart of critical research:

> Of any research tradition, critical scholars are the most likely to break with the notions of maintaining distance to achieve «objective» inquiry. Instead, critical scholars tend to share the values and even experiences of the human communities they are concerned with in their work, and to reveal their scholarly relationship to the research they have undertaken. (Byerly, 2017, p. 24)

In many of our numerous scholarly conversations, she always pushed me to trust my intuition when exploring new territories and think about how my work can expand upon existing theories and explore new paths in understudied research areas. Coming from an understudied culture, especially in regard to critical approach, I had so many challenges in identifying starting points. I always think about how a paper can inform the literature. Dr. Byerly's voice is always in my mind telling me to think critically about how my approach can produce new knowledge. Her critical perspective inspired me to work toward answers, amplify the voices of underrepresented groups, and challenge power dynamics in society.

Lastly, Dr. Byerly's dedication to empirical research, a data-driven approach, had a significant impact on how I conducted my own research. Despite being a qualitative and critical researcher, Dr. Byerly always stressed the significance of drawing on quantitative data to support qualitative investigations. This perspective has led me to adopt a triangulated approach to my data and data analysis methods, blending both quantitative and qualitative methods.

Dr. Byerly's intellectual legacy has not only inspired my study but also shaped who I am as a scholar. Her lessons have helped me understand the value of data-driven research, clear and understandable academic writing, a critical approach to power dynamics, and research ethics. It is an influence that continues to resonate in my work, shaping my scholarship's present and future trajectories.

## Continuing Dr. Byerly's Legacy

As a scholar, I have been dedicated to honoring Dr. Byerly's core principle of amplifying marginalized voices in the media. This commitment is not only an ethical obligation but also broadens the scope of discourse and deepens our collective knowledge of societal issues. In my research, I have worked on projects exploring women's status in my own culture, an understudied area to highlight these underrepresented views. Moreover, in my teaching, I enrich my students' learning experiences with diverse perspectives on communication and create an environment where all views are welcomed.

I have found Dr. Byerly's feminist critical approach to be especially useful as I apply her lessons to my research. My analysis and critique of power relations in Arab society have significantly benefited from her emphasis on examining the structural and institutional influences that shape media narratives. Her dedication to ethical research has also influenced how I engage with and understand the media, ensuring that I do my research with the utmost integrity and regard for my participants.

I am planning several projects inspired by Dr. Byerly's work and mentorship. One project is an in-depth examination of the Arabic-speaking digital environment—a topic that has intrigued me ever since I finished my dissertation. I've learned from Dr. Byerly's guidance that the digital sphere is not an isolated domain but rather a reflection of our society. By exploring the complexities of this digital environment, my study will provide new perspectives on the social norms and structures that exist within Arabic-speaking society. A society that is more to be explored. Another project, inspired by Dr. Byerly's passion for giving voice to the marginalized, focuses on the discourse around sexual harassment in religious places on Twitter (now called X). Specifically, I will be examining the stories that Muslim women construct when sharing their harassment experiences as part of the #mosquemetoo movement. Dr. Byerly's lessons are embodied in this project, which uses data-driven research through computational analysis to highlight these narratives while also questioning power relations and giving voice to those often silenced. As I continue to grow as a scholar, I am inspired by Dr. Byerly's commitment to challenging power dynamics in her research and activism. I aspire to continue in her footsteps, applying her teachings to my work, hopefully inspiring the next generation of scholars just as she has inspired me.

## References

Byerly, C. M. (2017). Feminist intersectionality research in communications: Origins, contributions and tensions. *Ex Aequo—Revista Da Associação Portuguesa De Estudos Sobre as Mulheres*, *35*: 23–32. https://doi.org/10.22355/exaequo.2017.35.02

Byerly, C. M., & Almalki, S. (2022). The other: Identity and difference in global, religious and gendered contexts. In P. Creedon & L. Wackwitz (Eds.), *Women in mass communication: Diversity, Equity, and Inclusion*, pp. 40–50. Routledge.

Russell, D. E. H. (1990). *Rape in marriage* (Exp. and rev. ed.). Indiana University Press.

14

# The Feminist Standpoint of Dr. Carolyn M. Byerly

TSOVINAR NAZARYAN

I had the honor to be Dr. Carolyn M. Byerly's student at Howard University, where I went to do a master's in Mass Communications and Media Studies through a Muskie Fellowship financed by the U.S. State Department, in 2009. She was my professor for two courses—one on Development Communication, and the other on Feminism, Communication, and Culture. She also directed my research for the master's thesis. A year after my graduation, Dr. Byerly generously accepted my request to volunteer to teach mass communication practices in advocacy campaigns to activists, mostly women, in several regions of Armenia. These common experiences, mostly based on shared values and interests, grew into a friendship in further years.

In this chapter, I will testify about Dr. Byerly's liberation teaching and humanist standpoints as a scholar, professor, and friend. To understand to what extent my experience at Howard University was eye-opening and life-changing, one should be informed about the context that will be introduced here. It was the first year of the presidency of Barack Obama, the first-ever Black president in the United States, when I moved to Washington, DC, a city predominantly populated by African Americans. I started my studies at Howard University, a historically Black university founded in 1867 and later an important part of the Civil Rights

Movement. Howard University opened up to me as a friendly space for learning and reflection that welcomed students with challenged backgrounds. The school is devoted to critical education. Being an ethnic Armenian from Armenia, this was my first-ever experience of being a minority among other minorities. Still, the pain of Black history resonated in the Armenians' historical survival struggle, which is well known to me. And the lived experiences of American women were largely relevant to me, as a woman.

## Liberation Teaching vs. Banking Education

Being born to and raised by a married couple involved in the Armenian anti-Soviet underground movement, I have always questioned the knowledge transferred through conventional education. In Soviet schools, questions were discouraged. The dominant teaching methodology made students memorize and reproduce the transferred knowledge for exams and oral presentations without questioning it. The knowledge created for Soviet students was in line with Soviet ideology and politics. After the collapse of the Soviet Union, the education system was slow to liberate itself, and although the content of the knowledge (mostly on history and social science) was changed, the pedagogy of transferring that content mainly remained the same. I would later learn, thanks to Dr. Byerly, that Brazilian educator and philosopher Paulo Freire had already named this the "banking" approach to education.

Applying for a master's degree program in the United States after 16 years working in journalism would become the best choice I have ever made in my life. I was about to discover another world of education where thinking was more appreciated than knowing (in times of the Web that knows almost everything). Howard University was devoted to cultural critical studies and greatly encouraged critical thinking. This was especially the case for the Mass Communications and Media Studies (MCMS) program at HU.

Dr. Barbara Hines, the head of the MCMS program at that time, recommended the Development Communication course to me, saying that Dr. Byerly was also working on a global study on gender equality in newsrooms in around 60 countries, including Eastern Europe, that appeared to have pretty much the same practices in newsrooms as in South-Eastern Europe, my region (she was referring to what would be published as *Global Report on the Status of Women in News Media*, Byerly, 2011). Dr. Hines knew my region well. She had worked with the IREX[16] office in the neighboring nation of Georgia. Soon, when I started the course with Dr. Byerly, I couldn't be thankful enough to Dr. Hines for her advice.

The course on Development Communication was taught by Dr. Byerly and one of her former students, Dr. Kerry-Ann Hamilton. We were only three students: two PhD students from Africa (Chad and Nigeria) and me, a master's student from the post-Soviet Caucasus. The syllabus took us to an eye-opening journey through the use of mass communication in the Third World, as brought by the most industrialized Western countries. We studied the application of modernization theory, the dominant paradigm of development, the liberation theory, and many more. This course made us discover the groundbreaking *Pedagogy of the Oppressed* by the Brazilian educator and philosopher Paulo Freire who promoted the idea of development *with* people, rather than *for* people. This book soon became a "bible" to me and I started translating extracts for Armenian activists. As Dr. Byerly would recall later, this was a life-changing book.

It was surprising to find out that the *Pedagogy of the Oppressed*, which promoted liberation from oppression through participatory education, had been a popular *samizdat* (home-published banned reading) in South Africa and many other postcolonial countries. The book had been neither officially published nor circulated as underground *samizdat* in the Soviet Union, which positioned itself as a protector of (former) colonies of the capitalist West. But a close reading of the book left no doubt that it could not be embraced by the Soviet system, where students were perceived as empty barrels for pouring propaganda into them. Critical consciousness (*conscientização* in Portuguese) could not be encouraged in Soviet education whose goal was to make people "more fully loyal" rather than "more fully human."

Paulo Freire writes:

> A revolutionary leadership must accordingly practice co-intentional education. Teachers and students (leadership and people), co-intent on reality, are both Subjects, not only in the task of unveiling that reality, and thereby coming to know it critically, but in the task of recreating that knowledge. As they attain this knowledge of reality through common reflection and action; they discover themselves as its permanent re-creators. In this way, the presence of the oppressed in the struggle for their liberation will be what it should be: not pseudo-participation, but committed involvement. (Freire, 2010, p. 69)

16 IREX—International Research and Exchange Board, the organization managing the Muskie Fellowship for the State Department.

Shortly I was determined to enroll in the next course taught by Dr. Byerly. It was the course on Feminism, Communication, and Culture, another eye-opening and life-changing experience thanks to Dr. Byerly's unique curriculum.

Carolyn M. Byerly's teaching was co-intentional and valorized every participating Subject. Her teaching was also thoroughly academic and thoroughly inspiring to become "more fully human." Students, being of different backgrounds, brought specific perspectives to the discussed subjects. We interacted with each other and asked each other's opinions whenever we felt that one's lived experiences could help to deconstruct and reconstruct our knowledge and analysis even further. We created a *praxis*, meaningful and conscious actions and practices, that was central to the liberation theory of Freire. Dr. Byerly was the teacher and the leader of the classroom but also, being very much interested in our insights into the discussed readings, as she sought to push boundaries of thought through everyone's contribution in the classroom. This created a very trustful space for critical thinking. When summing up our presentations on individual final papers, Dr. Byerly stressed how much she had learned from our work and how many more stories and aspects we had revealed to her. Some of us were happy to get assessed papers back with Dr. Byerly's remarks, to consider her suggested edits and to submit the paper for publication in a scholarly journal. I had never seen such appreciation for students' work before.

Dr. Byerly walked us through various feminist theories and disclosed many underestimated aspects of women's and minorities' struggles throughout history. Most of us fell in love with the feminist standpoint theory suggesting that a scholar should keep a distance from the center but also fold up their sleeves and get into the fight when it is inevitable. As Smith (2004, p. 31) states, "she cannot understand the nature of her experienced world by staying within its ordinary boundaries of assumption and knowledge." This was a fight against patriarchy that was for social solidarity and not a fraction. We knew that Dr. Byerly had actively participated in political movements, especially in women's movements, and even played some role in the civil rights movement. Still, in the classroom, Dr. Byerly kept an academic distance from her personal experiences. When asked, she would give a short reply as a witness and an extended reply as a scholar. We were encouraged to learn more through the research done in the field. Dr. Byerly also earned our respect for being honest with her answers to our questions.

The course load was greatly challenging but also very enriching and empowering in many ways. C. Byerly created an environment where students felt safe to disclose their personal experiences and pains related to the studied subjects. "Personal is political," the slogan of 1960s' feminist movement that later was theorized in many feminist studies, was a credo in her classroom. Human agency was central not only in the studied literature but also in the classroom where everyone was accepted as a historical subject and not a static object. It was in Byerly's classroom that I defined my position as a feminist. Once, an African American classmate disclosed that she was the first-ever member of her extended family to make it through college in the last 400–500 years. Such cases were typical topics for demonstrating ourselves and making us reflect on intersections between various aspects of discrimination—race, class, gender, social, and others. We came to understand Dr. Byerly's position: "I am a proponent of intersectionality scholarship, which defines my research and also my teaching. I believe one comes to intersectionality through consciousness born of lived experience as much as academic training" (Byerly, 2017).

Dr. Byerly was known as a demanding professor among students at Howard. Only those taking her courses knew how much more demanding she was of herself. She was always eager to support and orient students. Despite her load of work, she accepted my request to be my thesis advisor with enthusiasm. Further months were full of intense communication on my research which was on Armenia's alternative media during 20 days of censorship following a deadly crackdown on protesters in Armenia in March 2008 (Nazaryan, 2011). My emails were always answered between 8 a.m. and 10 p.m. Dr. Byerly gave feedback on every portion of my work and advised on the following steps.

With such a hard-working schedule, Dr. Byerly always kept a young zeal in her interactions with people which inspired many around her. I have never observed her taking things by default. She has never stopped being surprised and appreciating any effort for what she believes in, be it in research, study, or women's and minorities' rights and social solidarity. For the success of my thesis, I owe Dr. Byerly, as well as the two other members of my thesis committee, Dr. Anju Chaudhary and Dr. Clint Wilson. The last two have also been among those professors for whom I will always be grateful for their inclusive and inspiring teaching.

## A Feminist Scholar Folding Up Her Sleeves

A scholarly article co-authored by Dr. Byerly came out in the *Critical Studies in Media Communication* journal at the time. Her doctoral student Adam G. Klein was the first author. The idea for the research came from the various post-9/11 anti-war rallies across the United States. Dr. Byerly and her students examined how news coverage, identifying elements of public dissent which counter-framed the Iraq War (Klein et al., 2009). Its theoretical framework and methodology inspired me to come up with the topic for my master's thesis. But what inspired me more was the fact that my professor was also an activist and sided with her students as such. We had the privilege of having a curriculum that students did not have in many other U.S. universities. Dr. Byerly understood the pitfalls of this approach to teaching: "The classroom curricula we teach, the kind of research we undertake, the kind of questions we raise about the world and the academic processes we enter into will probably always put us at risk—even if we are nice people who work hard, do our jobs well and are meaningful contributors to our fields" (Byerly, 2011).

Dr. Byerly, along with other feminist scholars, had to "fold up their sleeves" and get involved in the fieldwork for women and for academia. In my notes taken in the classroom around 13 years ago, I found Dr. Byerly's remarks: "Academics must be really powerful to go into a field. It comes from Hegel: Who can have a standpoint? You have to earn it. You have to engage in a struggle." Yet as a student and later with her journalistic background, Dr. Byerly got engaged in the women's movement to stop violence against women. She made sure that the survivors' voices were properly reflected in the media and well heard by the public. She did it through handling the communications of an anti-violence center, in her role as the center's director. As Freire would say, Dr. Byerly and other feminist activists "named the world": They created a whole vocabulary to name the violence in its various stages and forms. I read in my notes from the classroom that what was called "rape victims" became "rape survivors"; what was a "pervert" became a "criminal." "Sexual abuse," "sexual harassment," "domestic violence," and many other expressions were adopted to define the violence.

We owe Dr. Byerly and her "sisters in arms" for this new language that is globally recognized as the legal vocabulary for sexual and domestic violence. Years later she would write that her academic path was defined by her feminist activism. "An activist academic is one who brings questions or approaches that advance fairness while challenging accepted knowledge and practices that constrain equality and the open expression of ideas within higher education" (Byerly, 2011). In the classroom, I also took notes of Dr. Byerly saying that lived experiences create a new language and help to analyze the phenomena as they are. This analysis, in turn, creates social agendas that may bring policy and life changes.

After graduation, I was involved in social-political movements for human rights in the military back in Armenia. For my efforts, I was awarded as the

Woman of Courage in 2012.[17] In this period, various informal groups were formed that were fighting for the environment, preservation of public spaces, women's rights, voters' rights, LGBT rights, and consumers' rights, as well as against government corruption and neighborhood gentrification. Through the Muskie fellowship, the alumni could invite their professors or mentors as volunteers to contribute to their field of activities. Dr. Byerly generously proposed and planned a series of workshops for mostly female activists on communication strategies in local campaigns. Later she would reflect on the teaching and activist scholarship in the context of the trip to Armenia that "pedagogy, scholarship and social action can interface in interesting ways as the times demand it and opportunities open" (Byerly, 2012).

The workshops on media and social activism took place in Yerevan, the capital city, and three in rural regions in the summer of 2012. They were full of meaningful interactions. The lively discussion about personal motivations in activism that was requested by Dr. Byerly from each participant is unforgettable. It was the first time that activists were challenged to disclose their personal "political economy." Dr. Byerly explained that this conversation was needed not only to create trust among the cohort but also, from her experience, it might reveal many aspects of the core problems that activists tried to address. At least, this was the case during the anti-violence movement in the United States. There were times when they would lock the doors and let none out until everyone told why they were there, Byerly recalled. When forced to speak, many unknown issues were disclosed. Our discussions also included a touching exchange of experiences between two seemingly different worlds and generations. Carolyn Byerly had developed communication strategy tools that she shared with activists for their further use.

During our trips, we visited some sights and enjoyed fresh food and sunshine. Dr. Byerly also visited the Armenian Genocide Museum, despite my discouragement. I feared that she would witness our longtime victimization story and she would get depressed. But my fears were in vain. Back in D.C., Carolyn Byerly recalled in her article: "The eyes of young Armenians are bright with determination and hope in spite of the challenges. [. . .] From the standpoint of teaching, I have rarely felt so fulfilled" (Byerly, 2012).

17 See See https://hetq.am/en/article/15156
https://editorials.voa.gov/a/honoring-rights-workers-in-armenia--158311965/1493343.html
https://www.osce.org/yerevan/91071

## Feminist Standpoint is the New Humanism

I have had the honor to know Carolyn M. Byerly not only as an inspiring professor and empowering feminist but also as a caring person. On July 27, 2010, when I was doing an internship at the Voice of America during the summer break, I received a call from my mother that would forever change my life. My brother Artak was killed during his military service as a lieutenant. I had to immediately join my family in Armenia. The investigation was being carried out in a shaky scenario, so I had to find lawyers and go public. My brother's death raised public outrage since I was known publicly through my work as a former journalist. (In 2022, the European Court of Human Rights issued a judgment establishing the violation of my brother's right to life and the failure of fair investigation in the country.)

I returned to Howard a couple of weeks after the academic year started. I was enrolled in Dr. Byerly's course on development communication. I had to study hard to catch up with the course while searching for housing and keeping up with the proceedings on my brother's case. The Arab Spring started right when I was overloaded with my final semester and my thesis. Still, I could not restrain myself from going to Washington DC rallies. Dr. Byerly, an activist herself, accepted my occasional late papers, once saying smilingly: "No more White House, OK?" How delicate she was with any students having a challenged background or passing through hardships. One would not see her demonstrating special treats but enjoy her care without even knowing about it.

After graduation, Dr. Byerly invited me to join a graduation party of professors and PhD students in her backyard. With her partner Kay, she hosted me again a couple of years ago in Spain where, as already good friends, we had nice walks across Toledo and meaningful talks on issues of common concern. We stayed in contact with Dr. Byerly, who I was honored to call by name Carolyn, thanks to her generous friendship. There were times when Armenian activists felt frustrated and useless as their efforts encountered closed doors. Carolyn's one email to me got my friends' energy and zeal back when I shared it with them: "I'm so glad you are so involved in making history. Stick with it, democracy comes slowly and is hard to maintain." She has empowered and inspired so many people who have known her. Later I also participated in a virtual session at a conference in Paris. There, Dr. Sarah Macharia presented her global study[18] on

18 https://www.comminit.com/media-development/content/global-study-gender-equality-and-media-regulation#.Yy4QgweIySI.linkedin

gender equality in media regulations across the world, a study for which I was the author of the country report on Armenia.[19]

Looking back on my life, I observe that women have played the biggest role in what and who I am now. It is women who never hesitate to invest in another person's personal and professional development. I must confess that Dr. Carolyn M. Byerly has had the biggest influence on me as a feminist scholar and activist and as a caring human. She lives what she teaches us: celebrating human agency, supporting women, immersing in inquiry, pushing boundaries of knowledge, and acting for humanism. I dare to state that Dr. Byerly's feminist standpoint and *praxis* are the new humanism.

## References

Klein, A. G., Byerly, C. M., & McEachern, T. M. (2009). Counterframing public dissent: An analysis of antiwar coverage in the U.S. Media. *Critical Studies in Media Communication, 26*, 331–350. https://doi.org/10.1080/15295030903176658

Byerly, C. M. (2011). Gender, critical scholarship, and the politics of tenure and promotion. In M. Meyers (Ed.), *Women in higher education: The fight for equity* (pp. 41–56). Hampton Press.

Byerly, C. M. (2011). *Global report on the status of women in news media.* IWMF. https://www.iwmf.org/wp-content/uploads/2018/06/IWMF-Global-Report.pdf

Byerly, C. M. (2012, Fall). Teaching in Armenia: Intersections of pedagogy, scholarship and activism. *Women's Words*, p. 7. https://nametheworld.files.wordpress.com/2012/11/fall2012cswnewsletterfinished.pdf

Byerly, C. M. (2017, June). Feminist intersectionality research in communications: Origins, contributions, and tensions. *Ex Aequo: Revista da Associação Portuguesa de Estudos sobre as Mulheres, 35*, 23–31. https://doi.org/10.22355/exaequo.2017.35.02

Freire, P. (2010). *Pedagogy of the oppressed.* Continuum.

Nazaryan, T. (2011). *Alternative discourse during the state of emergency in Armenia, 2008.* https://nametheworld.wordpress.com/2012/01/04/alternative-discourse-during-the-state-of-emergency-in-armenia-2008/

Smith, D. E. (2004). Women's perspective as a radical critique of sociology. In S. Harding (Ed.), *The feminist standpoint theory reader* (pp. 21–34). Routledge.

19 https://www.comminit.com/media-development/content/global-study-gender-equality-and-media-regulation#.Yy4QgwelySI.linkedin

15

# The Final Boss: Dr. Carolyn M. Byerly's Critical Empiricism

SHOLNN FREEMAN

## Coming from Journalism

I first met Dr. Carolyn Byerly as a graduate student at Howard University in 2010. She was my principal teacher in the master's program in mass communication and later advised my doctorate, which was completed in 2021. Before Howard, I had been born and bred in American newspaper journalism, and I was coming to the university with the hope of establishing a new life as an academic. I had a vague transition plan to pursue a PhD in communication. I viewed it as a way out of the doom and gloom of the journalism industry. The constant rounds of downsizing and reorganization had made me stressed and fearful. However, I soon learned that the path would be a lot more difficult than I had anticipated.

The new vision I had for myself came crashing down during one of my initial office hour meetings with Carolyn. I had come by to discuss a class paper I wrote about Nancy Pelosi and congressional politics. Carolyn had marked it up severely. In that office meeting, she criticized the paper as "journalistic" and lacking in evidence—refrains that I would hear often in our meetings. I believe she said that she considered the paper to be a piece of commentary, not scientific at all. She began pushing me to find a way to go beyond it. If not, she warned, I was probably in for a harsh time in the program, as it was one devoted to evidence and data and rigorous approaches to social science. The criticism cut deeply against the pride I had in my background in journalism—the profession I will always love and cherish.

## Embracing Change

As I dealt with my hurt feelings, it occurred to me that Carolyn's demanding nature would probably be the best fit for me in the program. I came to embrace her blunt effervescence as she came to take the role of something like the final boss in a video game. This was especially true in the dissertation process where she always loomed as the ultimate battle, the last level to clear before one could move on. For this, I will always carry a deep appreciation for Carolyn. She was the one who poured on the pressure, demanding that I develop a high standard for quality in my work.

With Carolyn's guidance over the years, I was able to forge a new academic and research identity. Slowly, I moved away from such a strong self-identification with journalism. Carolyn and I had some similarities. She had also been a reporter. We also shared political convictions based on similar humble socio-economic and family backgrounds. I grew up in the projects in Austin, Texas, in the inner-city crack cocaine years of the 1990s. In my neighborhood, there were only poor families, mostly Black and Mexican American. This background factored greatly into my approach to writing and reporting in journalism. I was taught early on that journalism was supposed to be the microphone for the powerless in society. I looked for stories that featured Black individuals and communities or analyses that addressed the struggles and cultures of everyday American working people.

It wasn't until I landed in graduate school that I realized just how little I had been taught in journalism school about how to intellectually approach social issues. I had learned virtually nothing about class relations or political economy, and how these dynamics affected debates in the national media about culture and politics. Ironically, these issues reached a critical point for me outside of the country in 2008 when I began a temporary assignment as an Iraq correspondent for *The Washington Post*. I was immediately taken aback at the amount of resources the newspaper had poured into the bureau. Thousands were spent to prepare me with personal amour and basic survival skills for a war zone. The bureau itself occupied a mansion in an affluent Baghdad neighborhood. I had never lived in such an extravagant house. And then there was the room they gave me. It was the biggest room I had had in my life. From that point, everything became really tight in my mind. How could it be that the biggest expense that America had ever really made in me was coming so far from home, and in the context of international war? I could not square the ideals and truisms about the United States as a positive force for democracy (which I really believed) with what I was seeing with my own eyes out in the world. When I was embedded with the U.S. military, I was stunned to see that most of the frontline American soldiers were black and brown people, and poor and white. I ended up learning far more about inequality in American society than about Iraqi society or the intricacies of international warfare. Later on, graduate studies in critical theory, international political economy, political communications, and international communications helped me make sense of these confusing observations.

## Discovering Critical Research

Carolyn instructed me in nearly all of the foundational coursework in mass communications. She gave me the first significant introduction to critical theory, historical materialism, and debates over Eurocentrism and Afrocentrism by Molefi Asante and Reiland Rabaka. In a media theory project, I opted to investigate Jürgen Habermas and *The Structural Transformations of the Public Sphere*. I came away with a lasting impression of how monumental change in world history leads to transformations in social theory. Carolyn's knowledge and understanding of feminist scholarship deepened my understanding. Along with Habermas, I also studied Nancy Fraser's question—*where are the women?*—which led to an essential extension of public sphere theory. Because I held full-time employment at Howard University, I had access to a generous employee tuition remission program. Carolyn encouraged me to use the benefit to delve into course work in other disciplines. I loaded up on courses in the history and sociology departments. I also studied literary theory, African philosophy, African Studies and Black psychology. This turned out to be important advice. The knowledge has added reach and depth to my perspective in media analysis and research.

Carolyn taught me the fundamentals of critical research inquiry. I often return to the lessons where she outlined the basic principles and methods of the field. Critical researchers start with a concern with the amelioration of a particular social problem. However, this is not what makes a critical researcher unique; as other types of researchers are similarly conscientious. Where critical stands apart are certain requirements for researchers to pay special attention to areas that might go unexamined in works by conventional social scientists. One of these dimensions is history. Oftentimes, social problems are decontextualized from their historical roots. Critical researchers must examine historical circumstances, acknowledging that a given social problem has a traceable historical development. Another dimension that Carolyn outlined was attention to social relations. Critical researchers are tasked with revealing the social arrangements and identities of the parties involved in social injustices or inequalities—which tend to exist at the heart of social problems. This concern is the great virtue of critical science as the identities of those who stand to benefit the most from social injustices are often well disguised, as are their strategies and practices. Critical inquiry is considered a landmark achievement due to its insistence that the prioritization of social justice values could lead to the enhancement of scientific inquiry, rather than its ruination.

## Charting My Own Way

As a student, my interest in critical theory was quite strong. Carolyn recommended that I develop my expertise in social theory and history. Courses by other Howard professors helped me as I pondered over the historical development of Marxist theory, especially debates within African and African American communities of scholars. I recall some of my classmates being relatively guarded about Marxist politics and schools of thought. Many simply could not embrace the approach because they felt it degraded the role played by race and racism in systems of oppression and injustice. They pounced on Marxist writings as Eurocentric. Carolyn encouraged back and forth in class debates. I spent a lot of time and energy struggling to understand how Africana scholars (Black scholars from around the world) viewed historical materialism and other forms of Marxism. I was also interested in how they used these ideas in their scholarship. I came to focus on the particular works by W. E. B. DuBois, C. L. R. James, and Frantz Fanon. I began to think that these works represent what can be seen as a stand-alone school of thought at race and Marxist theory; the term I continue to develop is "Africana Historical Materialism." Carolyn helped me talk through these ideas and never discouraged my own theoretical creatives—even though it began to take time away from doctoral and dissertation work, which was slowly beginning to materialize on a separate track.

Another requirement that Carolyn emphasized in critical research was self-reflexivity. This refers to the researcher's awareness of their own social identity, and how this identity influences the different facets of the scientific and research processes. Self-reflexivity pre-supposes that it is impossible for the researcher to stand apart, independently or objectively, apart from whatever research or social problem is under study. This is because researchers, like all other members of society, have social identities (the major aspects are race, sex and class) which influence why they care about a research problem, how they've been affected by it, and what kind of assumptions they already hold about it, including prior beliefs, biases, and attitudes. Habermas and others have argued that conventional Western science can be viewed as a tool of domination and control because racist, sexist, elitist assumptions tended to be deeply embedded in the larger culture. Thus, even researchers who proclaim their neutrality and objectivity can be culpable in furthering biases in social science if they ignore calls for self-reflexivity. Carolyn showed how these ideas are articulated and demonstrated in feminist scholarship. She introduced me to feminist standpoint theory, Black feminist theory and the Combahee River Collective in her course, "Feminism and Mass Communication." In undergraduate courses today, my lectures on Black feminist thinking and Second Wave Feminism are among the most popular sections. Carolyn's attentiveness to self-reflexivity and her drive to expose students to a wide range of critical material made a lasting impression. Personally, it helped me to deepen my awareness of how I had been using my own social identity (even as a journalist) in my intellectual output. However, the heightened intellectual understanding which Carolyn fostered provides the confidence and resolve to continue to do so as a communication researcher. I say "resolve" because critical scholarship might be one of the least attractive subdivisions for those seeking employment within the academy. Carolyn deserves immense credit for keeping these ideas alive.

## Empirical Commitments

Finally, and perhaps most importantly, what I profited the most from Carolyn was her trenchant commitment to empiricism in critical research. From that very first meeting, Carolyn had stressed the importance of data and evidence in scientific inquiry. She has sometimes referred to herself as a "critical empiricist," an appellation that I try to emulate and carry forward. In certain ways, journalists and editors in the United States are afforded extraordinary discretion over how phenomena are presented in the news. In many instances, we have an angle in mind before we even begin reporting out a story. The angle is generally developed after lengthy conversations with editors. Story angles were often pre-approved in these discussions. Sometimes, angles were simply handed down from even higher ranks of editors in the senior ranks of the newsroom. Thus, as reporters, we generally started out with a strong sense of what we wanted sources to say and what data points we needed to include. We used these different elements to construct a story driving home the angle we always had in mind.

Carolyn tried very hard to teach me how to avoid replicating this tendency as a researcher. The requirement for data and evidence seems like a no-brainer. But it can be very difficult for junior researchers and their research designs. A poor sense of data and evidence can cripple a research project at multiple points in the research process; these include the selection and investment of time and energy into a particular research topic, the formulation of meaningful and answerable research questions, choices of theories and concepts to apply, and all kinds of sampling and analysis questions, among other concerns. Unfortunately, I treated the question of data and evidence as an afterthought in my dissertation process. This made for very difficult meetings with Carolyn.

When I searched for a research topic, I looked for an issue that combined my interests in politics, journalism, and international affairs. At the time, I was following news about the U.S. presidential campaign in 2016. I had been paying particular attention to the controversy over Russian election interference. Something wasn't adding up in the news coverage. In the back of my mind, I kept returning to my experiences before the second Iraq War. Before the conflict, I had read the papers closely and observed how the George W. Bush administration had deceived the American public and manufactured a basis for war. The fact that major news organizations eagerly, and uncritically, went along for the ride had always bothered me. Part of my interest in traveling to Iraq was a desire to see first-hand what effect American foreign policy and media distortion had meant to the people of Iraq. I sensed parallels between the two separate media periods. The topic of my dissertation became Russian election interference in the 2016 election. Luckily, a Black media and politics angle emerged; the United States accused Russians of targeting Black audiences with political propaganda on social media. I struggled with data and evidence. I went through several phases. I contemplated a framing study based on political reporting, a critical discourse analysis of key U.S. documents, and even what would have been a cumbersome case of study of the different twists and turns of the relevant media discourse. Carolyn and the other dissertation committee members were not impressed. I kept my eye peeled for something better. Something began to stand out in the distance. I had downloaded a trove of Facebook ads that the U.S. government claimed had been used by Russians to manipulate American voters in 2016. By this time, I had fully absorbed Carolyn's warnings and dictums about data and evidence. I was finally able to take a deep breath because I knew I now had something to build around for a strong dissertation. Alas, Carolyn's insistence on data-driven science had pushed me forward in that final battle in my belabored journey from journalist to social scientist. I finally felt like a critical empiricist.

16

# #DOYOUSEEME: An Academic Search for "Self"—Inspired by Dr. Carolyn M. Byerly

NGOMA EVELN MOGHALU

The invisibility of West African immigrant students in U.S. academic institutions, and the invisibility of West African media scholars in U.S. media studies is felt heavily by those of us in these populations. While studies have addressed the invisibility and inequality of Black immigrants in the United States (Byrce-Laporte, 1972), there is insufficient research on how the invisibility of West African immigrant students in U.S. academic institutions impacts their academic search for "Self." My experiences with invisibility in U.S. academic institutions impacted my search for "Self" and shaped my identity as a West African immigrant social science researcher. In this article, I will show how Dr. Carolyn M. Byerly contributes to my visibility through her leadership, scholarship, and unwavering support for my success.

## The Invitation

This is my first invitation to participate in the honorable academic publication known as Festschrift. I was invited to contribute to this festschrift by Dr. Unwana Samuel Akpan, who is a West African media scholar/researcher from Nigeria, a published author, editor, and a former postdoctoral student of Dr. Byerly at

Howard University, Washington, DC. When I received my invitation to participate in this Festschrift, I was thrilled and excited, yet unsure of the process involved in writing a successful Festschrift chapter. My first instinct was to reach out to Dr. Byerly who has been a mentor, colleague, and friend since my graduate studies at Howard University. I expressed my desire to approach her Festschrift as a storytelling text to demonstrate how she inspires my academic search for "Self" because she always reminds me of Who I Am. In her true supportive nature, she said, "Ngoma! Do whatever makes you happy, and comfortable" (C. M. Byerly, personal communication, 2022). This is Dr. Byerly, a leader, a scholar, and phenomenal academic inspiration to her students.

## The Beginning

I am a first-generation West African immigrant to the United States of America from Nigeria. My academic search for "Self" heightened during my experiences with racism, ethnicism, marginalization, exclusion, and invisibility as a West African immigrant student in the United States. These experiences made me feel invisible, isolated, and displaced until I met Dr. Carolyn M. Byerly. Recently, during one of our many conversations, Dr. Byerly referred to me as "The Woman with Promise" (C. M. Byerly, personal communication, 2022). Dr. Byerly uplifts me by motivating me to persevere, and push through my challenges. This motivation started when I met her in 2004 in my first graduate course in mass communication theory. In the following section, I will discuss how Dr. Byerly's scholarship influenced my academic journey in media studies.

## The Scholarship

In Dr. Byerly's mass communication theory course, she laid the foundation of cultivating a sense of critical inquiry to analyze the media and by supporting this inquiry with critical methodology. I was introduced to scholars such as Tim Dant, Patricia Hill Collins, Larry Gross, David Croteau, William Hoynes, Denis McQuail, and Jürgen Habermas. In this course, there were topics that governed how theories are developed about the media namely public sphere, social critique, gender/race/sex misrepresentations and free press. Importantly, Dr. Byerly's class discussions on these topics shaped my sense of critical inquiry, and academic investigation on how negative media representations of West African immigrants in the public sphere heightens their invisibility in the United States, which impacts their search for "Self."

I enjoyed Dr. Byerly's thought-provoking discussions on critical theory because she challenged me to question social injustice, and racial/ethnic disparities in policies that negatively impact Black people, especially West African immigrants. Dr. Byerly's discussions started with the concern for media fairness and equality in the public sphere. According to McQuail (2000), the media should positively contribute to society by disseminating fair, and authentic information (McQuail, 2000). Additionally, Croteau and Hoynes (2001), argue that the public sphere should serve the interest of the public, and not profit the media (Croteau & Hoynes, 2001). Importantly, Harbemas (1962), argues that the media should contribute to the democratic process by creating a public space for social integration and public discourse; and where citizens regardless of race, ethnicity or class status can participate in politics (Habermas, 1962). The public sphere is a space where our collective interests should be represented.

In her class discussions, Byerly (2004), challenged us to use critical theory, and the social critique method to analyze media discourses, and practices about fairness and equality in the public sphere. In her research, Byerly (2018) utilizes "the critical paradigm where concerns about inequality are central and where scholarship is committed to enabling social change, thereby fulfilling the emancipatory potential of research" (Byerly, 2018, p. 28). My first introduction to critical theory was Tim Dant's (2004) *Critical Social Theory*, where the author used Sigmund Freud's and Karl Marx's works to explain social critique. Marx (1976) believed that our ideologies alone cannot change society; instead, we must understand how materialism, capitalism and power create oppressors and the oppressed, and produce the upper elite/class and lower class. To understand oppression, we must use critical theory to analyze oppressive institutions, and social/political structures. According to Dant (2004), "critical theory engages in a form of criticism of social formation" that does not engage in any form of political action until there is a rise in political failure, which will encourage social change and emancipation (Dant, 2004, p. 2). Freud (1962) believed that human beings suppress their emotions because of societal restrictions (religion, politics, class, etc.), but we can be emancipated if we free ourselves from the restrictions that prevent us from freely expressing ourselves. To achieve emancipation, Byerly (2004) argues that critical theorists must utilize the social critique method to analyze media discriminatory practices. Byerly's (2004) social critique method is as follows:

- Problematize the social phenomenon: Identify the injustice and inequality that exists in society.
- Identify the parties: The oppressors and the oppressed.
- Historicize the issue or problem: Explain the history of how the problem came to be in a time frame.
- Structure the problem: Verify how the problem came about and continues to exist in society.
- Emancipation: Define the road to social change. (Byerly, 2004)

Dr. Byerly's social critique structure is my blueprint for the critical theory methodology that I utilize often in conjunction with other theories (racial formation, intersectionality, critical race theory) to organize my research inquiries, ideas, arguments, and analysis. Furthermore, in my mass communication theory course, Dr. Byerly demonstrated the importance of familiarizing ourselves with the studies of critical theorists because they believe that social change is possible if citizens empower themselves to seek social justice for fairness and equality amid issues like capitalism, alienation, classism, racism, marginalization, sexism, and discrimination. For example, critical theorists Patricia Hill Collins' (1990) and Larry Gross's (2001) scholarship focuses on power relations and ways to seek social change for the misrepresented, marginalized, and underrepresented groups—in Collins' case, Black women, and in Gross's case, sexual minorities. Collins (1990) utilizes feminist critical theory to show how new racism prevents African American women from advancing in racialized white male-dominated social structures because the political economy of new racism relies on the commodification of Black bodies as property and commercialization of Black workers (Collins, 1990). In his work, Gross (2001) utilizes queer theory to analyze male heterosexual dominance in the media that alienates, and negatively misrepresents gay and lesbian communities on television (Gross, 2001).

Employing Byerly's (2004) social critique structure, Collins and Gross identify the problems as new racism, misrepresentation and alienation of African Americans, gays and lesbians. The oppressors are identified as white male heterosexual dominant social structures. The oppressed are identified as African Americans, gays, and lesbians. In historical context, the history of racism and white male dominance in America began during slavery, and racism continues today because of systemic oppression, and news stories controlled by white male-dominated media industries. Emancipation from racism, and oppression will happen when African Americans, gays and lesbians unite to fight for social justice, and seek equality from their oppressors. Dr. Byerly's social critique method allows me to think deeply about how to problematize social injustice, investigate news media bias, interrogate racialized misrepresentations, historicize social injustice, and seek ways to emancipate myself, my community, and the oppressed.

Lastly, Dr. Byerly challenged me to examine the concept of free press in the media, and how media market profit model systems control media content, which impacts the public interest. To serve our interest, we need reliable public broadcast systems that will allow our voices to be heard without being controlled by media conglomerates. Public broadcast systems rely on public-funded organizations to maintain their stations, which limits their potential to accommodate ample public generated programs. They need funding for extensive programs. To protect the public interest and limit the concentration of media power and wealth by the elite, the state must create laws, agencies, and policies to monitor and regulate media ownership, markets, and broadcast. Freedom of the press should be shared equally with the public, and not controlled by media conglomerates. Overall, Dr. Byerly's mass communication theory course has guided my research for the last 19 years. I continue to ask the tough questions about fairness and equality in the ways the media controls content and perpetuates negative narratives, and stereotypes about people of color, especially West African immigrants. In the following section, I will discuss how I am influenced by Dr. Byerly's leadership through her scholarship.

## The Leadership

As a researcher and West African immigrant woman, I am influenced by Dr. Byerly's leadership. She supports women and leads us through her scholarship. For example, Dr. Byerly's feminist theoretical framework examines the underrepresentation of women, especially women of color in journalism. On January 27, 2010, Dr. Byerly presented at the "Media Ownership Workshop on Diversity Issues" at the Federal Communications Commission (FCC), Washington, DC, where she argued that "media ownership in the United States today divides along the historical fault lines of gender and race" (Byerly, 2010, p. 1). To bridge this gap, Byerly (2010) argued that the FCC must serve the "public interest" by changing policies to empower women and people of color to become owners of media industries in their communities (p. 2).

Throughout her career she has advocated for women empowerment, visibility for women and people of color in the newsroom and placing women in positions of power in media industries (Byerly, 2004, 2006, 2010, 2011, 2013, 2014, 2016, 2017, 2018, 2021). In her earlier work, "News, Consciousness and Social participation: The Role of Women's Feature Service in World News," Byerly (1995) argued that women were excluded from male-dominated media industries, and women advocacy played an important role in bringing visibility to their efforts for inclusion (Byerly, 1995, pp. 105–106). In their book, Byerly and Ross (2008) applied the feminist political economy framework by analyzing ways in which "media industries have served to limit women's involvement in creative ranks, affecting women of color in particular" (Byerly & Ross, 2008, p. 8). The exclusion of women of color in media industries limits our representation on media platforms and silences our voices. Dr. Byerly's research on feminist theory highlights the importance of the representation of women in the media, which will bring visibility to women, especially women of color such as myself.

Byerly (2018) created her feminist theoretical framework as follows:

> By adopting a feminist critical political economy theory on media, which is grounded in Marxist assumptions, but which also factors in intersectionality concerns of gender and race relations. By examining the low rates of broadcast media ownership by women in the United States, where wealthy white men have had control of the nation's wealth, as well as the laws and policies regulating ownership that result from their ability to maintain control over Congress (which makes laws) and the Federal Communication Commission (which implements law through regulation). By using a combination of critical political economy and intersectionality to show that the material outcomes of neoliberalism in the United States and other nations are economic globalization and concentrated media markets, processes that have affected women's ability to own media and to advance into decision making ranks within news organizations. (pp. 26–27)

Overall, Dr. Byerly's leadership empowers me to use my voice through my research. Importantly, Dr. Byerly's leadership brings visibility to researchers of color who are marginalized and racialized in dominant social structures. Her leadership encourages women to demand fairness and equality in the ownership of media businesses, and representation in media industries. For example, in her study, Byerly (2018) "interrogates power in women's relationship to media, by seeking to identify patterns of enduring marginalization or change in the ways women are represented" (p. 27).

The marginalization of women of color by media industries is problematic because it impacts their equal rights to resources, and job opportunities, thus impeding their socio-economic upward mobility. As a leader, Dr. Byerly advocates for marginalized women who have been silenced. Further, she is an advocate for women scholars to use their scholarship to emancipate themselves from oppression. Importantly, her research emphasizes the importance of feminist communication theorists "naming" their own theory, because "feminist scholars have made minimal progress in naming their own theories to explain the women-and-language relationship (and, by extension, the women-and-media relationship)" (Byerly, 2018, p. 29). As a suggestion, Byerly (2018) argues that her idea of a "better theory building" . . . "requires naming our theories to reflect the phenomena we study, as well as setting forth their premises and structures" (p. 30). I believe that women scholars should create, develop, and name their own theories based on their research ideas, which will contribute to women, gender, and communication scholarship. I am inspired by the idea of naming a theory that will explain how the invisibility of West African immigrant scholars in U.S. academic institutions impacts their search for "Self."

Last, as a leader, Dr. Byerly serves as a mentor to her students. I have benefited from Dr. Byerly's leadership and mentorship, which gives me visibility, and helps in my evolution of "Self" as a West African immigrant researcher and public speaker.

## The Mentorship

As a mentor, Dr. Byerly laid the foundation of academic excellence and resilience that grounded my research. Her encouragement made me feel important, and proud of my work. When I started writing my thesis, I chose to use cluster analysis as my methodology. As the chair of my thesis Committee, Dr. Byerly helped me develop the cluster analysis methodology even though she was not familiar with this methodology. She did not complain or reject my thesis proposal because it was unfamiliar to her, instead, she worked with me until I mastered the methodology. To my amazement, Dr. Byerly shared my cluster analysis methodology with her students, and they reached out to me to learn how to use the methodology. I felt like a rock star academic researcher because of my skills with cluster analysis. My thesis has been cited in other academic research, and I owe it all to Dr. Byerly's dedication to the success of my thesis defense and graduation. Her encouragement did not end after I graduated from Howard University. She kept in touch with me and encouraged me to go back to school to get my PhD. I am blessed that she was able to watch me walk on stage, and to be hooded at my graduation ceremony as Dr. Ngoma Evelyn Moghalu. To celebrate my graduation, Dr. Byerly sent me a heartfelt card where she penned an encouraging and supportive message as follows:

> Dear, Ngoma, after all the years of determination, effort, and sacrifice, you become Dr. Moghalu. May the future be yours. (C. M. Byerly, personal communication, 2021)

I am grateful to Dr. Byerly for believing in me, and never giving up on me. Though Dr. Byerly is retired, she continues to include me in academic research opportunities, which gives me a platform to share my research interests with the world. This type of exposure brings visibility to my research. Dr. Byerly is very supportive of her West African immigrant students because she understands the struggles that African immigrant students encounter with racism, ethnicism, marginalization, exclusion and acknowledgment at academic institutions in the United States. I want to use this opportunity to give Dr. Byerly her Flowers because she is worthy.

## The Flowers

On the one hand, the act of giving physical flowers to someone is a popular way of appreciating the person. Guéguen et al. (2012) state that "flowers reflect our emotions and mood" and "receiving flowers elicits positive emotion in humans, especially in women" (p. 623). On the other hand, the notion of giving flowers metaphorically is an act of using words or praise to show appreciation for people you respect, and love while they are still here to receive their flowers. Dr. Byerly deserves her flowers because she has contributed immensely to the woman I am today. I believe that words have power, and when words are spoken in truth, words give life to the recipient of the flowers.

It is possible for teachers/professors to be generous, and genuinely support their students without ulterior motives to gain something from their students. I am an example of a recipient of this type of generosity from Dr. Byerly. She is not a "benevolent white–savior–teacher" (Bauer, 2021, p. 1). I did not need to be saved by Dr. Byerly, I needed a leader, and mentor to advise me on my research, and she dedicated her time to help me succeed. She has never asked anything of me but to engage in academic research of excellence. Dr. Byerly is real, in fact, she is a down-to-earth person. She understands that there is more power in unity than division, where women can use their voices to advocate for social justice.

Dr. Byerly believes in women empowerment, diversity, fairness, equal rights and freedom.

Thank you Dr. Byerly for leading by example through your scholarship, and mentorship. Thank you for dedicating your life to media, feminism, and political economy scholarship that inspires other scholars. Thank you for believing in your students and going the extra mile to help them succeed. Thank you for your relentless pursuit of academic excellence for your students. Thank you for never giving up on your students. Thank you for supporting the endeavors of your students. You are kind and generous with your contributions to making Humanity a better place. I am grateful for everything you have done for my academic career, especially your support for my family during our COVID-19 crisis. Thank you for being an example of academic success. Thank you for inspiring the next generation. Your academic and professional accomplishments inspire me to be successful, and I am proud to be part of your academic family. Thank You!

## The Accomplishments

Dr. Byerly's accomplishments are limitless because she is still contributing to academic scholarship through her journal and book publications, stewardship, leadership, mentorship, conferences, conventions, seminars, scholarship presentations, social activism, scholarly awards/honors/distinctions, and academic/professional service. I can copy and paste all her prestigious accomplishments from her 21-page curriculum vitae onto this article, but her CV is public information. Her real accomplishment is her genuine dedication to her students. In my opinion, Dr. Byerly's greatest accomplishment is positively changing the lives of her students that she has mentored, and motivated to accomplish their academic goals by passing her courses, defending their thesis or dissertation, graduating, and becoming mass media scholars.

## References

Bauer, N. K. (2021). What's love got to do with it? Toward a theory of benevolent whiteness in education. *The Urban Review*, *53*(4), 641–658.

Byerly, C. M. (1995). News, consciousness, and social participation. In A. Valdivia (Ed.), *Feminism, multiculturalism, and the media* (pp. 105–122). Sage.

Byerly, C. M. (2004). *Social critique structure* [Mass Communication Theory 552 course syllabus]. Department of Communication, Culture & Media Studies, Howard University.

Byerly, C. M. (2006). Questioning Media Access: Analysis of FCC Women & Minority Ownership Data. In *Does bigger media equal better media?* (Report) Social Science Research Council and Benton Foundation, http://www.ssrc.org/programs/media.

Byerly, C. M. (2010, January 27). *Gender-and-race-conscious research toward Eealitarian broadcast ownership regulation* [Conference Session]. Federal Communications Commission (FCC), 2010 Conference, Washington, DC, United States.

Byerly, C.M. (2011, March). *Global Report on Status of Women in News Media.* International Women's Media Foundation. (Technical Report).

Byerly, C. M. (Ed.) (2013). *Palgrave international handbook on women and journalism.* Palgrave Macmillan.

Byerly, C. M. (2014, April). Media Conglomeration and Women's Interests: A Global Concern (commentary), *Feminist Media Studies, 14*(2), 322-326.

Byerly, C. M. (2016) Stasis and shifts in feminist media scholarship, in C. Cerqueira, R. Cabecinhas & S. I. Magalhães (Eds.), *Gender in focus: new trends in media,* www.lasics.umi nho.pt/.../in.../cecs_ebooks/issue/view/193 .

Byerly, C. M. (2018). Feminism, theory, and communication: Progress, debates, and challenges ahead. In D. Harp, J. Loke, & I. Bachman (Eds.), *Feminist approaches to media theory and research* (pp. 19–35). Palgrave Macmillan.

Croteau, D., & Hoynes, W. (2001). *The business of media: Corporate media and the public interest.* Sage.

Collins, P. H. (1990). Black feminist thought in the matrix of domination. In Black feminist thought: Knowledge, consciousness, and the politics of empowerment (pp. 221–238). Routledge.

Dant, T. (2004). *Critical social theory: Culture, society, and critique.* Sage.

Freud, S. (1962). *Civilization and its Discontents.* Norton & Co.

Gross, L. (2001). *Up from invisibility: Lesbians, gay men, and the media in America.* Columbia University Press.

Guéguen, N., Meineri, S., & Stefan, J. (2012). "Say it with Flowers" . . . to female drivers: Hitchhikers holding flowers and driver behavior. *North American Journal of Psychology, 14*(3).

Habermas, J. (1962, trans. 1989). *The structural transformation of the public sphere: An inquiry into a category of bourgeois society.* Polity.

Marx, K. (1976). *Capital, Volume 1.* Penguin.

McQuail, D. (2000). *McQuail's mass communication theory.* Sage.

# Section IV

# Afterword

# Finding a Synthesis

CAROLYN M. BYERLY

The pages of this festschrift are filled with words about me from colleagues and former students whom I hold in high esteem and for whom I have great affection. It is more than an honor, it is greatly humbling that so many have taken time to recollect our relationship, what they have gained from it and, for several, what they believe I've contributed to the scholarship and pedagogy in the communication field. Of course, such relationships have been reciprocal, evidenced in the many ways we are still connected through shared interests, email messages, chats at conferences between sessions, and even collaborative projects of various kinds. I am close to many of the contributors—we have visited each other's homes and know each other's families. We have, in one way or another, helped to shape an intersectional vision of communication studies. I am especially glad for continued friendships with many of my former students—they inevitably taught me as much as I taught them. They used to laugh when I told them that, but it remains true even now, as I explain later.

My greatest thanks to Dr. Unwana Samuel Akpan for initiating this festschrift project and putting so many hours of his own academic life into bringing it to print. He served a postdoc visit with us in the Department of Communication, Culture and Media Studies (CCMS) several years ago, and we had many enjoyable discussions connecting his Nigerian experience to the American and African

American experiences. We talked about theory in many of our conversations, and I introduced him to Paul Gilroy's work, to feminist theory, and other topics. He told me about the Nigerian media, spoke to one of my seminars about Nigerian author Chinua Achebe's work, and gave a public lecture on an African culture theme. We never know what grows out of these encounters.

His invitation that I contribute to the festschrift allows me to answer questions that students have often asked about how I arrived at and have approached my intellectual pursuits these last decades of academic life. Hopefully this essay will provide a fuller and more personal context to the observations made by other authors in the book. Many readers already know that my academic life has always been bound up in my personal politics and early activism and professional work in journalism, yet they may know only snippets of these experiences. This essay attempts to map out some of the points through the years that mattered.

## The Conundrum

A scholarly life was never what I had in mind when I was young. I wanted to be a writer, and as that interest developed, I wanted to be a journalist. My life in journalism would be rather scattered and short-lived, but I embraced a love of the profession that would provide a thread of continuity through the years in one way or another. Mostly, I used the lessons I learned about writing from journalism in all of the jobs I would have after that—e.g., be accurate, keep to the point, write tight, use good grammar, be detailed. I will return to the life of writing momentarily, after some background.

It was the mid-1980s. I was intellectually hungry to learn more formally than experience alone could teach, and I was thinking of pursuing graduate studies. Having been out of college for 15 years, I went to an admissions counselor at a campus where I was living in Olympia, Washington, for some pointers on applying to graduate school. Where do I start, I asked her, and how do I decide what discipline or field to pursue? She asked me about my undergraduate studies and then told me to describe what I was most interested in. My undergraduate work had been in journalism and education. More recently, there was violence against women, the grassroots movement I had been working in full-time for the past five years, most of that time as a paid administrator of a women's shelter and rape crisis center.

In that role I had worked on legislation to protect child victims of sexual abuse and to lift the marital exclusion from the state's rape laws, among other things. There was also fundraising to do, educational talks to give, and professionals in law enforcement, schools, and hospitals to train on working with victims of sexual and domestic violence. There were also other aspects of feminism where I had given so much time, including advocating for equal pay for women. And, of course, there was journalism, something I had trained in during undergraduate studies and in which I had worked off and on at newspapers and in government. I had also applied my journalism skills in the feminist groups I'd worked in—writing press releases, organizing media events, helping survivors of abuse to give interviews to reporters and training grassroots activists in media relations.

The admissions counselor listened attentively. When I had finished reciting my background and interests, she looked at me thoughtfully and said, "I know there's a synthesis in there somewhere—your first step is to find it." As it turned out, finding that synthesis would not begin for another couple of years when I found critical scholarship. I had made a practical decision to apply to a communications graduate program at University of Washington, which I hoped would be flexible enough for me to pursue some of my scattered interests. After all, I reasoned, communication seemed central to all of them. I was energized by some of my classes, as well as communication conferences where I found feminist and other critical scholars and, inevitably, the context for my own work.

## New Paths

Being a scholar with a grounding in the Left tradition in the United States has long been precarious because it requires revealing an affinity for radical politics and intellectual pursuits. I had come to these through lived experience, most particularly my identity as a postwar child, feminist, and lesbian. These would leave indelible marks on my worldview, personality, and work, and also shape my struggles. Once in graduate school, one professor early on warned me: "You're a graduate student now, so it's time to give up those notions," with "notions" referring to the feminist-tinged questions I was raising in his class. Fortunately, I found other faculty more in sync with my questions and interests. Dr. Tony Giffard, a British South African and former journalist, taught seminars on international communication that revealed global-level debates over information inequality taking place in the United Nations Education, Scientific, and Cultural Organization (UNESCO) at the time. Tony's classes introduced me to the conflicts between developing nations and industrial nations such as my own over things like the Western bias in global news flow, and whether reporters should be licensed to practice journalism. These struggles had been named the New World Information and Communication Order (NWICO) debates, and they placed global politics squarely into the context of communication. When the United States, Britain, and Japan announced decisions to withdraw from UNESCO by 1983, Tony launched his study on the news coverage of the conflict and pull-out. He hired me as one of his two research assistants, something that whetted my appetite for research on real-life politicized events and gave me a path into my own international work. He would later also suggest my master's and dissertation research on the UNESCO-funded Women's Feature Project, and he would direct both my thesis and doctoral work. I later realized that I had conducted my department's first and second studies using feminist theory—my thesis in 1987 and my dissertation in 1990.

Mentoring from faculty like Dr. Gladys Engel Lang deepened my understanding of how women like herself had struggled for recognition in the shadow of the "great men" in the field they had worked with. Professor Ella Taylor, a British-Israeli critical scholar, recognized my search for radical traditions and suggested I might benefit from a course in "Marx, Foucault, and Feminism," being taught the next semester in a different department. That course—which required me to read a stack of books over the summer before it started, including Marx's *Capital*—would take me deeper into critical historical research and a critique of capitalism. Alongside required communication courses, I ventured into political science and sociology departments for additional work on Marx and critical theory. The synthesis I had been seeking on entering graduate studies was finally coming together.

## Emerging

As a child growing up in post-World War II United States, I was instilled with all the values of the Cold War, which embodied an unspoken denunciation of anything remotely associated with socialism, something seen as indistinguishable then from Stalinist communism and the Soviet Union's authoritarian regime. One of the Cold War's most abhorrent manifestations of the socialist taboo in the United States at the time was McCarthyism, something all too real to me. In the early 1950s, my brother and I had sat in front of our black-and-white console television and watched some of news coverage of the House Unamerican Activities Committee (HUAC) hearings and the Rosenberg trial, both broadcast to a nation obsessed with eradicating communism and communists—and, by association, socialism. While we didn't fully understand the politics of the hearings at the time, those mediated events fed into a broader narrative of anti-communism that permeated society. In the military milieux we lived in, both before and after my dad retired from the U.S. Army in the late 1950s, capitalism (or the free market as it was referred to) was bound up in a particular understanding of freedom and democracy. No one I knew questioned these assumptions.

The 1960s progressive social movements would turn much of this thinking on its head, though it would take me a while to fully grasp and bring my own thinking into line with the politics of that defining decade. My political awareness and ability to question my world would grow incrementally. My brother and I were children of parents whose families had barely scraped by during the depression. Dad would tell me later that he had joined the U.S. Army as a teenager to escape a future in the coal mines of Southern Indiana, where his own father had worked and developed black lung disease. He married my mother, who had worked in a Rosie-the Riveter type job in an airplane factory during the war, on a week-end pass not long after they met and courted. It was a wartime marriage that would have its ups and downs before an unhappy ending a couple of decades later. Both of my parents had quit school after eighth grade to work, something not uncommon for their generation. Yet, the military had offered dad a way to gain a high school diploma and take college courses so he could advance to officer status. Two years after the war ended, we were transferred to Germany, where we would stay for almost five years, being among the first military families allowed to live in that war-torn, occupied nation. My passion for the wider world of other languages and cultures probably dates from those years in postwar Europe, but my earliest political and racial sensibilities are owed to President Truman who integrated the U.S. armed forces in 1948, creating a multicultural milieu in which I would grow up.

## Consciousness

I was drawn to the early civil rights movement after then-Mississippi Governor Ross Barnett spoke at Colorado State University in the early 1960s. As a journalism student, I covered his speech for the student newspaper, wondering how anyone could spout such racist rhetoric and make a case for racial segregation. The positive aspect of my military upbringing had been living among and interacting with those of varied races, religions, and nationalities, and I had watched television coverage of early school desegregation after the Supreme Court's *Brown v. Board of Education of Topeka* case in 1954 with growing hope for change. The semi-rural community in Colorado we lived in through most of my public-school education was heavily Mexican American, and our school system was fully integrated. Racism and prejudice just never made any sense to me; but more important, I was drawn to those with identities and backgrounds different from my own White experience.

My deeper political consciousness remains forever indebted to the serendipitous fact of being born when I was, living through two decades of social movements in the 1960s and 1970s, and embracing the intellectual and moral convictions of those movements. A particularly significant chapter in that context came in the late 1960s when, as a college drop-out, I took a job as secretary for the Boulder, Colorado, YWCA. The pay was barely enough to live on, but there were other benefits, such as daily contact with many strong, intelligent, self-determined women who were involved in public life in ways that engaged the turbulence of the times. Through our YWCA, they organized public forums on anti-war activism, drugs, racism and civil rights, and women's rights. The elders among them had been suffragists, and some were retired YWCA executives who had lived in China and other countries. Several of them took me under their wings and encouraged me to finish school. Through them I gained my feminist voice and the conviction to stand up for myself, leave an abusive relationship, and apply to University of Colorado where I would finish my undergraduate work.

Boulder, in the late 1960s and early 1970s, was a hotbed of radicalism, what some called the Berkeley of the Rockies. Student life at the University of Colorado in 1968 was boisterous and noisy with student protests and demands of all kinds. I was stirred by classroom lectures by socially engaged faculty and by student activists in my classrooms. Professor Matthew Downy's U.S. History class of about 75 students was frequently interrupted by someone standing up and giving a mini-speech against the Vietnam War or something else—the amazing thing was that the professor accommodated these periodic interruptions and usually engaged the speechmaker in discussion. It was a model in teacher-student classroom interaction that would serve me years later when I began teaching. But students did not need professors alone to guide their thoughts in those days. A central feature of the University of Colorado student union cafeteria was a large roundtable near the back where a rotating population of students and non-students drank coffee, smoked cigarettes, and engaged in political debates throughout the day. I would sit as close as I could to listen, taking in the new ideas. Colorado's major minority groups are Indigenous (Native American) and

Mexican American communities. As a student, I took classes in Chicano politics and culture and supported the unionization of the farmworker movement (and their grapes and lettuce boycotts) led by Cesar Chavez and Dolores Huerta.

While finishing my undergraduate work, I supported myself by working for a local Boulder weekly newspaper, where my greatest experience, in 1969, was being sent to cover a noontime event at the large plaza on the CU-Boulder campus called "the fountain." Anti-war activist David Harris and his then-wife Joan Baez were appearing, only a few days before Harris was scheduled to report to prison for burning his draft card (thereby refusing to be drafted to fight in Vietnam). The two were touring the country to breathe even more energy into an already raging anti-war movement. Harris spoke passionately against U.S. imperialism and the Vietnam war, and afterward Baez sang *Amazing Grace* acapella, her voice reverberating off the brown sandstone walls of buildings surrounding the fountain plaza. It was an emotional, clarifying moment for me.

The moral arguments I was hearing convinced me of the wrongness of the Vietnam war—in fact, of all wars—and over the next several years my embrace of pacifism would develop alongside a more general critique of American capitalism and its imperialistic extension. I graduated from the University of Colorado in 1970, in the midst of a campus-wide strike by faculty and students who were protesting the U.S. National Guard's murder of four students at Kent State University that spring—students who were demonstrating against the war. That strike effectively shut down our campus, but the administration generously agreed to grant grades and, in my case, diplomas to those of us graduating. A few months later, I began working at a Boulder-based higher education think tank, which would be pivotal in my professional and political life. One colleague named Marie was raising money to bail out Black Panther Angela Davis, who was jailed in California on charges for which she would later be exonerated. Another colleague named Merry took me to Socialist Worker Party meetings and my first anti-war marches, and she gave me a small collection of pamphlets on feminism and Marxism. Others helped me find my way into organizational culture, something that would guide my survival on campuses years later.

In 1972, as part of my work at that think tank, I was sent to the first national conference on Equal Employment, something newly mandated by passage of Title VII of the Civil Rights Act of 1964. Title VII outlawed discrimination in employment based on race, sex, religion, and national origin. That conference, held in New York City, was attended by many civil rights and women's rights luminaries in education of the time, and both the notion of equality in employment and the explosive energy for change among participants felt revolutionary to me.

When I left that organization, I was open to a wider, more complicated world. It was 1973, and Richard Nixon was on the verge of resigning the presidency after the Watergate scandal. I needed a change. Taking my small savings, I headed to Latin America, the last year of which I would spend working at the *Brazil Herald*, Brazil's national English press, in Rio de Janeiro. Brazil was still under military dictatorship then, and our newspaper had a full-time censor who read all of our articles and headlines—mine were occasionally sent back for revision if they in any way sullied the government agencies or the paper's advertisers. Putting a neutral spin on things was often hard to do, such as the time when the Copacabana Beach was closed one week for raw sewage spillage.

The censorship situation was felt much more deeply by the Brazilian journalists like the ones who put out *Opinião*, the Leftist magazine housed in the same building of the Lapa district (Rio's inner city) as our English newspaper. As the story was told, the entire staff was arrested one night after an issue of the magazine criticized the military's political violence against citizens. The staff were all later released, but the retelling of that story put all of us in the news business on notice. The political repression at that time was so intense that I was warned not to be seen in public with one of my housemates who had been a student activist and was still connected to the popular resistance. Political conversations were carried on quietly or through innuendo everywhere but in trusted homes. Still, I loved many other things about Brazil, especially the walks along that famous black-and-white promenade of Copacabana Beach, days off at the beach or exploring small nearby towns, the diverse group of other ex-patriots and Brazilians I was getting to know, the good rich Brahma Chopp beer we drank at the working-class bars after finishing our work late at night, and that fabulous bossa nova music that seemed to be everywhere. I returned to the United States in the mid-1970s better grounded in my own life.

## Realignment

Once in graduate school 10 years later, I quickly realized that finding allies and creating networks were essential survival tactics in the academy, which I assessed as conservative. Early in my master's degree work, I found my way into communication associations where research on gender, race, and critical studies were just finding their ground. I developed collegial and personal friendships with women and men with whom to have intense exchanges and collaborate in various ways.

Many of them have become lifelong friends (and some are contributors to this book). My own research and teaching by the late 1980s were developing in feminist, critical, and international scholarship at a time when the first two of these were still considered marginal to communication studies. Stories also circulated about the difficulties critical and Marxist scholars faced in gaining and keeping employment, and my own dissertation advisor warned me not to "become too narrow" in my pursuits. I would later learn that this hold-over from cold-war politics had affected some prominent communication scholars like Dallas Smythe, a Canadian Marxist scholar, who had had difficulty securing a position at one U.S. research institution in the 1960s (Wasko, 2005). I encountered my own struggles, first as a faculty member at a state university in Virginia, then at a small private college in central New York. I experienced various kinds of push back at both, but at the second post, I was denied promotion and tenure in 2000 in what would be a messy, protracted situation.

I had submitted a strong tenure and promotion application, and received the vote of approval for tenure and promotion from my department personnel committee. However, my department chair and dean managed to find 43 student comments (out of several hundred) from course evaluations that accused me of "having an agenda" and "supporting gay rights and feminism." Other negative comments asserted that "human rights have nothing to do with the news" and similar absurdities. The dean, closely allied with the Disney Corporation and its subsidiary ABC News, was no fan of investigations into media conglomeration and its impact on newsrooms, something I had been studying. He saw me as a trouble-maker who did irrelevant research and questionable teaching. He ultimately attacked my teaching using this "evidence" from a few students' anonymous hand-written comments. Disapproval was all but guaranteed by the provost and president who read the dean's long, fictionalized accounts of my lack of suitability for tenure and promotion. Colleagues from all over the United States came to my defense and wrote letters to the dean and college president but these had no impact. As my appeals ran out, I found a civil rights lawyer in New York City and filed a discrimination lawsuit against the college. Colleagues from across the United States contributed to a Byerly Defense Fund that my dear friend and colleague, Dr. Joy Morrison, at University of Alaska-Fairbanks had set up. It raised several thousand dollars, but five years and $150,000 later, I lost my case, as nearly all faculty do who challenge tenure denial—particularly in so-called "right-to-work" states like New York. The old adage "some doors close, but others open" defines what followed.

## Moving On

Difficult moments are opportunities to rethink, reframe, and sometimes to relocate. Losing tenure and promotion was all of these. During graduate school in the mid-1980s, I had fallen in love and formed a lifelong relationship with a wonderful woman who would be my anchor in all the years to come. Dr. Kay McGraw and I would follow each other around the country with various job changes, as we sought to employ two PhDs in the family. We have leaned on each other in hard times, and we have laughed and celebrated in good times. She is the kindest person I have ever known, and in many ways also the smartest. We have collaborated in research, she loves to do statistics, me not so much, and we have read and edited each other's work. We have supported each other in our professional lives, and enjoyed each other's colleagues (and in my case, also my students). Kay is a marine biologist, and after my tenure denial, she took a job with the federal government and we moved to the Washington, DC, area. Being in a more urban environment with vibrant intellectual and political energy and multiple campuses around us opened new possibilities. For the next three years, I would teach communication theory and intercultural communication at University of Maryland, during which time I collaborated with a British colleague, Dr. Karen Ross, on two books. Life had clearly made a turn to more positive times.

## Synthesis Found

The Howard University chapter of my life began when I joined the School of Communications in 2004 to teach in a new graduate program in mass communication and media studies. Joining the faculty of a historically Black university provided a context where the synthesis I had spent much of a lifetime searching for would finally be fully found. At my new Howard post, I had colleagues with long histories in the civil rights movement and students who were already engaged in community work or politics. All of our work at Howard was concerned with racial justice, nationality, equality, and similar issues. A women's studies certificate program had been established on campus a couple of years earlier, and feminist research was carried on by colleagues across the campus. As one of few (at that time, only 15 percent) faculty not belonging to the African Diaspora, I was initially concerned about how a White feminist critical scholar who was also fairly open about her lesbian identity would fit in. With few exceptions, I found myself at home in class, as well as in meetings with my colleagues. We all worked hard and, I believe, felt a sense of common purpose.

Still, I was also very much a learner in the Howard environment. It was my syllabus and assignments that guided the seminars, for example, but it was the students' perceptions, analyses, and lived experiences that reflected and sometimes reframed ideas during discussions. They shared their lives openly, and in one doctoral seminar, I learned, for instance, that every one of the nine students present had had an encounter with mugging, some at gunpoint. The doctoral students, who were instinctively drawn to issues and problems in the Black community, Black families, or Black popular culture for research, challenged me to think more inclusively about theory and methodology. I pursued intersectional teaching and research with renewed zeal during my 17 years at Howard, expanding the content in race, ethnicity, gender, and critical theory in both scholarship and classroom teaching. I learned so much about myself in the process.

Other opportunities opened up for meaningful engagement with colleagues and students. When the Federal Communications Commission (FCC) proposed further deregulation of ownership in broadcast media, I became part of a media justice coalition, comprising activist-scholars in media like myself, as well as public interest attorneys like law professors Cathy Sandoval at Santa Clara University and Angela Campbell at Georgetown Law Center; and members of advocacy groups like Joe Torres at Free Press and Andy Schwartzman at Media Action Project, among others. At periodic strategy meetings, our group considered ways to address the problem of media ownership, which had seen the number of women and people of color who owned AM, FM and TV stations in the United States decrease severely through deregulation. Our coalition generated research data on the problem, met with FCC commissioners and their staff, gave testimony at FCC hearings, and, through the attorneys in our group, filed several legal challenges that became known as *Prometheus Radio Project vs. FCC I, II, II, and IV.* In addition to my participation in these efforts, I joined with two other Howard colleagues to form our own Howard Media Group, a collaborative of faculty and students who examined media regulations, wrote comments on proposed FCC regulations, and sponsored public panels on media regulations. Our HMG website contained our FCC comments, other articles, and information on media regulation and ownership—sadly, the group disbanded around the time of my retirement in 2021.

Around 2012, colleagues from three other Howard departments and I joined together to form the Howard Initiative on Public Opinion (HIPO), with the goal of conducting polling in Black and Brown communities on current issues. With modest grants from organizations needing specific data, and space and telephonic equipment for calling provided by Howard's Graduate School, our HIPO collaborative conducted polls related to sickle cell anemia, the Black vote in Georgia, and covid stigma in Black and Brown communities, among other things.

A particular highlight in those years was working with students doing research for their theses and dissertations. In all, I directed 7 masters' theses and 27 doctoral dissertations, and, in the process, I was the professor-learner, accumulating new knowledge of things I did not know. Among these were the use of cellular technology in health care delivery in Kenya, men's interference in Nigerian women's organizations, misogyny in hip hop, Russia's alleged interference in the Black vote in the 2016 U.S. presidential election, the role of "grime" music in London's Black youth culture, the Black press's coverage of a prominent women's organization, online abuse of women in the Mideast-North Africa region, and the role of citizen action in reshaping telecommunications policy in Philadelphia. More than one dissertation issue was resolved on my patio or around the kitchen table, and more than one formal seminar led to collaborative published research. I received a teaching award from the Graduate Student Association in Arts and Sciences, as well as a Graduate Faculty Exemplar award in my Howard years. Those were good days.

When I became chair of the Communication, Culture and Media Studies Department in 2014, I had a particular goal of refining the curriculum. We had formed this PhD department during a School of Communication restructuring a few years earlier by merging two previous PhD programs in the school. What resulted was a broad, loosely defined program with too many courses, some of which had not been taught for years. One of the most enjoyable memories of my time as chair were those curriculum meetings with the CCMS faculty, hammering out the new program with three clearly defined tracks—one in media studies, one in communication technology, and one in health communication. We suspended courses that no longer fit and proposed new ones to flesh-out our new tracks. These played to our strengths as faculty, and they met the needs of students applying to the program. Today, it is a sound program that has guided many doctoral students through to their degrees. Just before my retirement, my colleague Dr. Wei Sun tracked the statistics and found that our PhD program graduated the greatest number of Black PhDs of any other communication doctoral program in the United States. It was a moment of pride.

## Reflections

So many things were possible personally and intellectually for me in my Howard years. But, as I write, all is not well out there in the larger U.S. academic world. Those teaching and advocating for knowledge related to race, class, and gender are presently under assault in the United States, as seen, for example, in the current case of Florida politicians' and educational leaders' attacks on critical race theory, intersectionality, and even the use of language related to LGBTQ identity. In January 2023, the presidents of Florida's 28 community colleges issued a joint statement declaring that they would eliminate any requirement or program that "compels belief in critical race theory or related concepts such as intersectionality" (Thomason, 2023). This might be seen as the extension of conservative movements in the academy to quash diversity, equity, and inclusion, to steer research toward conservative interests, and to undermine and eliminate tenure. The last of these represent the academy's longstanding guarantee of faculty rights to free speech and inquiry.

The push to suppress progressive voices, research, and teaching has been fueled by the likes of Koch Brothers Industries, which have poured millions into endowments, research, scholarships and fellowships to support the promotion of "free-enterprise" (i.e., capitalism) (Levinthal, 2014). The movement began in the 1980s when neoliberalism emerged as a dominant philosophy in the United States. What an odd situation, this backlash, coming on the cusp of so many cultural shifts in the United States—a population that will be majority non-White in a few years, a vibrant and successful transgender movement that has fought for and won (and also lost) so many battles for their civil rights, a resurging multi-racial movement for justice through the Black Lives Matter Movement's leadership, and a rejuvenated feminist movement striving to protect women's reproductive rights.

Intellectuals in the Left tradition are once again targeted for seeking to broaden academic attention to equality/inequality, justice/injustice, racism, homophobia, sexism and similar issues that run through our society. However, students across the United States are leading the challenges to exclusionary policies that seek to eliminate race, class and gender in their curriculum, as well as demanding better laws to stop gun violence that has taken so many lives in school shootings (Aldrich, 2023; Beck, 2023; Schneider, 2023). In the dialectical process, the struggle never ends. And, as the celebrated abolitionist leader Frederick Douglass is said to have observed more than a century ago, the only reward for being in that struggle is being in the struggle. I will continue to do my part through my writing for a few more years, but the in-person challenges will now be led by younger (and hopefully smarter) rabble-rousers than I. There are strong leaders prepared to move ahead on this front and take up the work to be done. I know many of them. In fact, some of those leaders have chapters in this book. It's their time to carry on.

To end with my earlier mention, it is such an honor to have the latter days of my career marked by the honors bestowed by this festschrift. My heartfelt thanks to Dr. Unwana Samuel Akpan and to all who took up his invitation to contribute and then found the time in their own crowded schedules to write chapters. I also want to acknowledge those who expressed regrets at not being able to contribute due to other commitments, and to many others who might have been included if space had allowed. The landscape of trusted, admired colleagues seems vast when I survey it, and in this, I am incredibly fortunate and rich.

## References

Aldrich, M. W. (2023, April 3). *Nashville students rally for tougher gun laws, as governor seeks armed guards for every school.* Chalkbeat. https://tn.chalkbeat.org/2023/4/3/23668031/nashville-school-shooting-walkout-march-lives-capitol-protest-gun-safety

Beck, C. (2023, March 20). *IPS students protest "Don't Say Gay" bill.* Indianapolis Star. https://www.indystar.com/story/news/education/2023/03/20/ips-students-walk-out-in-protest-of-dont-say-gay-bill/70029824007/

Levinthal, D. (2014, March 28). *The Koch brothers' influence on college campus is spreading.* Washington Post. https://www.washingtonpost.com/news/answer-sheet/wp/2014/03/28/the-koch-brothers-influence-on-college-campus-is-spreading/

Schneider, S. (2023, March 27). *Pitt students plan to protest what they call transphobic events organized by other student groups.* WESA 90.5. https://www.wesa.fm/education/2023-03-27/pitt-students-plan-to-protest-what-they-call-transphobic-events-organized-by-other-student-groups

Thomason, A. (2023, January 18). *Florida's state colleges say they'll ban promotion of critical race theory.* The Chronicle of Higher Education. https://www.chronicle.com/article/floridas-state-colleges-say-theyll-stop-promoting-critical-race-theory?cid=at&source=&sourceid=

Wasko, J. (2005). Studying the political economy of media and information. *Comunicacao e Sociedade, 7,* 25–48.

# Gallery

Dr. Carolyn M. Byerly.

Pinning ceremony to honor our CCMS students' acceptance into doctoral candidacy, 2022. Left to right: Dr. Chuka Onwumechili, Dr. Carolyn Stroman, Tanya Gardner, Shoaa Almalki, Bryan Jenkins, Dr. Carolyn M. Byerly, Dr. Frances Gateward, Dr. Wei Sun.

Dr. Byerly and Dr. Kay McGraw, hiking at Pipestem National Park, West Virginia, 2012.

Dr. Carolyn M. Byerly and Dr. Dafna Lemish, Washington, DC, at the annual International Communication Association conference, 2018.

Dr. Unwana Samuel Akpan and Dr. Byerly in front of the CCMS department bulletin board, Howard University, Washington DC, USA, 2019.

Dr. Karen Ross and Dr. Byerly, in Dublin for the annual International Communication Association conference, 2013.

Dr. Martha Allen, director, Women's Institute for Freedom of Press, and Dr. Byerly, demonstrating at the U.S. Federal Communications Commission in favor of a policy on internet neutrality, 2017.

Dr. Byerly with Tsovinar Nazaryan, Gyumri, Armenia, 2012.

Dr. Khebuma Langmia, Dr. Wei Sun, Dr. Byerly, Dr. Unwana Samuel Akpan, Dr. Chuka Onwumechili and Dr. Yong Jin Park, after Dr. Akpan's postdoc public presentation, Howard University, Washington DC, USA, 2019. Image courtesy of Dr. Colin Campbell.

Dr. Byerly with Margaret Gallagher and Ammu Joseph in Paris, for a UNESCO consultation on world media trends, 2013.

CCMS faculty and students on the first day of the academic year, 2019. From left to right sitting: Dr. Yong Jin Park, Dr. Carolyn Byerly, Dr. Unwana Samuel Akpan, Dr. Carolyn Stroman, Dr. Wei Sun, Dr. Natalie Hopkinson, and CCMS doctoral students. Image courtesy of Dr. Colin Campbell.

Dr. Byerly speaking to a Congressional Black Caucus meeting about media conglomeration. Image courtesy of Dr. Ashla Hill Roseboro.

# Biography and Published Works

CAROLYN M. BYERLY, PH.D.

Carolyn M. Byerly was born in Greenville, Alabama, in May 1945. She attended public schools in Munich, Germany; Mountlake Terrace, Washington state; Augusta, Georgia; and Colorado Springs, Colorado. After high school graduation in 1963, she studied journalism at Colorado State University for three years, then transferred to University of Colorado at Boulder, where she received a Bachelor of Science in Education. She worked as a researcher and writer, news reporter, government public information officer, and director of a women's shelter and rape crisis center before pursuing graduate studies. She completed graduate work at University of Washington, Seattle, receiving her Master's of Arts and Doctor of Philosophy in communication in 1987 and 1990, respectively.

In her academic life, Dr. Byerly held faculty positions in journalism and communication at Radford University (Virginia), Ithaca College (New York), University of Maryland (Maryland), and Howard University (Washington, D.C.). She retired from Howard in 2021, after 17 years, the last 7 of those as chair of the Department of Communication, Culture, & Media Studies, a doctoral-level program. While at Howard, she directed 7 master's theses and 27 doctoral dissertations, in addition to teaching and research. She holds the title of professor emerita at Howard University, a historically Black research institution in Washington, D.C., USA.

She lives in Olympia, Washington, with her spouse Kay McGraw, and their bouncy Samoyed, Koda. She continues her research and writing, and engages in community-level activism.

## Books

Byerly, C. M. (2024). *Intersectionality, political economy and the media*. Routledge.

Byerly, C. M. (Ed.) (2013). *Palgrave international handbook on women and journalism*. Palgrave Macmillan.

Byerly, C.M. (2011, March). *Global Report on Status of Women in News Media*. International Women's Media Foundation. (Technical Report).

Byerly, C. M. and Ross, K. (2006). *Women and media: A critical introduction*. Blackwell.

Ross, K. and Byerly, C. M. (eds.). (2004). *Women and media: International perspectives*. Blackwell.

Byerly, C. M. (1997, 1992, 1985). *The mother's book: How to survive the molestation of your child (*editions 3, 2, 1). Kendall/Hunt Publishing Co. [NOTE: Japanese edition, Ashoki Shoten Publishers, Tokyo, 2010.]

## Journal Articles

Moody-Ramirez, M., Byerly, C. Mishra, S. Waisbord, S. R. (2023). Media representations and diversity in the 100 years of *Journalism & Mass Communication Quarterly, Journalism & Mass Communication Quarterly, 100*(4), 826-846.

Byerly, C. M. Sha, B.-L., Nielsen, C., Grant, R. L., Daniels, G. L., Pevac, M. (2023). The versatility of intersectionality in journalism and mass communication research, *Journalism & Mass Communication Quarterly 100* (2), 249-263.

Byerly, C. M. (2020). Incels online: Reframing sexual violence. *Communication Review*, pp. 1-19. https://doi.org/10.1080/10714421.2020.1829305

Byerly, C. M. (2019). Gender equality and media structures. In A. Vega Montiel & S. Macharia (Eds.), *Setting the gender agenda for communication policy*. Paris, France: United Nations Educational, Scientific & Cultural Organization (UNESCO). Available in open access at https://en.unesco.org/gamagandunitwin

Lamb, Y. R. & Byerly, C. M. (2019). Kerner @ 50: Looking forward, looking back. *Howard Journal of Communication, 30* (4), 317-331.

Byerly, C. M. (2017). Feminist Intersectionality Research in Communications: Origins, Contributions and Tensions. *Ex Aequo* (European journal), pp. 23-32. Available at http://exaequo.apem-estudos.org/artigo/35-feminist-intersectionality-research-in-communications-origins-contributions-and-tensions

Byerly, C. M., Harman, S., & Lewis, A. (2016, Jan-March). The legacy of Stuart Hall (overview chapter for special section on Stuart Hall, edited by C. M Byerly & S. Harman), *Howard Journal of Communication*.

Byerly, C. M. (2014, April). Media Conglomeration and Women's Interests: A Global Concern (commentary), *Feminist Media Studies*, *14*(2), 322-326.

Byerly, C. M. (2013, March) Media conglomeration is women's business: FCC reports female broadcast ownership below 8%, *Media Report to Women*, 24/20-22,

Reviere, R. & Byerly, C. M. (2012). Sexual messages in Black and White: Discourse analysis of *Essence* and *Cosmo* advice columns. *Feminist Media Studies, 1-17,* . DOI:10.1080/14680777 .2012.680195.

Byerly, C. M. (2012). Gender, justice and the media: Shifting our agendas to media ownership. *Derecho a Comunicar* (Revista Científica de la Asociación Mexicana de Derecho a la Información), *4*, 22-32.

Byerly, C. M. & Hill, M. (December 2012). Reformulation theory: Gauging feminist impact on news of violence against women. *Journal of Women and Gender (Symposium Issue).* https://www.academia.edu/2247510/Reformulation_Theory_Gauging_Feminist_Impact_on_News_of_Violence_Against_Women

Byerly, C. M., Park, Y.J. & R. Miles. (2011). Race and gender-conscious policies: Toward a more egalitarian communications future. *Journal of Information Policy, 1*: 425-440.

Tyree, T., Byerly, C. M , & Hamilton, K.A. (October 2011). Representations of Black masculinity: A newsmaking case study. *Journalism: Theory, Practice & Criticism*, 467-484.

Byerly, C. M. (2011). Behind the scenes of women's broadcast ownership. *Howard Journal of Communication, 29*(3), 24-42.

Klein, A., Byerly, C. M., & McEachern, T. (2009). Counterframing public dissent: An analysis of anti-war coverage in the U.S. media. *Critical Studies in Media and Communication*, 331-350.

Byerly, C.M. and Wilson, C. C.II. (2009). Journalism as Kerner turns 40: Its multicultural problems and possibilities. *Howard Journal of Communication 20*(3), 209-221.

Byerly, C. M. (2009). Women, the economy and news: Analysis of the 2008 U.S. primary coverage, *St. John's Journal of Legal Commentary 24:*2, 387-402.

Byerly, C. M. (2007). War resistors and public dissent: In the pursuit of enlightened reporting, *Global Media Journal* (Mediterranean edition) *2*(2), 30-36.

Byerly, C. M. (2007, Fall). Tabloid television: America's shift to the sensational, *Gender & Media Diversity Journal, 42-46.*

Byerly, C. M. (2007, Fall). Tabloid television: America's shift to the sensational, *Gender and Media Diversity Journal*, 3, 42-46.

Byerly, C. M. and D. L. Walker. (2007, Summer). Ignoring International Women's Day: A case study of U.S. news coverage, 2005. *Media Report to Women*, 35,(3), 13-21.

Byerly, C. M. and Walker, D. L. (2007). An invisible celebration of International Women's Day in U.S. media," *Sciences de la Société*, special issue on International Women's Day news, *70,* 165-178.

Byerly, C. M. (2006). Feminist research in an era of globalization, *Redes.com (Revista de Estudios para el Desarrollo Social de la Comunicación* (special issue on gender and media), 3, 39-52.

Byerly, C. M. and Ross, K. (2006, March). Women's media activism: cross-cultural research and theory. *Gender & Media Diversity Journal*, 40-44.

Byerly, C. M. (2004, November). After September 11: Formation of an oppositional discourse, *Feminist Media Studies*, 5(3), 281-296.

Byerly, C. M. (2001, Winter). The deeper structures of storytelling: Women, media corporations and the task of communication researchers, *Inter/Sections* (journal of International Assoc. of Media & Communication Research), 63-68.

Byerly, C. M. (1997, Summer). Review of Les Switzer, *South Africa's Alternative Press: Voices of Protest & Resistance*, 1880-1960, *Journal of Communication, 47*:3, 140-143.

Byerly, C. M. and Warren, C. A. (1996, Spring). From margin to center: Organized Protest in the newsroom, *Critical Studies in Mass Communication, 13:1*, 1-23.

Byerly, C. M. (1996, Winter). Review of Rodger Streitmatter's *Unspeakable: The Rise of the Gay and Lesbian Press in America, Journalism Quarterly, 73*:4, 1021-1022.

Byerly, C. M. (1994, Spring). An agenda for teaching the reporting of rape. *Journalism Educator*, 49:1, 59-69.

Byerly, C. M. (1990, May). Taking a stronger hand: Women and the making of world news, *Development* (journal of the Society for International Development).

## Book Chapters

Byerly, C. M. (2024). Finding a synthesis. In U. S. Akpan (Ed.), *Moving the marginalized to the center: Dr. Carolyn M. Byerly's Research and Pedagogy*. Peter Lang.

Byerly, C. M. (2023). Gender dimensions of communication industries: A political economy analysis. In A. Vega Montiel & M. Gallagher (Eds.), *Handbook on gender, communication and women's human rights*. Wiley-Blackwell.

Byerly, C. M. & Almalki, S. (2023). The Other: Identity and difference in global, religious, and gendered contexts. In P. J. Creedon & L. A. Wackwitz (Eds.), *Women in mass communication: Diversity, Equity and Inclusion* (pp. 40-50). Routledge.

Byerly, C. M. & McGraw, K. A. (2020) "Axes of power: Examining women's access to leadership positions in the news media," (pp. 191-232) in M. Djerff-Pierre & M. Edstrom (Eds.), *Gender Equality in the Media*. Nordicom.

Byerly, C. M. (2019). Gender, media and ICT structures. In L. French (Ed.), *Gender, media and ICTs: New syllabi for media, communication and journalism*. UNESCO

Byerly, C. M. (2019). Neoliberalism and women's right to communicate: The politics of ownership and voice in media. In M. Meyers (Ed.), *Neoliberalism and the media*. Routledge.

Byerly, C. M. (2019). Gender, research and media development: A feminist perspective on media structures. In N. Benequista, S. Abbott, P. Rothman & W. Mano (Eds.*), International media development: Historical perspectives and new frontiers*. Peter Lang Publishing.

Byerly, C. M. & Simon-Roberts, S. (2019). Women, journalism and labor unions. In C. Carter, L. Steiner & S. Allen (Eds.), *Journalism, gender and power*. Routledge Taylor & Francis.

Byerly, C. M. (2021). Gender and political economy of the media. In K. Ross (Ed.), *Encyclopedia of gender, media and communication*. Wiley-Blackwell.

Byerly, C. M. (2018). Theorizing women and communication: Progress and challenges. In D. Harp, J. Loke & I. Bachmann (Eds.), *Feminist approaches to media theory and research*. Palgrave Macmillan.

Byerly, C. M. (2017). Feminist activism and U.S. communications policy. In V. Pickard & G. Yang (Ed.), *Media activism: Charting an Evolving Field of Research.* Routledge.

Adams, T., Patterson, **Byerly, C. M.,** Morris, L., R., Patterson, R., Plaisime, M., Roseboro, A. H. (2017). *National Poll of African Americans on Sickle Cell Disease Awareness* (Report). Howard University study, funded by Pfizer Company.

Byerly, C. M & Valentin, A. (2016). Women's access to media: Legal dimensions of ownership and employment in the United States. In R. Lind (Ed.), *Race and gender in electronic media: Challenges and opportunities*. Routledge.

Byerly, C. M. & Valentin, A. (2016). Feminist perspectives on critical information needs. In M. Lloyd & L. Friedlander (Eds.), *Communication policy and how to fix it.* Palgrave Macmillan.

Byerly, C. M. (2013). News and public discourse: The limits of feminist influence. In C. Armstrong (Ed.), *Media (dis)parity: Battle of the sexes* (pp. 207-216). Lexington Books.

Byerly, C. M. (2013). Women and media control: Feminist interrogations at the macro level, in C. Carter, L. Steiner & L. McLaughlin (eds.), *The Routledge Companion to Media and Gender*. Abingdon, UK: Taylor & Francis/Routledge, 105-115.

Byerly, C. M. (2012, Sept. 10). Overview: Women and Media, A Global Perspective, *IIP Digital*, U.S. Department of State, http://iipdigital.usembassy.gov/st/english/publication/2012/09/20120905135625ael0.4823986.html#axzz29UQ3WO2U.

Byerly, C. M. (2008). Sexism in media. In W. Donsbach (Ed.), *The Blackwell international encyclopedia of communications.* Blackwell.

Byerly, C. M. (2008). Woman as sign. In W. Donsbach (Ed.), *The Blackwell International Encyclopedia of Communications.* Blackwell.

Byerly, C. M. (2008). The dialectical relationship of women and media. In M. Meyers (Ed.), *Women in popular culture: Representation and meaning* (pp. 257-276). Hampton Press.

Byerly, C M. (2007). Situating the other: Women, racial and sexual minorities in the media, in P. J. Creedon and J. Cramer (Eds.), *Women and mass communication* (3rd ed.) (pp. 221-232). Thousand Oaks, CA: Sage Publications.

Byerly, C. M. (2006). Questioning Media Access: Analysis of FCC Women & Minority Ownership Data. In *Does bigger media equal better media?* (Report) Social Science Research Council and Benton Foundation, http://www.ssrc.org/programs/media.

Byerly, C. M., Langmia, K., & Cupid, J. A. (2006). Ownership matters: Localism, the ethnic minority news audience, and community participation. . In *Does bigger media equal better media?* (Report) Social Science Research Council and Benton Foundation, 2006, http://www.ssrc.org/programs/media.

Byerly, C. M. (2004). Shifting sites: Feminist, gay and lesbian newsroom activism, in the U.S. context. In M. deBruin and K. Ross (Eds.), *Gender and Newsroom Cultures: Identities at Work.* Hampton Press.

Byerly, C. M. (2004). Women and the concentration of media ownership. In Rush, R.R., Oukrup, C. and Creedon, P. (Eds.), *Women in journalism and mass communication*: A 30-year summary. Lawrence Erlbaum Associates, 245-262.

Byerly, C. M. (2002). Gender and the political economy of newsmaking: A case study of human rights coverage. In E. R. Meehan and E. Riordan (Eds.), *Sex and money: Intersections of feminism and political economy.* University of Minnesota Press, 130-144.

Byerly, C. M. (2001). Women. In E.K. Thomas and B. Carpenter (Eds.), *Mass media in 2025: Industries, organizations, people and nations* (pp. 151-165). Greenwood Publishing Group.

Byerly, C. M. (2000). News, feminism and the dialectics of gender relations. In M. Meyers (Ed.), *Representations of women in encyclopedia of women's studies* (pp. 383-402). Hampton Press.

Byerly, C. M. (2000). Women's Feature Service. In E. Burt (Ed.), *Historical dictionary of women's press organizations* (pp. 265-272). Greenwood Press.

Byerly, C. M. (1995). News, consciousness and social participation: The role of Women's Feature Service in world news. In A. Valdivia (Ed.), *Feminism, multiculturalism* and the media. Sage Publications.

Reprinted in Sreberny-Mohammadi, A., Winseck, D., McKenna, J. &Boyd-Barrett, O. (Eds.). (1997). *Media in Global Context: A Reader* (pp. 248-258) Arnold.

Byerly, C. M. (1995). Strategies for integrating practical journalism experience into teaching and scholarship," in J. Polumbaum (Ed.), *No Shrinking Violets: Anticipating Beijing* (Conference proceedings from World Women and Media Conference, March 23-26, 1995). University of Iowa.

## Theses and Dissertations Directed

### *Theses:*

Carla Brooks
Ngoma Iroabuchi
Rolake Bamgbose
Meagan Ford
Tsovinar Nazaryan
Teshonne Powel
Ashley Lewis

### *Dissertations:*

Kehbuma Langmia
Muhammad Hamisu Sani
Maria Nghidinwa
Gwendolyn Bethea
Candace Calloway
Kerry-Ann Hamilton

Bellarmine Ezumah
Imani Cheers
Russell Robinson
Desrene Vernon
Annie Duru
Jayne Cubbage
David Olanipekun
Christopher Jackson
Carmen House
Janice Smith
Sheila Brooks
Laounodji Mbairessem
Dominique Harrison
Ashley Lewis
Tamanika Ferguson
Alisa Valentin
Ashla Hill Roseboro
Florence Didigu
Jasmin Goodman
Sholnn Freeman
Shoaa Almalki

## *Service on Journal Editorial Boards:*

Journalism & Mass Communication Quarterly
Journal of Communication
Journal of Communication, Culture & Critique
Howard Journal of Communication
Feminist Media Studies
Journal of Culture & Media Politics
Global Media Journal (Mediterranean Edition)
Ex Aequo

# Notes on Contributors

UNWANA SAMUEL AKPAN is a multidisciplinary media scholar-practitioner with over two decades of broadcast experience. He has been a visiting scholar at the Department of Communication, Culture and Media Studies (CCMS), where he completed his Postdoctoral Studies in the School of Communication and Media Studies, Howard University, Washington DC, USA. He is the Editor of the University of Lagos Communication Review. He started his career with The Federal Radio Corporation of Nigeria, and was deployed to The National Broadcast Academy, its training arm, after obtaining his PhD in Mass Communication. He's presently a lecturer in the Department of Mass Communication, University of Lagos, Akoka, Nigeria. He has been a visiting scholar in the Department of Communication, Culture and Media Studies, Howard University, Washington DC, USA, where he completed his Postdoctoral Research. He has publications in the form of book chapters and research articles in prominent national and international journals. He has delivered several research papers at international conferences, and has published journal articles, book chapters and books in both prominent local and international journals and publishers such as Lexington, Palgrave Macmillan (Springer Nature), Routledge (Taylor and Francis) and Peter Lang. His classes are where research, teaching and learning interface, and he's dedicated to making students succeed in the classroom and beyond. His research and teaching investigate and explore Broadcast Contents, Sport Communication, African Communication Systems, Diaspora Communication Studies, Media Aesthetic.

SHOAA ALMALKI is an Arab feminist scholar whose research is focused on amplifying marginalized groups' voices in the health, organizational, and digital communication fields. She works as an FDA postdoctoral research fellow at Howard University exploring best practices in creating culturally sensitive recruitment messages for clinical trials. Her other research projects include culture-based health communication interventions, safety on social media, and corporate social responsibility.

MEENAKSHI GIGI DURHAM is a professor and CLAS Collegiate Scholar in the University of Iowa's School of Journalism and Mass Communication, and University Ombudsman. She earned her Ph.D. from the University of Florida. Her research addresses gender and sexuality in the media, using an intersectional feminist approach to analyze embodiment, intersectional identities, and youth cultures. Her articles have appeared in leading communication journals, and she serves on many editorial boards. Her books include *MeToo: The Impact of Rape Culture in the Media*, *Technosex*, *The Lolita Effect* and *Media and Cultural Studies: Key Works*. Among her numerous honors are the Teresa Award from ICA's Feminist Scholarship Division and the University of Iowa's May Brodbeck Distinguished Achievement Award for Faculty.

STINE ECKERT is an associate professor in the Department of Communication at Wayne State University, Detroit. She is Chair of the Helen Award Committee for Emerging Feminist Scholarship of the Feminist Scholarship Division (FSD) of the International Communication Association (ICA). She is co-editor of *Reflections on Feminist Communication and Media Scholarship: Theory, Method, Impact* and Co-PI on the NSF ADVANCE WSU-GEARS grant to advance gender equity through retention in STEM. Her research and teaching foci are journalism studies, gender media studies, and communication theories and publics.

SHOLNN FREEMAN is a media scholar who specializes in ethnocentrism and racism in American and international politics. He holds a doctorate in mass communication from Howard University in Washington, DC. He is a former journalist who has worked for *The Wall Street Journal* and *The Washington Post*.

MARGARET GALLAGHER is an independent researcher specializing in gender, media and communication. She started her career at the British Broadcasting Corporation (BBC), before moving to the Open University where she was Deputy Head of the Audiovisual Media Research Group. She has worked as a consultant for the United Nations and its agencies, the European Commission, the Council of Europe, international development agencies and broadcasting organizations. She serves on the editorial boards of *International Communication Gazette, Feminist Media Studies,* and *Media Development*. She is an Advisory Board member of the European Communication Research and Education Association (ECREA) and an international steering committee member of the Global Alliance on Media and Gender (GAMAG).

AMMU JOSEPH is an independent journalist and author based in Bangalore, India. Among her many publications are six books. She has been on the visiting faculty of several institutions of media education and is a founder-member of the Network of Women in Media, India.

DAFNA LEMISH is a distinguished professor and dean of the School of Communication and Information at Rutgers University, the founding editor of the *Journal of Children and Media*, and a Fellow of the International Communication Association (ICA). She is author and editor of numerous books and articles on children, media and gender representations, including *The Routledge International Handbook of Children, Adolescents, and Media* (edited, 2022); *Children and Media Worldwide in a Time of a Pandemic* (co-edited with Götz, 2022); *KakaoTalk and Facebook: Korean American Youth Constructing Hybrid Identities* (with Park, 2019); *Fear in Front of the Screen: Children's Fears, Nightmares and Thrills* (with Götz & Holler, 2019); *Beyond the Stereotypes: Images of Boys and Girls and Their Consequences* (co-edited with Götz, 2017).

MARIAN MEYERS is professor emerita in the Department of Communication and a former affiliate of the Institute for Women's, Gender and Sexuality Studies at Georgia State University. Her research has focused on the mainstreaming of neoliberal ideology in the media, as well as the media's portrayal of women and other socially marginalized groups from an intersectional perspective. She is the author of four books, including *Neoliberalism and the Media* (Routledge, 2019), and dozens of articles and book chapters.

NGOMA EVELYN MOGHALU (Dr. M.) is a wife, mother, social science researcher, public speaker, and an avid advocate for race research, women, African immigrants, and Autism awareness/acceptance. Dr. Moghalu's research is informed by her experiences as a Black woman, first-generation Nigerian immigrant, and mother to her handsome son with Autism. Dr. Moghalu received her Bachelor's degree in political science, and Master's degree in mass media and communication studies from Howard University, Washington, DC. She received her PhD in sociology from Texas A&M University, College Station, Texas. Dr. Moghalu enjoys sharing her academic and personal experiences through public speaking engagements, and podcast platforms. She started her Webinar Series titled "The Conversation—#DoYouSeeME," to bring awareness to the experiences of African/Black families living with ASD. In her spare time, she enjoys exploring her interests in film, documentary, video production, creative content creation, and networking with people who share similar interests.

AIMÉE VEGA MONTIEL is a Mexican feminist scholar. She holds a doctorate in Communication and Journalism Studies. She is a Researcher at the Center of Interdisciplinary Research in Sciences and Humanities at the National Autonomous University of Mexico (UNAM). She is a feminist scholar, expert in women's human rights and communication. She has worked in the fields of communication rights, media policy and advocacy. She has conducted international research that has informed legislation, policy, education programs and transformative initiatives in and through media and digital platforms. She is Co-Chair of the UniTWIN on Gender, Media and ICTs, Chair of the Global Alliance on Media and Gender (GAMAG). She has been Vice-President of the IAMCR and has served as an expert to the Council of Europe Recommendation of Gender Equality for the Audiovisual Sector (2017).

TSOVINAR NAZARYAN holds an M.A. in Mass Communications and Media Studies, Howard University. She is an organizational consultant, activist, independent journalist, and researcher on projects related to gender equality in media regulation, the Armenian diaspora, police violations of freedom of expression, electoral practices, anti-corruption, and other issues. She was Dr. Byerly's student at Howard University between 2009 and 2011, where she took courses on feminism, communication and culture, and development communication. Byerly also directed her master's thesis on alternative discourses in times of censorship. After returning to Armenia, Nazaryan engaged in civic movements for democratic change, especially for human rights in the military. With a grant from the U.S. State Department, Nazaryan coordinated a series of workshops in 2012 in which Dr. Byerly trained Armenian female activists in community organizing.

LANA F. RAKOW is professor emerita of Communication at the University of North Dakota, where she also was the Founder and Director of the Center for Community Engagement. Rakow earned a B.A. and M.A. at UND and a PhD in cultural studies at the University of Illinois, Urbana-Champaign. A feminist activist even before her academic career, Rakow helped found the Feminist Communication Interest Group of the International Communication Association, chaired the Committee on the Status of Women of the Association for Education in Journalism and Mass Communication, and served on numerous other state and national committees and boards. She is the author or editor of five books and dozens of book chapters on feminist theory, democracy, and technology.

ASHLA C. HILL ROSEBORO is an assistant professor of communications and media in the Alabama State University Department of Communications. She received her PhD in Communication, Culture and Media Studies and graduate certificate in Women's Studies from Howard University. Other degrees she holds are from Virginia State University (M.S.) and James Madison University (B.A.). Her research is on women in media, organizational communications and digital media, including a study on African American college-educated women and the Black press. Her recent publications include a book chapter on "HBCUs Access to Digital Media: An Intersectional Content Analysis of Black Women Social Entrepreneurs."

KAREN ROSS is a professor of gender and media in the School of Arts and Cultures, Newcastle University, UK. Her teaching and research are focused on issues of gender, media and society including aspects of social media and political communication and gender and news. Her latest monograph *Gender, Politics and News* was published in 2017 (Wiley-Blackwell). She was Lead Researcher on an EU-funded project on Advancing Gender Equality in the Media (2017–2019). She is Editor-in-Chief of a major new reference work, the *International Encyclopaedia of Gender, Media and Communication* (Wiley-Blackwell, 2020) and is the UK and European coordinator of the Global Media Monitoring Project 2020. She has written 8 books, edited a further 13 and written 80+ journal articles and book chapters. She has an international reputation as a leading scholar in the domain of gender, politics and communication, and gender and media.

CATHERINE J. K. SANDOVAL is a tenured Law professor at Santa Clara University, specializing in Communications and Energy law. She has served in government roles as a U.S. Chemical Safety Board Member, Commissioner of the California Public Utilities Commission, and Director of the Federal Communications Commission Office of Communications Business Opportunities.

ELIZABETH L. TOTH is professor emerita, APR, Fellow PRSA, and professor and past chair of the Department of Communication at the University of Maryland, College Park. She was previously the Associate Dean of the S.I. Newhouse School of Public Communication at Syracuse University. She is past president of the Association for Education in Journalism and Mass Communication. Toth has produced more than 90 refereed journal articles, book chapters, monographs, and conference papers on public relations. She co-authored and co-edited 10 books, including *Women and Public Relations: How Gender Influences Practice* and *The Future of Feminism in Public Relations and Strategic Communication: A Socio-ecological Model of Influence*. She was editor of the *Journal of Public Relations Research*. Toth has received numerous awards, including the Institute for Public Relations Pathfinder Award; the PRSA Jackson, Jackson & Wagner Behavioral Science Prize; the PRSA Outstanding Educator Award; the PRSA National Capital Chapter's Diversity Award; and the PRSA College of Fellows Sage Award. She has received three NCA PRIDE awards for her scholarship.

# Index

# Tabular Gratulatoria

Unwana Samuel Akpan

Shoaa Almalki

Ingrid Bachmann

Julie Burton

Meenakshi Gigi Durham

Stine Eckert

Karen Fraser

Sholnn Freeman

Audrey S. Gadzekpo

Margaret Gallagher

Ashla C. Hill Roseboro

Ammu Joseph

Dafna Lemish

Marian Meyers

Ngoma Evelyn Moghalu

Aimée Vega Montiel

Tsovinar Nazaryan

Stella Okigbo

Lana F. Rakow

Karen Ross

Catherine J. K. Sandoval

H. Leslie Steeves

Ingrid Sturgis

Elizabeth L. Toth

Kristi Warab

Clint Wilson